THERE'S A HIPPO IN MY CISTERN...

**One Man's Misadventures
On The Eco-Frontline**

PETE MAY

Collins

Collins
An imprint of HarperCollins Publishers
77-85 Fulham Palace Road
London W6 8JB

www.collins.co.uk

Published in 2008 by HarperCollins Publishers Ltd

Reprint 10 9 8 7 6 5 4 3 2 1

A catalogue record for this book is available from the British Library

ISBN-13 978-0-00-726431-5

Design and typeset by seagulls.net
Printed and bound in Great Britain by Clays Ltd, St Ives plc.

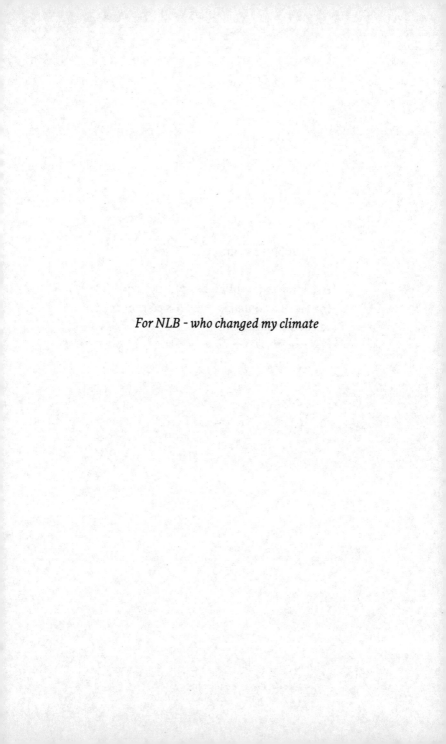

For NLB - who changed my climate

A Note About the Title

A Hippo is an inflatable plastic bag
that is placed inside a toilet's cistern
to conserve water.

CONTENTS

ACKNOWLEDGEMENTS

Firstly, a massive thank you to my wife Nicola for support, ideas, unpaid subbing, and allowing me to write about our lives without censure. And, of course, restraining herself from emptying the contents of the compost bin over my head for satirising her green mates.

Special thanks too to Claire Kingston at Collins for listening to my ramblings on fruit flies and chickens and, for some reason, agreeing to publish them.

My agent David Luxton deserves praise for his perseverance in ensuing we finally got the synopsis right and refusing to talk about all that literary stuff during meetings, instead sticking to important matters such as the fortunes of West Ham and Leeds United.

Thanks to all at Collins for their efforts, in particular Liz Woabank for poring over the manuscript with a green pen, Katherine Patrick for publicity and Bernice Davison for copy editing. Also worthy of commendation are Phill Jupitus, Justin Rowlatt, Joe Norris, Nicolette Jones, Nicholas Clee and junior proof readers Lola May and Nell May. Thanks also to any editors who have published my thoughts over the years, including Steve Platt, Bill Williamson, Becky Gardiner, Steve Chamberlain and Susie Steiner.

And finally, thanks to all the Greens out there. You only have to look at the likes of Hugh Fearnley Whittingstall to realize that most deep Greens are in fact marvelous English eccentrics. Some may be offended by my satire on earnest lives, but I am afraid that the comic opportunities were too good to omit (my own Green mishaps included).

This book might not save the planet, but hopefully it will raise enough chuckles to perhaps power a metaphorical long-life light bulb.

CHAPTER 1
Don't Ever Date an Eco-Bunny

The last months of 1993 are for me a kind of male nirvana. My short-life flat in Elephant and Castle certainly smells like team spirit. Shin pads drying above the gas fire, footie shorts on the back of the kitchen chair. My ideal weekend starts with Friday night TV and the blokeish repartee of *Have I Got News For You* and *Fantasy Football*. Saturday it's down the Hammers, *Match of the Day* in the evening and on Sunday, five-a-side beneath the Westway.

Division One has become the Premiership and Sky has begun to televise live matches on a Sunday, ideal for a post-game pint in the boozer. It is possible to spend an entire weekend watching and playing football. It feels a bit like being Arthur Seaton in Alan Sillitoe's *Saturday Night and Sunday Morning*. Arthur couldn't believe that after post-war austerity he could now drink endless pints of beer and mugs of tea and

1

knock off a married bird; here in Elephant I can't believe there's football almost every day on the telly.

By day I'm 'Sidelines', the gossip columnist for *Time Out* magazine and you'll always find me out to launch. The invites come from flirtatious PRs and I'm happy to trek to various revamped warehouses and bars all over London in search of a story. CDs, videos, books, T-shirts, computers and numerous over-packaged consumer durables are relentlessly promoted over free beer, Chardonnay and nibbly things served by waitresses in black and white uniforms. My flat is full of freebies. And through *Time Out* I get to review every new *Doctor Who* video. My collection of fifty Whovian titles is filed chronologically in a new video stand I've just purchased from the Virgin Megastore.

James Brown and Tim Southwell are plotting a new men's magazine to be called *Loaded* and I'm called in for consultation meetings and subbing shifts. With my pals Denis and Andrew I'm attempting to sell to publishers a book idea called *The Lad Done Bad*, detailing sex, sleaze and scandal in football. We think it perfectly captures the zeitgeist, to use the current buzz word so beloved by media-prats wearing trendy narrow glasses.

There's regular work writing the *London Spy* column in *Midweek* magazine, numerous features to be written about fat balding blokes playing for Sunday league football clubs in *FC*, a magazine that specialises in Sunday league football, and my column in the West Ham fanzine *On A Mission From God* – all enough to keep me in Dr Martens shoes, Gap chinos and a navy-blue bomber jacket with orange lining. Another factor enhancing my writing prospects is that everyone in the media is now affecting an Essex accent; only I don't have to, because I'm the real thing.

Much of the 1980s and early 1990s were spent in a peripatetic tour of London, among dodgy gaffs and even dodgier landlords at Turnpike Lane, West Kensington, Hammersmith, Parsons Green, Fulham Broadway, Camberwell, Neasden, Westbourne Park, Victoria and now Elephant and Castle. I've reached my thirties without owning a home or getting coupled up and my parents are probably convinced that in London I lead a secret life of the Julian Clary kind. They're probably already saying to their neighbours, 'It's funny how he never married'.

They're retired and living up in Norfolk now. When I ask my dad, a former tenant farmer who received a nice little earner when the M25 sliced through his farm, why he's still worried about the price of a pint he replies, 'But I'm a cattle dealer!'. My own finances, based mainly on passing large sums of cash to satellite dish, CD and VHS video manufacturers plus brewers and curry houses, must be a deep disappointment to him.

Still, there's been a good run of form with women recently, even if they do tend to wash and go with the regularity of West

Ham signing journeymen strikers. To my great joy, women in their thirties are suddenly much less choosy who they go out with. My back pages from the nineties contain a probation officer with two children, a teacher, a charity worker, and a literary bird with a daughter. Nothing that's got beyond mid-table mediocrity or flirting around the edges of Europe, but there's always another pub and party, another can of over-priced Stella Artois, or another freelance sub to pursue.

As Billy Joel might have put it, I'm living in a white bread world. A downtown guy waiting for an uptown girl, who then usually goes off with some poncy TV person with their own car. But then, my flat isn't exactly a *GQ* or *Arena*-style pulling pad; it's more *Men Behaving Badly*.

My life is not all work and socialising in London. I've been on the road with Jack Kerouac twice in recent years. Travel is the right of my generation. I retreated to Australia and New Zealand for lengthy periods in 1989 and 1992. Flying is exciting and helps create the illusion that I'm the last of Morrissey's famous international playboys. Internal flights, flights over Ayers Rock, flights to the top of Mount Cook, the more the better. The backpacker generation wanted to booze their way around the world; I'd travelled twelve thousand miles to discover that Kings Cross was in Sydney and full of English people. But it didn't matter; I'd fallen into spinifex at Ayers Rock with a woman from Camden and snogged a Surrey girl on Sydney Harbour

Bridge. Beer, CDs, videos, women, freebies, flights, football – the world is truly my lobster.

But then something happens which might just mark the end of my carefree, live-for-today-for-tomorrow-may-never-come existence. I meet a girl. Another of my jobs sees me sub-editing two days a week at the *New Statesman*. It's a boozy sort of place, with long pub meetings preceding the days before it becomes the Blairite house journal. Editor Steve Platt is a mate of mine from *Midweek* days and a big Port Vale fan.

Prime Minister John Major is suing the *Statesman* because the mag has written about rumours he's had an affair with a cook. Major claims the magazine was not correct about this matter. Years later we'd discover that he had, in fact, been rogering Edwina Currie, an image that still makes most people of a certain age feel queasy. The girl I meet is fund-raising to help our case. Nicola organises lunches among Lefty types to raise money and stop the magazine being bank-rupted by this pernicious prosecution.

Nicola isn't my usual sort of babe. She cycles to work and wears an exhaust-stained Gore-Tex jacket, a peculiarly eth-nic brown waistcoat covered in reindeers and snowdrop patterns, black drainpipe trousers and scuffed Kickers. It's hard to tell her form, if any, under the packaging. She has Ben Elton-style big brown glasses and twiddles her dark hair as she speaks. Linda the chief sub says that Nicola likes me.

Our eyes meet over my red pen and a page proof of a Ken

Livingstone article. Her accent is BBC toned down to lefty Estuary football-speak for my benefit. We chat by the juddering old filter coffee machine in the utility room. For the previous two years Nicola has been working as a VSO volunteer in the Solomon Islands. She's come home skint and says she wants to be an environmental writer and is taking an MSc in Environmental Management. Despite having no idea what this is, I try to sound impressed. A carbon footprint is something my old manual typewriter used to leave, and the closest I've come to recycling is trying to go out with someone else's girlfriend.

But Nicola does have something. Will she be interested in the Elephant man, though? It's worth a try. Having at times dated Red Wedgers, social workers, Labour supporters, Socialist Workers and women in black polo-neck jumpers, an environmentalist will surely be easy to cope with.

Several months after that first meeting we go on our first sort-of-date. Well it might be a date, or it could just be a friend asking another friend to watch a football match. That's my reasoning, just in case she has no interest in penetrating my ozone layer and it all becomes embarrassing. Nicola has read Nick Hornby's best-seller *Fever Pitch* and is now interested in football, she keeps telling me in the *Statesman*'s utility room. She's even seen Arsenal play; she lives in Highbury, close to the ground. The new middle-class interest in football is all a little bemusing to me, having spent years trying not to mention the sport in intelligent circles or in front of women, because they treated football fans like some sort of rabid, racist sub-species. Still, why not use this new-found love of *When Saturday Comes* and soccerati writers...

My photographer mate Dave Kampfner has invited a group of mates over to watch the Holland v England World Cup qualifying match. Dave accuses me, probably quite accurately, of 'always sniffing around Lefty women', usually with various degrees of distress. But as Dave and myself know, concerned, caring women are often extremely attractive and up for a raunch-fest with downwardly mobile writers too. And in 1993 you don't get too many babes at Young Conservative meetings.

'Is Wrighty going to play? You can see at Arsenal that he's so much quicker than the other players,' says Nicola as we open pre-match cans of designer lager.

'I think Taylor should play him. But as long as Carlton Palmer doesn't play I'll be happy,' I reply, ruminating upon Taylor's turnips, as the *Sun* has dubbed his side. Football coverage was becoming much more fanzine-like in its blokey humour. When England had lost to Sweden, the *Sun* came up with the unforgettable headline of 'Swedes 2 Turnips 1'.

It all goes wrong. England hits the post, then Ronald Koeman brings down David Platt but the referee doesn't send him off. Graham Taylor is haranguing the referee in the style of a very irate grocery shop owner. 'Taylor's lost it,' says Nicola. Correctly ascertaining that Taylor 'had lost it' impresses me. However, she does insist on referring to the England players' kits as 'uniforms'. Deflated by a familiar England defeat we take the Tube back and depart for our separate lines, still unsure if we're friends or potential lovers.

When we next meet Nicola takes a Taylor-esque route one approach. She phones me up and suggests we meet in Pizza Express at the Angel. That morning Nicola had watched the *New Statesman* versus VSO match at Regent's Park, a game she organised through her contacts at the volunteer service. Clearly she's been impressed by the firm man-to-man marking job I performed on her mate Morgan, a Carlisle United fanatic who was in the Solomons with her.

I haven't followed up the first date as yet. There's also a charity worker in Brixton I've been dating, and it's all too tiring doing *Time Out* shifts seeking stories to fill the diary page and there are just so many football matches to fit in. But having just been dumped by Brixton woman (probably for watching *Match of the Day* during a romantic mini-break in Shropshire) Nicola's call is a boost.

Over dinner Nicola tells me about her plans to move north, to stay with friends in Yorkshire for a couple of months, so that she can finally get down to writing a novel based on her volunteer work in the Solomons. I volunteer the story that after a number of failed liaisons, I'm not looking to go out with anyone at the moment. I'm thinking of taking time off from women and devoting more waking hours to football. All in a faltering, commitment-phobic fashion. This doesn't seem to bother her, which is promising.

After a nervous pizza date we end up taking a taxi to her flat in Highbury. Result. Up the tattered carpet on the stairs towards the top floor. Only inside her flat, there appears to be no heating. Maybe her boiler has broken down. There's a bike on the landing surrounded by helmets and luminous sashes. The kitchen has a copy of *Gaia* by James Lovelock on the chopping board. A huge edifice constructed from plastic bags full of wine bottles and old *Guardian*s is dumped on the floor. It resembles my flat, with its empty bottles, piles of crumbling newsprint and crumpled beer cans. But hers haven't just been tossed aside. They're apparently going to be taken to the recycling bins. The walls on the stairs are covered in hunting prints and a display of ethnic masks from various obscure parts of the globe.

It's a little disturbing to spot several ring binders bulging with stuff on European environmental law by her bed. But after a bottle of Chardonnay my main area of reflection is based on the fact that here is an attractive woman who wants to sleep with embryonic *Loaded* man. Do I not like that.

The next morning we kiss goodbye with affection as I try to memorise her instructions on how to get to Drayton Park station. I'm due at the *Loaded* office to work on a dummy issue. And for some reason Nicola has a flower behind her ear.

'Pete, you remind me of my horse,' she says at her door.

'What, a stallion?' I ask hopefully.

'No, my old horse Cass, she had a face like yours. And she was calm, with big teeth, creaking joints, a floppy lower lip...'

'Is this a compliment?'

'Of course it is. I've had horses all my life. And I used to work for *Horse & Hound*.'

'Is that how you know so much about IPC?'

'Yeah, I was in that tower block for years, long before *Loaded*. Then I went to the Solomons and everything changed.'

On board the train I indulge in that self-satisfied, knowing sensation that I've bedded a new woman in a new part of town while everyone else is reading their morning papers. I'm feeling groovier than Paul Simon. But as the stations pass I remember that she's going away and though last night might be a beginning it's looking more likely to be the end. It's never going to work with her writing her saving-the-planet novel on a mist-shrouded moor in Yorkshire and me down here in London living the *Loaded* life, now is it? And surely I've given up on girlfriends, haven't I? Haven't I?

Two days later there's one further furtive assignation over lunch at the *Statesman* and a snog in Hoxton Square, which we hope that Linda the chief sub and Nyta the features writer who suspects something won't see. Two days later Nicola decamps to Yorkshire, just like a latter-day Sally Bowles.

Surprisingly, I find myself thinking of her at unguarded moments, such as the ads break when the Sky game is on. But she writes to me. A good sign, from someone I'm not involved with. Long stream-of-consciousness letters that make me laugh. 'Oh my God, you're not going to believe this, I went to use a duster and I discovered it's a fox's brush!' she writes in a quick scrawl that seems to sum up the speed of her thoughts.

Details emerges about the family she's staying with. Fleur is the granddaughter of a legendary Conservative Cabinet minister and her husband is master of hounds in the local hunt. All non-PC enough to get us both excommunicated from the *New Statesman*.

After a fortnight she returns to London for a long weekend because she's attending a party in Kemble, which I'd always thought was a planet on *Doctor Who*. And she wants me to come too. I'm imagining cans of lager and a party tape.

As the train shuffles through the Gloucestershire country-side the market towns become leafier and more prosperous. We take a minicab from Kemble station for several miles down country lanes and emerge at a large detached house with stables.

Nicola then tells me that her mate Diana is in fact a Lady. Not the Lady Diana, but still a genuine Lady. She seems friendly in an earthy, county-ish way and at least doesn't send me round to the tradesman's entrance. Nicola tells me she used to go to school with her.

We are shown to our room and later emerge for dinner in the Aga-fired kitchen. Some of the other guests have arrived. Women in Puffa jackets and chaps called Johno.

'Nicola I've got nothing in common with these people,' I blurt as we have a moment's respite in our bedroom full of crisp white linen.

'Nonsense, they're too polite to be rude to you. Just be yourself and tell them you're a writer.'

Maybe she's right. The kitchen is homely, there's a dish called kedgeree that's good, although I furtively have to observe the other guests to make sure which knife and fork you use, as there's enough cutlery on the table to feed the Third World. Everyone tries to be friendly. But conversations tend to end once Nicola refers to me as a football journalist. There are several men here, all apparently in the Army and they're all, of course, fans of rugger. And I'm the man who arrived wearing a navy-blue bomber jacket with an orange lining.

I'm not the only one struggling though. One of the guests has brought a dog with her and it's yapping away by the table.

'What an annoying dog, why don't you have it shot!' says Nicola politely to its owner. 'Oh sorry, sometimes I speak without thinking,' she giggles, as there's a bemused silence. Is she rude, mad or just drunk on champagne? I realise I find her fascinating. Strange, different and horribly fascinating.

But what am I doing here with these people, with her? Dinner over, we collapse into the fine linen and it all feels very *Brideshead Revisited*. Surely our relationship will end soon. We come from different classes. I'm not posh enough for her. She's living all over the country. And I appear to be playing the Mellors to her Lady Chatterley. Where can this possibly be going, and do I want to be on this journey anyway?

The next day we get a lift with Lady Diana's husband Tim, a man of typically English diffidence, who drives us to the station in a horsebox. It's the first time I've ever used such a mode of transport. It feels like being Harvey Smith. I find myself rather enjoying it all. Horses, dogs, posh girls. And then it's back on the train to London covered in straw.

Once I'm back on the city streets I realise I'm not getting that usual 'back home' feeling. Something has changed. I know things are different, because although I'm back in my world, I find myself thinking about Nicola's.

After several weeks at the Yorkshire farmhouse, Nicola returns to London and announces that she's renting out her flat in Highbury and moving to Oxford. Why? Because it's the epicentre of the Green movement. Her plans change more often than Graham Taylor's formations.

We watch *Four Weddings and a Funeral*, a British film that's becoming a huge hit. Hugh Grant is brilliant as the diffident, very English, Charles. I tell Nicola that I once met Hugh, when I was interviewing his girlfriend, actress Elizabeth Hurley round at their Earl's Court flat. In fact *Loaded* has just found some very tasty shots of Liz in lingerie for the first issue, but best not mention that.

When Hugh's rushing to beat the alarm clock in the first scene it reminds me of life with Nicola, always dashing to make a train or appointment in the mornings. She cries at the end of the film, and indeed during it when W H Auden's 'Stop All the Clocks' poem is read out at Gareth's funeral. She's a strange mixture of earnest Green and utterly sentimental romantic. And where does she feature in my life? Is she Andie MacDowell's Carrie, Vomiting Veronica or Duckface? Will *we* one day agree not to get married? I realise, with a mounting sense of terror, that I'm thinking about getting married. Or at least, about the possibility that we might not get married. Why am I even thinking this?

Nicola is no rock chick. I try to play her some of my CDs but her interest in music appears to have ended when she left York University in the early eighties, when she did at least like 'Soul Mining' by The The. She likes reggae and Lucky Dube in particular, because he was played all the time in the Solomon Islands. But she covers her ears when I play early Clash and Buzzcocks to her. She says she can see why Joy Division's Ian Curtis killed himself because they were so bloody awful to listen to. She hates the mournful dirge of REM and thinks

Radiohead's Thom Yorke should just cheer up, stop whining and get a girlfriend.

I am slightly surprised, but pleased, to discover that I have got myself a girlfriend. *Loaded* lad has fallen for posh eco-bunny. By the spring of 1994 I'm helping my peripatetic girlfriend move her possessions via the Oxford Tube, the hourly coach service that runs between Oxford and London. As we leave her flat she turns out the pockets of her exhaust-stained Gore-Tex jacket, looking for her tube pass. Inside are crumpled receipts, bank statements, bus tickets, an apple core, some conkers and a hastily-scrawled address. We race across London and she insists we call at the home of Gareth, a freelance writer for the *New Statesman*. She emerges from his doorway with a black bucket full of water. I glimpse inside the bucket and take a step back.

'What the hell is that!' I exclaim.

'It's Terra.'

'It's a bloody great big monster!'

'No it isn't. He's lovely. Gareth's going to work for the *Daily Star* in Lebanon [no, not the sleazy British paper] so Terra's going to come and live with me.'

Inside the bucket a terrapin is splashing around, trying to scale the shiny plastic walls. Perhaps it is all virtual reality. No, it's still there.

'We're taking that to Oxford? Nicola, you're wearing green Wellington boots and carrying a bucket with a terrapin in it. Oh, and your pockets are full of conkers. Have you ever thought you might be eccentric?'

We board the coach with the bucket veiled by her coat. Is what we are doing legal? Somehow we survive the two-and-a-half hour coach journey with a bucket at our feet containing an irate terrapin. If he'd escaped and savaged the driver it might have caused one of the M4's worst-ever disasters.

She carries the bucket down a side street while I follow with her bags like a faithful retainer. Her new home is in her friend's mum's house, situated by the River Cherwell. She's renting a small room with a damp shower area, plus a living room with French windows, several ancient armchairs and a pleasing air of Oxford donnishness. Terra the terrapin is housed in a borrowed fish tank, although I'm all for putting him in the Cherwell and never mind the ecology.

As spring passes into summer, we spend long weekends here by the river. We go to see the film *Shadowlands*, the film about C S Lewis and his doomed lover Joy Gresham, which is set in Oxford. There's not much sex in it though. And *Forrest Gump*, where Nicola cries five times, and it's really embarrassing. Blokes don't cry unless their team wins the League or gets relegated. Why are women so susceptible to the fact that life is like a box of chocolates?

We visit tea rooms, saunter around the ancient colleges, and gaze at artefacts from the South Pacific in the Pitt Rivers museum. We spend a dreamy summer picnicking by the

River Isis watching punters wobble their way along the water and stopping for real ale in bucolic pubs. If you travel far enough you can even catch Sky in some of the less cerebral boozers. 'Love Is All Around' by Wet Wet Wet, the theme song from *Four Weddings and a Funeral*, is on all the juke boxes. And maybe it is in the air for us too. The man who wrote the original hit for The Troggs, Reg Presley, now spends his time looking for evidence of aliens making crop circles. I'm quite surprised he isn't a mate of Nicola's.

It's not very laddish at all out in misty, academic old Oxford. When *Loaded* has its annual day out at Brighton races followed by karaoke, I find myself turning down the offer of some cocaine in the loos on the pier, pleading that I have to work the next day when actually I'm catching the Oxford Tube and really I think that real ale is better than drugs anyway.

Nicola joins an Oxford writers' circle and soon establishes links with the Oxford Greens. In fact the entire Green movement, all twelve of them, seem to be in Oxford. They can be found playing Ultimate Frisbee in the parks and resolutely not talking about football.

Soon Nicola is making eco-waves. She's running a tree-saving charity called the Forest Management Foundation (FMF), via a phone/fax machine she's bought. That's the important thing about being a Green. Through her tree-hugging work on the FMF I discover that there's only one thing Greens value more than saving hardwood in Papua New Guinea, and that's having an acronym.

Back in London I'm spending my week days in Colindale newspaper library searching through old copies of the *Sun* for our book on soccer sleaze. It doesn't feel like I'm plugging the hole in the ozone layer, but it's fun.

Amazingly, *Loaded* is suddenly the publishing sensation of the year. Most people thought it would last for only a few issues. It's selling hundreds of thousands of copies. Now the staff are stars and there are regular subbing shifts, my contributions to write for the Greatest Living Englishmen column (Brian Clough, Steve Jones, Patrick McGoohan, Tom Baker, the Brigadier off *Doctor Who* and Robin Askwith all prove popular) and interviews with footie icons Julian Dicks and Karren Brady.

Inadvertently, through dating Nicola, it seems I've cracked a *Loaded* fantasy. Editor James Brown often asks, in his strong Yorkshire accent, 'Eh, are you still going out with that posh bird?' and offers me more shifts.

Despite *Loaded* attracting much ire from *Guardian* and *Independent* commentators, Nicola seems pleased that I'm part of something successful and exciting. The lads in the office aren't exactly environmentally aware though. One afternoon at the IPC offices, where *Loaded* is based, the building is besieged by placard-waving protestors. They're campaigning against the cruelty of angling. It turns out that IPC also produces fishing mags. The *Loaded* staffers respond by making paper darts from pieces of A4 printer paper. They write messages on them reading 'Cod and two chips please' and 'There's a plaice for us' and then fly them at the irate demonstrators. Juvenile, but very funny after lunch in the Stamford Arms.

It's strange commuting between London and Oxford. Soon I'll have to make a choice. Can I keep laughing as I throw paper out of a window while Nicola fights to save trees? Oasis and Blur are battling for Britpop supremacy in the charts. *Loaded* has Noel Gallagher on its cover. 'You Gotta Roll With It' wouldn't inspire the Oxford Greens to holler an Oasis anthem into the night. They'd ask if the roll was organic.

In my new Oxford circles the guru of the Greens is George Monbiot. Everyone speaks about him in awed tones and refers to him as simply 'George'. He's a Fellow (is that the academic version of being a lad?) at the university and writes columns for the *Guardian*. Nicola already has his books on Kenyan nomads, persecuted tribes in Irian Jaya, and displaced indigenous peoples in the Amazon. According to the publisher's blurb he's been caught by hired gunmen, beaten up, shot at by military police and shipwrecked. The most dangerous thing I've ever managed is an away trip to Millwall.

George is one of the Frisbee players Nicola hangs out with. He's the most intellectual man I've ever met. His parents are rumoured to be keen Conservatives, but then so are mine. George is a radical with a great grasp of figures and an incisive mind, dedicated to fighting planetary pollution. He wears steel-rimmed glasses and in his *Guardian* column regularly attacks corporate eco-vandalism and climate change doubters.

He isn't exactly a football fan though. He says he went to an England game at Wembley once and it epitomised everything he disliked about xenophobia and nationalism. At one post-Frisbee picnic we discuss TV. George says there's so much he can do without watching TV. He could write a column every day, there are so many issues to research. He claims that TV is like a boxed fire in the living room. Humans used to tell stories around the campfire but now that oral tradition has been lost.

One of George's best mates is Oliver. He comes from a strong environmental background – his dad advised Mrs Thatcher on the environment. Oliver is an endearing eco-warrior, a friendly, large-framed man with wild red hair and permanent stubble on his chin. He's a lovely geezer, Nicola really likes him, but like most Greens he's completely unaware how eco-eccentric his lifestyle can appear to a mere civilian.

He's the only man I've ever met who wears a pouch around his waist, in which he keeps his cash. He lives in a house by the river and just as in Nicola's flat, the walls are covered in masks from indigenous peoples he's visited around the world. His front room is one giant office, covered in tottering towers of eco-faxes.

Oliver's toilet has pieces of newspaper instead of loo roll, something I haven't seen since watching *Steptoe and Son*. I admire his commitment, but surely this is taking paper saving to an unacceptable extreme. As we might put it at *Loaded*, it's a bunch of (sore) arse.

Some of Nicola's Green friends take their 'back to nature' beliefs to unusual extremes. Even she laughs about the time one of them answered the door wearing shorts and holding a sprig of comfrey, his legs smeared in goose fat. He'd bruised his leg hedge-laying, he explained matter-of-factly. Goose fat and comfrey was apparently the traditional method of healing bruises. He then wrapped the comfrey leaves around his goose fat-covered leg and secured it with a red bandanna. Normal behaviour to a Green.

Another of her eco-pals, George Marshall, wears a battered trilby and long overcoat, speaks in clipped received pronunciation, and is trying to turn his former council house into a carbon-neutral home. He's another fine eco-eccentric and a delightfully non-PC Green, a man always prepared to talk about his search for a suitable eco-babe (eventually ended after meeting his wife while working for the Rainforest Foundation in New York) as well as the imminent disaster awaiting Bangladesh when the sea levels rise.

He is typical of the people in Nicola's world. Everyone is either writing about GM foods or making programmes for *Costing The Earth* on Radio 4. Nicola's mate Matthew

21

Wenban-Smith works for the FSC, the Forest Stewardship Council. He's a nice guy, although after a few drinks I keep thinking of him as Whambam Smith. Matthew says he can trace the Wenban-Smiths back to medieval times. Nicola says she can trace her family back to 1066. I can trace my family back to 1966.

Nicola met Debs and Thomas through her writing group. Thomas edits a subversive video news series called *Undercurrents* and is George Monbiot's cousin. *Undercurrents* contains numerous reports from eco-protestors around the world, including one memorable piece on Carmageddon, where a group of crusties take a fleet of old cars to Scotland and bury them vertically to form a modern version of Stonehenge. Thomas's wife Debs is American, full of energy and novel ideas, and is the only person I know who keeps a writer's journal, although, astonishingly, she does have to ask who Eric Cantona is during one discussion.

At least Nicola has a sense of humour about Greens like the media-friendly Jonathon Porritt, head of Forum for the Future, coming from toff backgrounds. 'Of course they can cope with turning the heating off and wearing an extra jumper, they're used to it in their stately homes,' she jokes.

I discover just how different the Oxford Greens are to my usual acquaintances at a dinner party one night. I play Essex Man to their Ethics Men. Everyone speaks of PNG (Papua New Guinea to the uninitiated) as if it's a suburb of Oxford.

The après lentil-bake conversation moves on to private schools and bizarre initiation rituals. One of our party mentions something involving a cardboard box and a banana. When my turn for an anecdote comes I have to confess that actually my school didn't have an initiation ritual. George Monbiot is fiercely anti-public school and decries them for producing 'emotionally stunted' members of the ruling class.

'That's not true,' says Nicola. 'Pete's emotionally stunted and he went to a comprehensive.'

'I'm not emotionally stunted!' I complain. 'I'd probably cry if West Ham won the league.'

'See what I mean?' she smirks.

The revelations about my state school education cause some interest. Suddenly I'm studied with as much interest as if I was an indigenous person from some obscure tribe; which in a way I suppose I am.

Back in London I sit with my mate John, drinking pints of real ale in Borough High Street. He's the Terry Collier to my Bob Ferris. We discuss my fears that maybe the Greens are just too scared to be Tories. Was it easier to be a Green and not really upset anyone? What if Nicola demands that I wear a Barbour jacket? Or grow dreadlocks? But maybe that's too harsh. The Oxford Greens seem sincere enough, even if their parents are loaded. But still, their lifestyle seems extreme. John and I think that electing a radical Labour government will end all our problems, especially after our third pint.

Surely we can't go back to a pre-industrial world? And global warming hasn't yet been proved beyond all doubt.

Green puritans are new to me. They grow organic vegetables on allotments, refuse to shop in supermarkets, and visit white people with dreadlocks at places called Tinker's Bubble. They advocate urinating on garden plants to encourage growth. They dress in waistcoats. They are different from you and me.

Recently I'd read a piece by Matthew Parris claiming that Greens were simply part of the natural human tendency to always prophecy that the 'end of the world is nigh'. Maybe he's right. Would the Green movement go the way of CND in the eighties? We were all terrified of global annihilation, we went on marches to Trafalgar Square in our thousands, but the Cold War ended and it never happened. But what if they're right? What if my loo paper is responsible for killing the planet? But I have other things to worry about. It's time to meet Nicola's parents.

They live in Hertfordshire, in the country, and I find the whole thought of visiting them terrifying. We're from such different worlds. Nicola boarded at a girls' school where they even had lessons in table manners. She explained you had to talk to the person on your left first, over the starters and then the person on the right during the main course. Or was it the other way round? My school merely insisted you didn't throw food at your peers.

Maybe that's why our ambitions differ. Us comprehensive types are content to be earning enough to buy the odd CD by a new band called Oasis who want to live forever; Nicola is constantly traumatised that she hasn't become the head of the United Nations. Her personality is a strange mix of confidence and insecurity; she wakes early in the morning, when I'm half asleep, wondering if her novel will be good enough, can she make it as an environmentalist, should she go back to the Solomons to stop the logging companies, and how can she halt global warming?

But when I do finally visit her parents there's no horse-whipping from her old-Etonian dad, despite my being a property-less, car-less man who thinks that 'In the City' is a single by the Jam rather than a description of a job. Their house has five bedrooms and a swimming pool, but it's not the stately home I feared, even if there are numerous portraits pointing to a grander past. Some of Nicola's ancestors did own large chunks of Bath, but in true *Loaded* style, they managed to lose most of the dosh through high living, drinking, gambling and death duties.

Her dad Angus is having chemotherapy for cancer, and in the circumstances he's friendlier than I ever imagined he'd be to a football fan frolicking with his daughter. I'm beginning to see where she gets some of her quirkiness. Angus owns a waxworks in York and used to own a Dracula Museum in Whitby. He shows me his coppicing in the family wood and the horses in the top paddock. The only land I held in stewardship is the window box Nicola had installed in my Elephant and Castle short-life pit.

Nicola's mum Fiona has the same energy as her daughter; always working in the garden, putting the cover on the swimming pool, preparing meals and running the house. As we load the dishwasher she tells me that she was Green long before it was fashionable, because she and Angus had to make do and mend as they put their children through private school. Fiona is always smart and keeps her house tidy; Nicola is all flyaway hair, ethnic waistcoat and untidy bedrooms.

Her brother Drew is staying too and he's a big fan of *Loaded*. He's carrying a CD. Angus picks it up and asks "Sorted for Es and Whizz'? What's all that about then?' It might be OK here. I drink whisky, which Angus seems to approve of, even if my coppicing is, as yet, uninspired.

So in turn I take her to visit my parents, who now live in King's Lynn. She's a little bemused that my mum does all the work and that we eat at six o'clock and no-one speaks during meals. Her family are normally arguing, telling stories, swearing or laughing throughout dinner, which is at eight. 'I'm not a performing monkey,' I tell her, 'we don't do raconteurs in my family.' She's no doubt spotted that we call the living room the lounge and the loo the toilet.

My dad is baffled at meeting an assertive woman. Nicola

quite enjoys challenging his opinions. He has no sympathy with the Greens. A retired farmer and lifelong Tory he tells us over a pint of home brew, 'There's no such thing as global warming, it's invented by people who make a living out of it. They've all got college jobs, they rely on it to sell their books. And if the ocean level rises a foot what effect will that have on us?' He then produces an article from *Farmers Weekly* that proves that organic food is a waste of time and that nitrates are really good for the land.

She must be committed to this relationship to be listening to this here in Norfolk with me. She copes with my dad's views with hitherto unknown levels of diplomacy.

'Thank you for putting up with this. My dad enjoys telling people they're wrong.'

'I've heard it all before from my relatives. And I was enjoying counting how many ways he could insert "Well, if Pete had gone into farming" into a conversation.'

'Can you imagine me as a farmer?'

'I can't imagine anyone worse. You're completely cack-handed at anything practical!'

There's a small blip when she tells him to slow down in his car - no one in my family has dared criticise my dad's driving - as he drives past a pheasant, but no disasters. She puts up with lots of things that irritate her, such as watching television and always having to drive to pub lunches. No-one does that simply out of politeness. She's doing it for me. I want to believe she's doing it for me.

Meanwhile my Oxford commutes continue. My true inauguration into the Green set comes with an invitation to George Monbiot's party. No one drives to this venue. In the front garden of George's two-storey house is a huge mountain of mating bikes. Racing bikes, granny bikes, mountain bikes. Piled on top of each other like a bizarre cyclical sculpture. The sort of thing the EU should do something about.

Inside it's squeezing room only. In one corner of the living room stand a group of bearded Newbury veterans and members of the Donga Tribe, jamming on bongos, violins and harmonicas singing in pseudo-folkie voices and occasionally blowing tin whistles.

Many guests appear to have been issued with ethnic trousers with drawstrings. A man in a rainbow jumper is slumped on the stairs. Fashion has clearly never penetrated Oxford. Collarless shirts, tweed jackets and endlessly patched trousers are everywhere. This party would never feature on a glossy magazine's lifestyle pages. Not a high heel, short skirt or a glass of champagne in sight. We're soon introduced to a local novelist, a woman doing a project on bananas and a man who was working for Sting's Rainforest Foundation. George is unfailingly friendly, performing introductions as if he's on *Question Time*.

'Ah, yes, this is Nicola who's an environmental journalist and director of the FMF, and this is Pete who's a journalist doing some very interesting work with, erm, football, and this is Tim Pears who's just written a fantastic novel and this is Piers who's back from PNG where's he's campaigning on logging issues.'

The guests appear impressed by a commissioned book, but there's a silence when I mention it's on something called football. At times it feels less a party and more like a convention of anthropologists. No wonder we have global warming; it's because the Oxford Greens are doing so much flying around the world studying deforestation, indigenous tribes and Fairtrade fruit.

It does make me wonder if my split existence can really continue. It's football and TV versus Frisbees and story telling, showbiz parties in London versus tin-whistle affairs in Oxford. Is love worth a future of drawstring trousers? The only solution is to try and not think too hard about it and to gratefully sup several bottles of organically-brewed beer.

A couple of weeks later we're on another big night out and as we're on the wrong side of Oxford we end up sleeping at Oliver's house, dossing down on the floor of his office. We're awoken at the unbelievable time of 6.30 am by the sound of something mechanical swishing. Light cascades into the previously dark room as an organic hangover batters my cranium.

'Oliver has automatic curtains. He likes to get up with the sun,' explains a strangely awake Nicola. She thinks the automatic curtains are a brilliant invention.

Ten minutes later Oliver emerges munching a bowl of muesli and wearing headphones. Where's the coffee? Sodding 6.30 am. Who wants *Gaia* and a perfect sense of elemental nature at this time? It's neither day or night.

'Oh, I'm sorry,' booms Oliver. 'I was just listening to yesterday's *Archers* on my personal stereo.'

'Do you know what is the biggest problem about saving the planet?' I ask Nicola.

'No.'

'The hours.'

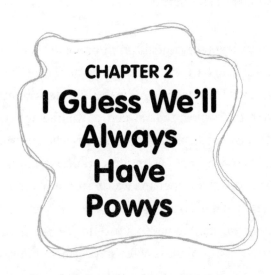

CHAPTER 2
I Guess We'll Always Have Powys

In the outside world Radiohead have the Bends, Paul Weller is the Changingman and Oasis say the sink is full of fishes. Eric Cantona's away with the seagulls and trawlers after being suspended for kung-fu kicking Crystal Palace fan Matthew Simmons. John Smith is ushering in a New-ish Labour and Jarvis Cocker wants to do what Common People do. Meanwhile I'm marooned inside a roofless cottage, desperately trying to restrict my bowel movements through fear of using the compost loo.

Gazing at the hole in a piece of wood intended for my backside and the accompanying bucket of sawdust, it seems that Green life is perhaps beyond me. Or more accurately, beneath me.

An updraught of cold air chills my buttocks. Cobwebs cover the bare stone walls of the bathroom. Outside, half a metre away from the condensation-drenched bathroom window, is a slab of bare and decidedly damp rock.

The house has been dug into the hillside in an attempt to keep out the winds that sweep down the valley. Ernest Shackleton must have felt a little like this when he was immobile on the *Endurance*, sitting in darkness for months, not having a proper loo either and waiting for the pack ice to close in and crush the life from his vessel.

Nicola has invited me to a meeting of like-minded eco-warriors in Powys, Wales. We're staying in the house of a man called Chris. He looks a prototype Green. He's got a light beard and the thin wiry frame of the perpetual cyclist. No sign of a paunch, just a six-pack stomach from a diet of vegetable stir-fries and much mountain biking. From the evidence of the ropes and karabiners in his garage Chris knows a lot about climbing and abseiling. There's a canoe too. Chris works in some capacity at the Centre for Alternative Technology (CAT) in Machynlleth, known affectionately as 'CAT' to CAT people.

We visit CAT after finally leaving the train that spent several eons perambulating gently through the wintry hills under grey skies. Set in an old slate mine, CAT has a hydro-powered cliff railway, lots of solar panels, a community wind turbine, geodesic domes (whatever they are), a straw-bale theatre, an eco-playground and recycled glass tableware.

It's all good, worthy planet-saving stuff. As an eminently unpractical man I could never design anything propelled by water, not even a paper boat. So maybe I'm a cynic for knocking environmentally-aware people simply trying to promote a sustainable non-polluting lifestyle. Yes, everyone at CAT is doing a fantastic job. It's just Chris's alternative loo technology that presents a bit of a problem.

Chris lives with his partner Jane in an old farmhouse that they've bought for the price of a London garage. This sounds a good deal on paper, until you discover that it's, as the estate agents say, in need of some refurbishment. The cottage itself is reached by driving in Chris's Land Rover across a river, up an improbably steep and winding road for three miles and then down a long muddy track. It's perched at the bottom of the valley and at times it does look inviting, when there's a rare burst of sunlight. Chris and Jane are busy turning it into an eco-home. Which means that it doesn't have any tiles on part of the roof. Just a tarpaulin slung over the rafters.

'At least the Oxford Greens have roofs,' I mumble to Nicola.

'Oh shut up, it's lovely. And the insulation will be going in soon and when the roof is finished they're going to have solar panels and a wind turbine.'

It's the coldest weekend of my life. We're staying inside a work in progress. Several of the windowpanes have holes in them. They will be replaced with double glazing one day we're told, but at the moment it's make do and don't mend. Chris is clearly a very hardy (and Hardy-esque) environmentalist – a model of low-impact living.

I'm reminded of an old classic black-and-white TV series, *The Survivors*, which can be dimly remembered from my youth. Nearly all the population had been destroyed by a plague and the few survivors are trying to cannibalise what technology they can still find and construct a new society while growing vegetables and avoiding outlaws. There are no papers here, no TVs, no means of finding out the football results. Civilisation could easily have collapsed in the outside world.

We go for a long walk across muddy hills in a squall and then return to huddle before the log burner in the living room. Several old armchairs lie before a partially collapsed inglenook fireplace. Large pieces of ancient insulating material are hanging precariously above the burner.

We eat toast, hoping the bread will remain warm long enough to thaw fingers now devoid of all tactile sensation. It's all reminiscent of the arrival of Withnail and I at Uncle Monty's cottage in the Lake District.

But my major problem here is not the cold, it's the sanitary arrangements. Green life is starting to seem like a major cistern error. Especially when I discover that the only loo is of the composting variety. Using the compost loo involves defecating into the abyss, and then sprinkling sawdust upon your deposits.

The whole contraption is more than a metre off the ground, meaning you have to climb on top of it and then rest your feet on a piece of wood. It's like some kind of fiendish interrogation device. Less waterboarding, more faeces skimming.

You can't urinate while standing up because the whole structure is so precarious. In some kind of act of feminist revenge, all men have to sit down to pee or retreat into the fields outside. And however much you try not to look down into the pit of doom, some irresistible perverted wish means that you can't help but glance down into the depths – viewing sawdust, horrible bits of scrumpled paper and biodegrading turds.

Small flies retreat into darker quarters of the odorous wooden box. This sewage sludge also contains numerous tiger worms, silently composting our faeces. Chris stands by the compost loo looking down into the depths and admiring his worm's work.

'Greedy buggers, aren't they?' he says cheerily.

They are diminutive tiger worms, admittedly. But they could get bigger. Remember the giant maggots made from condoms that menaced Jon Pertwee in *Doctor Who*? My subconscious registers some forgotten primeval fear of white buttocks being clamped by all sorts of creatures emerging from the dirt.

But at least it's helping me appreciate some of the innovations of modern life. Thomas Crapper was a genius. Defecating into a box of malodorous turds and sawdust was never going to be preferable to the glorious clear water of Crapper's fabulous flushing closet. Perhaps I'm a bad person for not being able to tackle a compost loo. They save countless litres of water, provide fertiliser (although I'm still not sure I'd want to eat crops grown with 'humanure') and are essential in places without sewage systems. Maybe it's because I'm an anally retentive, pathetic wuss, as the Australians might put it. It's just that I've never worked in the Third World or remote islands, or disaster zones and refugee camps, unlike all of Nicola's friends. My whole life has been spent using conventional lavatories. And I never realised just what a luxury they are.

I'm trying to get into this, honestly. Chris and Jane are friendly people and attentive hosts. It's just that they seem oblivious to cold. They even give up their bed for us. And it's the perfect bed for an 'eco-bunny', as Nicola calls her Green friends. Jane has attached four silver birch trunks to each corner of the bed and created a rustic four-poster bed. She's entwined fairy lights among the twigs, creating a sort of *Lord of the Rings* meets *The Woodlanders* ambience.

I'm not sure my mates at football would be that impressed. But as long as I make a big effort to unleash my inner Hobbit then the fairy bed is fine, really. If only Jane and Chris had given the same amount of attention to the window, which looks as if one push would remove the whole crumbling frame from the wall.

The next morning we eat muesli, feet chilling on the stone floor of the kitchen. In order to shower we have to boil the kettle several times and then stand in the bath beneath a bucket with holes in its bottom. In the living room there's a sort of stable door, which leads directly out to the fields and a vista across the hills. As soon as she's up, Nicola opens the top section of this door, ensuring the glorious chill of March frost permeates the room.

She's loving it, and is irritated by my shivering. I suggest a walk among the sheep, hoping it might be warmer outside and on the move.

When we return two of our old Oxford Green chums have colonised the living room. Oliver is lying in a hammock, all booming voice, sure opinions, wild hair and bristly chin. He's wearing a red-check, padded lumberjack shirt and his pouch. He is also the only man I had ever seen lying in a hammock, if we exclude the odd viewing of *South Pacific*.

Sitting in an ancient armchair is bespectacled, woolly-jumpered George Monbiot. I realise that George and Oliver's conversation is as indecipherable to me as my discussions about football must be to Nicola. They mention acronyms in every sentence. Their talk is all of Carmageddon, *Undercurrents*, the Diggers, park-and-ride schemes, food miles and things George said to John Gummer. They're bemoaning the tragedy of the commons and then they mention Enclosure.

'Yes, I've seen the movie, Demi Moore was great,' I declare enthusiastically. They both look a little puzzled.

The morning passes with more Lapsang tea and eco-jargon. I shuffle closer to the wood burner, still wearing my Polartec fleecy jacket, jumper, shirt, T-shirt and thermal vest.

Then it's a group walk, admiring the sensuous curves of the hills (at least that's how Nicola describes them, her inner poet inspired by this arctic expedition). We walk to a waterfall and then admire a set of sustainable wind turbines upon a distant hill. The windmills remind me a little of the effigy the islanders create in *The Wicker Man*. I start to wonder if the Greens sacrifice non-virgin men who write for lad mags, like football and have problems with compost loos in giant wicker turbines.

That evening Chris puts *Bob Dylan's Greatest Hits* on the cassette and 'Blowing in the Wind' has rarely sounded more appropriate. Then he takes off his trousers. Underneath them is another pair.

'Just how many pairs of trousers are you wearing?' I ask.

'Only two and a pair of thermals,' he answers, as if multi-trousering is a completely normal dress code.

If my host is wearing three pairs of trousers then I'll always struggle to be a proper Green. I refuse to live anywhere, however scenic, that requires three pairs of trousers. Never has a return to London's carbon-dinosaur-generated asthma-inducing soup of smog seemed more enticing. Nicola will surely dump me soon; my lack of commitment, and trousers, must be showing.

The evening continues. We cook rice and stir-fry. That's the other thing about Greens. They don't eat enough junk food. The house is stocked with enough pulses and grains to feed a small nation. A return to the composting loo looms and this time I may have to use it.

After dinner we chill, in every sense, over glasses of red wine. Someone asks about my work in London. Chris looks genuinely surprised that someone can earn a living from reviewing *Doctor Who* videos and writing about football, when there's global warming and deforestation to be fought. The fact that I've also just completed co-writing *The Lad Done Bad*, a book on footballers behaving badly, doesn't make my case any more convincing. He's creating certified sustainable energy sources, while I'm watching TV and reading the *Sun*.

'I know it's not saving the planet, or saving trees or Nigerians from exploitation by multinational oil companies, but there's a talent in writing about cult TV in a humorous fashion,' I plead, warmed a little by several glasses of wine, 'Life is made up of pointless but brilliant memories of trivia. That's what makes it great, and I get free videos!'

'He is amusing sometimes,' admits Nicola as if she's discussing an aberrant pony she's about to sell. I still feel a little like a pornographer at an Andrea Dworkin lecture.

Finally, after twenty-four hours of bowel restraint, I have to use the compost loo. Resistance is useless. I feel like Joe Simpson's companion cutting the rope in *Touching the Void*. Relief... The lavatorial deed is done. Nothing leaps out of the loo to attack me. I try to scatter the sawdust without looking down. If nothing else, my turds are now mingling with those of some of the finest minds in the environmental movement.

There's no chance of watching *Match of the Day*, because Chris and Jane's TV can only get one wobbly channel and in any case they only use the TV for videos. When the TV detector van man called they proudly told him that they're among the few people in Britain who don't have to pay for a TV licence, because they genuinely don't use it except for watching videos.

And so it's a big night in watching the fire. Eventually we retreat upstairs to the bedroom. Nicola is unimpressed with my lack of eco-ardour and tells me so. I admit it. I'm not sure that this relationship is, as they say, sustainable, and nor is she. There's only one place to go.

The fairy lights sparkle in our tree-bed. We snuggle together for warmth beneath the blankets and duvets, still wearing our thermal underwear. Wind whistles through a broken windowpane. A spider crawls across the wall. The tarpaulin over the rafters flutters in the wind.

Turning towards Nicola, I mumble, 'I guess we'll always have Powys.'

*

There's trouble when we return to London.

'You were pathetic, a bit of cold never did anyone any harm.'

'I'm sorry, Nicola. I was exhausted, I've been trying to write a book to a deadline. They are good people. But it was the three pairs of trousers... I guess I'm just the urban space-man, baby. I can't cope with somewhere where it's 27 miles to get a newspaper.'

'And we don't go away enough.'

'What?'

'We don't go away enough!'

'Are you joking? You're always arranging things. Oh no, we haven't been anywhere this year apart from Oxford, London, Wales, Dinan, Penzance, Yorkshire, Hertfordshire, King's Lynn, the Lake District, Edinburgh, York, Glasgow and about fifty other places!'

'But it's me who has to do the organising...'

'I would, it's just that you organise everything first!'

I write for *Loaded*. So it's natural to be a loafer. But maybe she's right. Her life might be driven, mine is PR-driven. When I sit at home PRs ring up at short notice and within hours or days I'm at the theatre, a launch or on a press trip to Pisa. Things just happen.

'*And* you organise your life around football!'

That's it. She's gone too far, I can feel my rage building.

'Do you know how difficult it is to organise your life

around football matches? ' I holler dramatically. 'Do you know how difficult it is when Sky keeps altering the dates and kick-off times? Do you know how hard it is to add extra Coca-Cola Cup ties to the existing home fixtures, and how the FA Cup draw isn't made until January and how you have to make allowances for replays and possible away trips and the fact you might enjoy a bit of groundhopping and pencil in the FA Cup Final and the Coca-Cola Cup Final just in case and allow for postponements because of inclement weather... careful, Nicola you're smiling.'

'Have you ever thought about how much carbon you use travelling to football?'

'I use the tube, mainly. Well, unless we get into Europe and then there might have to be some flights. Still, we can do a deal. If you agree to tolerate football I'll try to be Greener.'

'Really?'

'Yes, really. And I've organised a special trip for you tonight, all the way up the stairs to the bedroom. I'm afraid there are no fairy lights on the bed yet. But it is relatively warm... and we do have a roof.'

And so we carry on our relationship between London and Oxford through 1995. Nicola phones at unearthly hours like seven in the morning to say that the fritillaries in the meadows are looking beautiful in the mist. She busies herself working with the Forest Management Foundation, sending endless faxes to the Solomons and Papua New Guinea, going to meetings, freelancing and entering a series of essay-writing competitions. She tries to persuade me to enter a few, but the odds are so slim it hardly seems worthwhile. And now I'm taking part in a radical Green counter-offensive. We're on St George's Hill being buzzed by a low-flying police helicopter. Nicola wanted me to be Greener, so now I'm on the front line, dodging golf balls and choppers. It's partly the fault of Billy Bragg. He wrote a song called 'World Turned Upside Down' in which he told us that in 1649 on St George's Hill the Diggers attempted to cultivate untilled land before the army came to cut them down, or something like that. And if Billy wrote a song about it then it must have some rock 'n'roll credibility and so I'm there with an elite force of Greens.

The Diggers were led by Gerrard Winstanley, a religious geezer who thought that Jesus Christ was the head Leveller and that the Church should adhere to all that 'The meek shall inherit the Earth' stuff. So now the Oxford environmentalists are returning to the site of the Diggers' original action, attempting to plant organic vegetables on what is now an exclusive housing estate and private golf club in Surrey.

I'm becoming more familiar with changing eco-fashions. In the sixties and seventies it was all Cat Stevens's 'Where Do The Children Play' and communes and squats and copies of *Small is Beautiful*, *Gaia* and *Silent Spring*. Back in the late 1980s everyone was worried about the hole in the ozone layer and CFCs in fridges. The nineties has seen attacks on road building and now it's hip to do guerilla gardening. A group called Earth First is keen on digging up patches of motorways and putting plants on them. Now we're all becoming modern-day Diggers. When I visited Australia, a root was a euphemism for sex, not something you stuck in the ground. Now I'm stuck in some sort of industrial evolution. We're leaving the city to reclaim our jobs in the fields. Not that I'm worried about my ability to stick an onion into the ground; just the fact that I might soon be buying *Farmers Weekly* instead of *Q*.

A dozen or so Greens, armed with trowels and plants, manage to enter the golf club's private road without too much difficulty. Nicola is wearing a huge scarf and Peruvian hat, with long dangly bits drawn down over her ears, and is carrying a small garden fork. I'm reminded of the Knights Who Say Ni! in *Monty Python and the Holy Grail* and their demands for a shrubbery. Equipped for horticultural mayhem, we'd be just the people to steal it for them.

'Make sure you hold the flower pots upright,' Nicola whispers.

St George's Hill is a horrible place. Gated houses surrounded by a course for the world's most boring sport. It's where Terry and June would go if they won the Pools.

But now the horticultural revolution is imminent. We're stalking our way past tees and fairways and bunkers. 'If anyone asks us questions, we're looking for golf balls,' commands Oliver, in the fashion of a Green Andy McNab. He looks purposeful, no doubt ready to defend himself with a rolled-up copy of the *Independent* should he be apprehended by security guards.

We drift through woods and past pairs of golfers. A golfer eventually challenges us and Oliver replies 'We're looking for golf balls!' Luckily his received pronunciation appears to win us some time. Did the Dam Busters feel like this? We're deep in enemy territory now – the heartland of *Daily Mail* readers.

We carry on skulking in the undergrowth looking for our fellow 20th-century Diggers. But then there's the drone of a helicopter engine. It appears overhead, hovering. It feels like we're in the Vietnam War. We run for the safety of the woods, wondering if we're soon to be strafed by machine-gun fire as Wagner plays over the soundtrack. Maybe we could throw golf balls at it. We embark upon a strategic retreat, trowels and plants in hand.

At the gatehouse to the golf club a uniformed security man is surprisingly friendly. 'We had reports there were stalkers outside Cliff Richard's house,' he explains in a mystified tone.

'Nicola, you're just a Devil Woman,' I tell her.

The ignominy. Being mistaken for a Green Digger was tolerable – but a Cliff Richard fan? Gerrard Winstanley would have scarpered immediately if it had happened to him.

It's not been as dramatic as a Greenpeace action. But it was my first outing as an activist, and I realise I felt kind of proud to have carried a plant pot into action. We were there, and we were prepared to dig, and it took a police helicopter before we threw in the trowel.

But was this real commitment? And if so, to what? To the Green cause, or to my Green girlfriend?

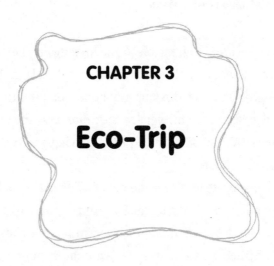

CHAPTER 3

Eco-Trip

'I'm the joint winner of the David Thomas Prize!' exclaims Nicola, tearing open a newly-arrived letter.

'Great, brilliant, but who does David Thomas play for?'

'No you idiot, it's the prize I entered...'

'The one I said was a waste of time? Well, I'm a complete durr brain. You're a genius. Let me give you a hug. What's the prize?'

'My essay gets published in the *Financial Times* and there's a prize of £5,000 that I can use for an FMF project to promote sustainable forestry in the Solomon Islands! Isn't that brilliant. And I get to go to the Solomons again!'

It turns out that David Thomas was a *Financial Times* journalist who was killed while on a foreign assignment; his family set up the prize in his honour. This year it's being awarded to whoever wrote the best piece about 'development issues'.

Nicola's written a great piece on logging in the Solomon Islands and it's won the prize and I'm really pleased for her. Although, of course, this may not bode well for our relationship. The last time she went to the Solomons she stayed for two years. Will she want me to go? And what good would Pete May be in a canoe?

We celebrate and over the next few days Nicola finalises her plans. She wants to take a study group of Solomon Islanders to a project in Papua New Guinea that has already been certified by the Forest Stewardship Council (FSC) as practising sustainable forestry. What's sustainable forestry exactly? She tries to explain, and it seems it's where you tell the bloke with the chainsaw to chop down only selected trees. Nicola's ability to organise new projects is always surprising to a man like me who struggles to order his sock drawer. She keeps saying that I should open a credit card account with the Co-operative Bank because it doesn't invest in the arms trade, but I haven't even managed to do that yet.

Nicola is still besotted with the Solomon Islands. She plans to take a flight there, via Australia, pick up her islanders and then take them on to PNG. After that she's been offered a job helping with the administration of the FSC-certified project somewhere in the remotest bush of PNG. She's going to be away for five months and everyone agrees long-distance relationships don't work. She says that I can come and live with her there if I want. Or if I don't, then that's fine too.

'What do you think I should do?' I ask my mate John in the pub.

'Women don't ever mean what they say,' says John, sagely. 'When they attack you for not squeezing the bottom of the toothpaste tube you know it's really for something else. So if she says you don't have to go then it probably means you do.'

'But I'm not sure I want to leave everything. I've got a book to write and columns to write, I'm getting published in *Time Out*, *Loaded*, *Midweek* and *FC* and everything's going really well,' I sigh into my pint of IPA. 'And I'm useless in the heat.'

'Well, maybe you should compromise. Agree to stay with her for a few weeks. That way at least you've tried it.'

'Yeah, good idea. That way it's a holiday and not an exile. And there might be loads of models from James and Tim's photo-shoots throwing themselves at me while she's away. Women who wear make-up. And don't mind if I eat take-aways and turn the heating on. Do you want the same again?'

Should I be so reluctant to leave Britain? My travel experience is mainly in safe English-speaking countries such as Australia and New Zealand. Living in places that didn't have bars or Sky TV is, to be honest, quite terrifying. So Nicola and I end up agreeing that she'll go to the Solomons first and then I'll fly out to visit her for three weeks.

We go to the David Thomas Prize ceremony at the *FT*. It's

full of people who know about development stuff and I feel proud of Nicola as I consume their white wine and kettle crisps and chat to previous winner Nick Clegg.

It does occur to me that soon we'll be flying to the other side of the world and emitting tons of carbon during this tree-saving sojourn, but surely it's worth it to save the rainforest? Blimey. I'm in danger of thinking like a Green.

A week later I travel with Nicola to Heathrow and kiss her goodbye at the departure gates as she heads for the Solomons. After two years with her, I'm suddenly alone in London, living the life of the *Loaded* lothario. But it's not like the stories I've been subbing. Isn't London full of babes? Well, no, not in N5. Life continues as previously, working till late most nights filing copy, attending PR dos, but it all feels a little lonelier. Nicola sends faxes to me and phones; I send her the news about Hugh Grant. He's been arrested by the police after being caught asking prostitute Divine Brown for a blow job in LA and girlfriend Liz Hurley isn't happy. He'll surely be number one in *Loaded*'s Platinum Rogues, a monthly top ten of bad behaviour. He looks suitably embarrassed in the police mug shots. But at least Hugh has been tested by temptation. Single life doesn't seem quite as good as in the lad mags.

My columns are written in advance and in August 1995 it's time to fly to the Solomons. It takes three days, via a night sleeping in a Brisbane hotel. After a month apart we embrace in the stifling heat of Henderson Field airport on Guadalcanal. It's good to see her; maybe I've been missing her ethical monitoring of my life. And maybe, soon, I'll be able to match the Oxford Greens and their tales of PNG with my own stories of the SI.

But first I have to cope with one of my main phobias about travelling to equatorial states – my body's capacity for exuding large amounts of sweat. You don't want to smell my sandals. Nicola has arranged a gentle introduction, a three-night stay at a beachside resort north of the capital, Honiara. It's undoubtedly a beautiful country. Coconuts on the beach, white sand, blue sea and all that. Everyone moves slowly because of the heat and the Solomon Islanders seem even more laid back than Bryan Ferry after a three-martini lunch. The pace of life is pleasing. Everything runs on 'Solomon time', which means things get done when people turn up. All times are moveable. It's almost as if the *Loaded* editorial team is running an entire country. Another plus is that although hardly any houses have televisions, everyone knows Premiership football. Big matches can be watched at a bar in Honiara and luckily I've arrived with a stock of football magazines such as *90 Minutes* where I'd done some freelance subbing. They're like hard currency in the Solomons and Nicola's local friends are very pleased to receive them.

We sit drinking beers in a shaded bar by the beach and it all seems ideal – at least until nightfall. As ever, we clash over sleeping arrangements in our beach hut. At home, she wants to sleep with the window open. Here, she feels 'trapped' by the mosquito net over our bed. So she removes it. I soon realise that her body is cold-blooded and possibly reptilian. Mine is hot, sweaty and deliciously salty. Mosquitoes adore it, and spend the night feasting on my flesh. In the morning I'm covered in itchy bites; Nicola is untouched. For her, I'm a one-man mosquito repellant. But for my course of anti-malarial tablets, I'd surely have died a lingering death in the fashion of some Victorian missionary.

After three days at the beach we return to Honiara, staying in a local guest house. From there we take a walk to Bloody Ridge, so named because of the thousands of soldiers who perished there in fighting between US and Japanese troops during the Second World War. We have lunch with Nicola's friend ML, a journalist with *The Australian* newspaper who's researching a book on the civil war in the nearby island of Bougainville. I'm not sure what my own field of research is, although ML does supply some useful information about a riot following an offside goal in the Guadalcanal/Malaita Island derby match. Aggro is universal, it seems.

We take a motorised canoe across the waters to the volcanic island of Savo. As we arrive a group of Solomon Islanders in traditional dress are performing tribal dances. Is this for me? Erm, no, a group of Swedish tourists are politely applauding. Nicola can speak Solomon pidgin (the English/

Portuguese hybrid that developed when Europeans first visited the islands), and this helps negotiate our passage. She introduces me to several useful phrases such as *'What kinda Mary u tu ya? You makem me karange for good now!'* which translates as 'What kind of woman are you, you make me permanently crazy!' – sentiments that had often occurred to me in London.

We spend the night with a local family in a traditional hut made of leaves, sleeping on plaited leaf mats. The local taboos take some getting used to; such as women not being allowed to show their thighs (thighs matters?) and the fact that at nightfall the entire village goes down to the sea to wash and, if necessary, go to the loo on the beach. Is there no lavatorial indignity Nicola won't put me through? At first I think we're supposed to try to defecate in waist-high waves. When I discover it's on the beach in the dark, that's even worse. The tide is meant to wash everything away, but even so, group pooing is a little over-familiar for this Englishman abroad. Maybe if I don't eat too much there will be no need for a loo trip until Honiara.

The next morning George, a local guide, takes us on a guided walk to the volcano, along with his dog. He carries a huge bush knife and chops away foliage in the casual manner of the Solomon Islander. George strides effortlessly through river valleys and then up a steep sharp ridge towards the volcanic peak. Dense rainforest is all around us. George stops to show us a snake sitting on a vine, just as I'm about to put my hand on it. He yomps up ever-steeper hills in flip-flops and a vest with the air of a man on a Sunday stroll.

My outfit is an entirely appropriate pair of luminous green surfing shorts, as modelled by English lager louts abroad, a navy-blue Fred Perry T-shirt, trainers and a baseball cap. Soon poor Fred Perry is saturated with sweat later analysed as containing 90 per cent beer. Here is my personal Bloody Ridge. My thoughts turn to the Second World War battles fought here and how hellish it all must have been. The heat is relentless and Nicola and I find ourselves drinking copious amounts of water. They don't train you how to be an explorer at comprehensive school or, indeed, during days at *Loaded*. It's worth the effort though, when we finally reach the summit and find a plateau of smouldering sulphur, boiling streams and hot geysers.

Our next trip is a flight to the island of Bellona in a tiny twelve-person light aircraft. We fly over idyllic islands covered in coconut palms and surrounded by sand and coral reefs. The islands are only a metre or so above sea level and the huts are built on stilts. 'They'll be the first to go when the sea level rises,' says Nicola. If it's true, if the sea level really is rising because of human-created global warming, then this is the consequence of Westerners sitting in centrally-heated flats wearing just a T-shirt in winter. Other people's homes became obliterated.

We fly on, over taller, conical islands. They're still covered in rainforest, but from the air, you can see the ugly red scars of logging roads. Nicola tells me of islands where clear-felling has occurred. Without the protection of the rainforest, the fertile soils leech into the sea, swamping the coral reefs and ruining the villagers' fishing grounds.

Bellona's airport is a stretch of grass. It's all rather pleasing after Heathrow – and the whole island has turned out to greet the plane, a vital source of supplies. The terminal building is one open-air stall selling instant coffee. It's windier than on Guadalcanal, and the welcome breeze keeps the mosquitoes away.

Nicola has booked us into a cave with a double bed. The cave doubles as a hotel room. We're met by John and Nita, the owners of the cave hotel, and several of their children. They're hugely hospitable throughout our stay. First we walk for an hour through the trees. John points out various giant spiders sitting in huge webs spanning coconut trunks. His son Edmond shins up a gigantic coconut palm in roughly two seconds and presents us with a fresh coconut.

Reaching some cliffs, we descend steep coral paths and find our cave, standing some ten metres above an angry sea. John and his family own the cave and use it to shelter in whenever cyclones hit the island. Eventually he had the idea of turning it into a hotel. It's certainly more salubrious than some of my short-life addresses have been. A double bed rests under a coral overhang, with a tarpaulin above it to keep off any drips from the rocks. A rock plateau in front of the bed area forms a natural balcony overlooking the sea. It has several chairs and a shelf of books. Our view is of white breakers. We can glimpse a bay below where thousands of green coconut crabs – capable of crushing a coconut with a squeeze from one immense pincer – congregate during their breeding cycle. At night the room is lit by candles resting in natural rock shelves.

The cave has a 'drop loo', a Tardis-like cabinet in the corner of the plateau area. It's basically a bog seat set over a twenty-foot drop. Again I can't look down it, for fear of testicle-crushing pincers grabbing my privates. What if the coconut crabs climb the rocks? Unfortunately I'm old enough to remember The Macra Terror, a *Doctor Who* adventure from the Patrick Troughton era, where giant crab-like creatures menace a human colony, probably having infiltrated through the sewage system.

Toilet terrors aside, our nights are comfortable and indeed, romantic. Candlelight flickering on coral, stars flickering over the sea. I'm a tanned cave man in a Fred Perry shirt. John takes me through a tiny hole into the rock into an adjoining bat cave. We're covered in slimy mud. His torch reveals hundreds of the things, upside down.

The food is wonderful. Nita, John and various children arrive as part of 'cave service', carrying cassava, yams, taro, sweet potatoes, fish and many other delicacies, all stored in traditional baskets made from the fronds of coconut palms. For three days we chill. John sits and talks about UK politics and religion; his son Edmond is very impressed to receive a copy of *90 Minutes*. Nita and her daughters paint a tattoo of a bonito (a tuna) on my arm, the symbol of their island. It looks good with the shell necklace Nicola has bought me. My life is all getting a bit Robinson Crusoe, but without constant threats to our survival. At least until our final night.

Nicola thought it would be romantic to spend my birthday in a cave when she organised our trip. For all our differences, she thought it worth making a real effort for the world's worst adventurer. A man whose foot odour could probably finish off an entire indigenous species. She's bought a pair of turtle-shell rings ('it's endangered so we mustn't tell anyone,' she warns). The ring is a nice burnished brown colour. But then I start to wonder if this is some huge token of commitment. A sign of some sort of mental engagement. Maybe it means we're already married on the Solomons? No, no, it's just a ring, that's all. I think.

We spend a mellow morning brewing real coffee on the camp stove. I read Norman Mailer's *The Naked and the Dead*. Nicola is sitting in her lava lava (the local version of a sarong) reading up on PNG forestry. I am finally relaxing in this laid-back eco-friendly sort of loafing. We have lunch and then lie in bed away from the sun. We're making love, listening to the breakers, when 'SNAKE!!!!! SNAKE!!!!! It's up there! DO SOMETHING!!!!'

What, a trouser snake? No something worse. Bizarrely, a snake is dangling from the top of the cave's arch.

'It's a sea snake – they're poisonous!!! ' screams Nicola, whose worst phobia is close encounters with either snakes or worms.

'OK. Stand back, keep calm, don't panic, ' I mutter uselessly, hopping from foot to foot, wondering if I should throw a flip-flop at it. For God's sake! What do you do when confronted with a snake? I try to remember how they coped with Ka the sneaky snake in *The Jungle Book*. Captain James T Kirk would, of course, roll over on the ground and then fire off his phaser. But I'm armed only with a plastic sandal and am totally useless. The snake falls from the roof and slides towards a fold in the rock.

At this moment, Nita and John arrive with more food, and seem unfazed by the slippery visitor.

'It must have been dropped by a seagull, that's the only way it could could have got out of the sea,' says Nicola, suddenly lucid in all aspects of snake lore.

Our Solomon Island friends take a calm approach to the problem. First Nita throws rocks at the snake until it disappears into a crevice. John waits, ponders and then returns with a kettle of boiling water and a tube. He pours the boiling water down the tube into the crevice and claims to have killed the snake. It's not exactly a World Wildlife Fund-approved way of removing a snake, but it makes Nicola feel a little better. We spend an uneasy final night, wondering whether the snake is really dead and what else might be crawling through the coral passages.

We're up at six the next morning to walk to the airport with, seemingly, the whole island there for the plane's arrival – only it's four hours late, as the plane had been chartered to move a body, a common practice in the Solomons. Maybe the unfortunate cadaver was another victim of flying sea snakes.

Our hosts have been superb, it's a beautiful place, but it's not right for me, not as a place to live. The Greens speak lovingly of wildernesses and the untapped knowledge of indigenous peoples. Being hunted by mosquitoes, coconut crabs and sea snakes has left me desiring nothing more than the iffy cigarette sellers and gridlocked sprawl of the snake-free Holloway Road. Out there in the other world where they have TV, Kermit the frog is singing about how it's not easy being Green. I know just what he means.

We continue to island hop. Munda has a bit more lad credibility, as it's full of Second World War memorabilia. Rusting troop carriers still lie in the sea and the road the Japanese built to the airport is pot-holed but still intact. We visit a 73-year-old islander called Alfred who has a Second World War relic shed. He reminisces about his old English commanding officer, 'Mister Bolton' and Nicola takes a snap of me wearing a *Loaded* T-shirt, grenade in hand, US helmet on head.

We arrive at Choiseul Island only to be attacked by swarms of mosquitoes, forcing me to repel them with Rambo-esque towel attacks. It's a further hour-long canoe ride to visit Chris and Maggie, Australian and English development workers. We stay in the old hospital next to their house, and Nicola has bad vibes about dead souls around us. In their traditional Solomon-style house Maggie and Chris have solar panels and are self-sufficient in energy. Once again, we shower standing under a bucket filled with hot water. For some reason Nicola is under the impression that I can snorkel. Chris takes us out over the coral reef. My swimming is equal to my snake-catching abilities. I flounder and discover just how sharp coral is. The next day is spent indoors, clad in a lava lava, countless plasters on my torn legs.

'But you said you could snorkel!' exclaims Nicola.

'No, I said I once did an hour's diving off the Barrier Reef in Australia. That was OK. We had oxygen tanks. I've never bloody snorkelled in my life and I can't do it.'

Ernest Hemingway I am not. Helping indigenous people fight loggers clearly requires what Thomas Gradgrind would term 'an eminently practical man' – and I am an eminently unpractical one.

We miss our first return flight back to Honiara because Nicola refuses to board the small plane in a thunderstorm, as she is sure it's going to be struck by lightning. But rule one of a successful relationship is to never question your partner's emotional intelligence. Or emotional stupidity if you're worried you'll never leave the Pacific.

After a further day's wait we finally return to Honiara. We stay with friends of Nicola's, a lovely hospitable local family and their *wantoks* (extended family). In one final dashing of my lad credibility, they tell me I look very like Prince Andrew.

On my last day in the Solomons we visit Matanikau Falls. Nicola has told me to be careful not to fall from the rocks at the top of the waterfall – one man stumbled a few years ago and his body was found two miles downstream. Oh, and there are crocodiles in the river.

After a sweltering walk we take extra care on the rocks. We view the falls from a safe distance, climb down to a lower area and relax by a rock pool. The surface is level here and a mere handful of centimetres above the pool, so there's obviously no danger now. That's until my sandal somehow slips on an apparently solid rock and my body is propelled through the humid air and plunged straight into the rock pool. Cold water surrounds my pathetic form as I'm completely immersed. Then from underwater my body emerges like some Arthurian apparition, holding my sodden Canon Sure Shot camera above my head. It's whirring uncontrollably, the film is rewinding in demented fashion, and the flash bulb is going off. The camera hasn't appreciated its dunking. Nicola is laughing uncontrollably, clearly not appreciating how close to death I've come.

'I told you not to fall!' she chortles.

'It was my sandal! Look, I'm hurt!'

Desperately I swim the metre to the edge of the pool and clamber out. My camera refuses to work and the film is probably now useless. My right foot has hit a rock and is missing a small square of skin. Maybe it's an inept explorer's equivalent to a bullet wound.

Luckily, I'm departing these humid and dangerous parts that night, returning to London. Nicola's flying on to PNG with her team of fact-finding Solomon Island community foresters, and then staying for a further three months.

' I love you,' she says, at the airport.

'Even when I'm falling in waterfalls?'

'Even then.'

'I love you too.'

What am I saying? Has the soaking affected the lad side of my brain? She'll be working on an isolated project in the bush. And they'll probably ask her to stay longer. And she won't be able to say no because she loves the tropics. And there's bound to be some hunky forestry-type man involved in the project who'll impress her with his knowledge of tropical hardwoods.

'Come on, you'd better go through.'

'Bye, I'll see if I can salvage the film.'

The flight to Brisbane is at the horrible time of ten past two in the morning. Then it's a six o'clock internal flight to Sydney. I book into a youth hostel on arrival and immediately place my sodden clothes from the waterfall debacle into the YHA's washing machine. Sleep can come later. The sweat-encrusted clothes go through their cycle and I remove them, only to find my trousers still have my camera in them. If it hasn't been destroyed by its saturation in the Matanikau Falls it certainly has now.

Exhaustedly, I stare at my pile of laundry and my sodden camera and think that I've failed. Failed to be a global citizen. I'll never be able to mention 'PNG' or 'SI' at Oxford Green parties or talk about 'development issues'. Development issues to me are when your pictures don't come back from Boots because they've been immersed in a waterfall, not anything to do with saving the planet.

Foreign languages are too difficult, and I don't want to seek wilderness or be like indigenous people. My girlfriend wants to save the rainforests and that's good, but I need my urban space, my consumer durables and an open pub.

Looking at my ruined camera, it seems that my flirtation with the Greener side of life may be at an end. It seems my sodden relationship may be over too.

CHAPTER 4

The Cold War

Back in London my work life shifts into place. Columns to catch up with, launches to attend, commissions to be written, subbing shifts to be done.

Nicola and I communicate mainly by fax. Occasionally I manage to ring her in PNG and her voice has changed; it's suddenly all relaxed instead of full of energy. Her boss Max keeps a wallaby and an emu as pets, as you do. She's way out in the bush, her lodge has leaf roofs and open walls instead of windows. Every night she says there's the noise of insects and animals all around her. 'It's like sleeping in a rainforest,' she tells me. At least her scope for meeting other men is limited. She's isolated and a long way from Port Moresby, where it's too dangerous for a woman to walk out alone at night.

Perhaps I should visit her in PNG if I can find the cash. Or maybe I should make an effort to appear Greener. Perhaps my videos of *Men Behaving Badly* might help. There's one episode where Tony hears that Deborah likes people who want to help others. He's so desperate to impress Debs that he pretends to develop an altruistic streak, working for charity, helping out in old people's homes. No, that will never work. Nicola would never believe it if I suddenly joined Earth First.

But after two months she suddenly announces that she's returning home. And she plans to come and live in her London flat with me. She gave up her room in Oxford before leaving for the Pacific and has now decided to move back to London. More than that, she has decided that she thinks we do have what it takes to make a serious relationship. No more Frisbee playing with the Oxford Greens. We are an official couple. I feel a wave of relief, followed quickly by several smaller waves, all tinged with something pretty close to panic. Isn't commitment something I expect to see on the football field?

I meet her at the airport. She's looking brown and slimmer and for once she's not wearing her exhaust-stained red Gore-Tex.

'So you were missing me?' I ask hopefully as we hug at arrivals.

'No, Pete, my visa ran out.'

'Oh.'

'And I don't love PNG, I love the Solomons.'

Show me a man who can contemplate cohabitation without fear and I will show you a liar. What if she wants a flowery duvet cover? No, she won't, not Nicola. Or fills the bathroom with make-up? She won't do that either.

But I do know she likes to have baths in the dark surrounded by candles. In Upper Street there's enough candle shops to keep her going in perpetuity, which is worrying. What is it about women and candles? And why don't they want to see their bodies when they're in the bath? How do they cut their toenails, eh? If I then use her water (she likes this as it's a good use of resources, although I'm not so sure) she gets cross if I blow her candles out and turn on the light. It's all very illogical.

Before she has time to fully unpack, we're away for Christmas at her mum's and then we spend New Year's Eve in Wiltshire. The parents of Thomas, the maker of *Undercurrents* videos, have a place there. We're accompanied by 15 Oxford Green types, people with names like Hux. We play charades and eat communal meals of vegetarian chilli and baked potatoes.

On New Year's Day 1996 we're awakened by the loud mooing of cattle outside. That morning we travel to Avebury to look at the standing stones. They're fantastic today, shrouded in mist, mysterious and, well, all stoney. Like all proper men, I love standing stones. But not in the manner of the Greens, who caress them lovingly and feel electro-magnetic forces and vibes from beneath the earth.

Were the stone circles for religious ceremonies or just big raves? Or more likely something that could encourage a huge collective effort, like sport? After all, there is an avenue of stones that leaves Avebury and leads to the man-made Silbury Hill. In fact the flat top of Silbury Hill, Britain's version of the Pyramids, looks an ideal spot for a presentation to be made to the winner of the Avebury and District versus Beaker People Challenge Cup.

We retreat into the village pub and listen to 'Zombie' by the Cranberries on the jukebox. After a couple of pints I begin to wonder if in Neolithic times they had stones protestors chanting 'No more stones!' and claiming that we had quite enough stone circles already and in fact Avebury was a site of special scientific interest. Maybe inside Silbury Hill was a gigantic network of tunnels where the protestors hid to prevent the extension of the avenue to meet up with the Ridgeway bypass?

My first night's sleep of 1996 is disturbed by the sound of an American anthropologist and shamen speaking loudly on the landing. He's telling an eco-hippy that he can't sleep because of the dead bodies he's sensed are buried beneath this house. I contemplate adding his body to the collection of dead souls apparently beneath our feet.

It's back to London and serious coupledom. Compromises have to be made. But mainly, it seems, by me.

The bedroom is the first area of dispute. Nicola has spotted my radio alarm clock, with digital figures showing the time.

'You can't have that by the bed!' she announces.

'Why not?'

'It's full of electro-magnetic radiation. It will give you cancer if it's so close to your head.'

'Is that something from the *Ecologist* or *Resurgence*? You've been reading too many eco-scare stories. Anyway, I've had it since I was at university...'

'I don't care, it's going!'

'Oh no it isn't! It's my oldest friend... and it never asks me to light candles in the bedroom!'

Eventually we compromise and I place the radio alarm on the floor, a metre away from the bed with the numbers turned away from us – thus rendering it 90 per cent useless in terms of being able to wake up and see the time with my contact lens-free eyes.

Nicola insists on leaving the bedroom window partially open all night, even in winter. 'You live longer if you have fresh air!' she beams, sounding more than ever like Flora from *Cold Comfort Farm* organising Seth and co.

One inadvertent side effect of this fresh air policy is an alarming plague of moths in our wardrobe on the landing and in our bedroom drawers. These winged asylum seekers take grateful advantage of the lack of all border controls. There's little chance of being a woolly-jumpered intellectual here, as the contents of our drawers soon disintegrate.

'It's not wild moths that lay eggs in the drawers,' chides Nicola.

'Well, someone bloody has. Can't we just blitz them with pesticide?'

'No, we'll just have to use cedar wood moth balls...'

Heat, starring Robert de Niro and Al Pacino, is a big hit at the movies. But heat is certainly not a major player in our flat. Nicola soon has her reluctant Green boyfriend placing silver foil behind the radiators. 'It'll reflect the heat back into the room,' she tells me. This is of course dependent on the central heating actually being turned on – and it rarely is. Nicola gleefully turns the thermostat down to zero, or stands over me while I set the timer, ensuring we only have a minimum period of heat in the early mornings and evenings.

'Just wear another jumper if you're cold!' she demands.

'I can't, they're full of moths!'

'Oh for goodness sake! We have to cut our carbon emissions and half of those come from things we can directly control, like household heating , driving and flying. Just put them on!'

And so I take to wearing deeply unfashionable holey jumpers from the Shetland Isles and Iceland. It makes me think of one of my adolescent heroes, Elvis Costello. Everything she says really does mean less than zero.

We certainly save on burning unsustainable carbon-emitting gas. Even though we both work from home we're not allowed any central heating in the daytime, not even for lunch. Occasionally Nicola goes out for the day and I furtively turn on the heating for an hour, judging when she'll be back and whether the radiators will have cooled enough to avoid suspicion, feeling as guilty as a man playing a pornographic video while his partner is away.

It's not the warmest of flats, even with heating. We're on the third and fourth floors of a Victorian house. The bedrooms are in the old attic and have sloping ceilings. A thin layer of plaster and roof slates keep the rain off our bed, but do little in terms of insulation. Several small cracks have opened up in the external walls. The insurance company thinks we might have subsidence and its surveyor has put studs in the walls to monitor any movement.

When you look at the windows of the living room from the street they're disturbingly crooked. The glass in the sash windows rattles worryingly whenever the wind blows and fierce draughts sweep through gaps in the crumbling woodwork of the window frames. Eventually we screw plastic sheets over them, but it has little effect on the general temperature. Probably because Nicola still insists on 'airing' the upstairs rooms each morning by leaving the windows open.

Things must be bad because we go to stay with Chris and Jane in Wales and their house feels warmer than ours. The roof is now on and they've installed central heating. They've repaired the inglenook fireplace and the wood burner is much more effective. It's actually starting to feel quite homely. And now they have central heating they don't appear scared to use it.

Meanwhile I'm suffering the open windows and the lack of central heating, which are keeping me in a state of near-permanent dormancy. When Nicola is in Oxford I zap the thermostat up as high as I want. The bills might be bigger, but for once I'm warm.

My new life reminds me of the opening scenes of *Withnail and I*. Each morning I get up, stumble down the stairs in my thick dressing gown and secretly turn on the rings on the cooker in a desperate attempt to get warm. If Nicola arrives in the kitchen I can always claim to be about to heat up our organic porridge.

As in *Withnail*, it's tempting to wear my coat indoors. Why has my head gone numb? Perhaps, like Withnail, I'll soon be getting up and immediately reaching for the dregs of last night's wine, then standing in my underpants and coat desperately massaging Deep Heat into my body with rubber-gloved hands. Or maybe I'll be drinking lighter fuel?

But we are not struggling thespians waiting for calls from our agents; we're the cold-hearted pioneers of something called voluntary simplicity. To paraphrase Withnail, we have renounced the thing that other members of society class as their right; heated indoor space.

Should I leave? Or seek counselling with Relate? The therapy sessions might be interesting.

'Tell me Pete, how do you feel?'

'I just feel cold.'

'Emotionally, yes, I understand, a lot of men have this problem...'

'No, I just feel cold and she's too cold too... in fact her toes are tinged with permafrost every time she gets into bed.'

But at least we spend a lot of time in bed together. It is, after all, the warmest place in the house. Once I spent my life in pursuit of hot dates – now it's just a relentless search for body heat.

'What do I get out of this relationship?' I find myself mumbling in the cold as Nicola reads her copy of *The Indigenous Voice* (Vol 1).

'At least I'm low maintenance. You never have to buy me clothes or say 'No your bum doesn't look big in that'. Or say I'm beautiful,' she answers.

'I did say you were beautiful – in 1993, I remember it. And your bum never looks big in anything. You're far too busy to ever get fat. And I know my bum won't look big in anything as I have to keep moving around so much to keep warm.'

The only time she'll allows me to put the heating on for more than two hours at night is on Tuesdays, when we have guests round for her 'Chooseday soirées'. Her energy has to be admired. She's trying to turn London into Oxford.

'DIY culture is the post-modern thing, we should all be making our own entertainment,' she says. And so each week a person is invited to give a talk to selected guests over Chardonnay and nibbles. Amazingly lots of her friends, and even a few of mine, turn up. Nicola gives a talk on ecological

design and I do *Doctor Who* (with a video screening of Jon
Pertwee classic 'The Dæmons') and the Neolithic monuments
of Avebury (postulating it was all a giant sports stadium). We
have author Anne Coddington speaking on women in football, Oxford Green Hugh Warwick on pangolins and Nicola's
brother's mate Charles on a bluffer's guide to wine.

'Nicola, I think you've created our very own Bloomsbury
set,' I tell her, still a little shocked to be hosting a salon, 'You're
the Virginia Woolf of Highbury.'

She is forever working at some project or another. At one
stage Nicola decides that she's going to give everyone in the
street window boxes to green the neighbourhood. She manages to get a grant from Arsenal's Gunners Fund to pay for the
window boxes and fill them with compost and red geraniums
('because they go on forever'). She then knocks at every door
seeing who wants them and astonishingly the street is soon
full of her flowers.

Before meeting Nicola my idea of a shopping trip was to
visit HMV or the Virgin Megastore, with maybe a yearly venture into Shelly's in Covent Garden to buy a new pair of black
Doctor Martens shoes. But now I'm in strange and unfamil-
iar territory.

'We'll have to go to Westbourne Grove and look at Planet
Organic,' Nicola says enthusiastically.

'Is that a science fiction bookshop like Forbidden Planet?'
I ask.

'No you idiot, it's London's first organic superstore. It'll be great. People are starting to get the message about pesticides at last.'

And so we trek to that well-known vale of pastoral dreaming, Westbourne Grove. Planet Organic is right opposite Khan's, where I've eaten many a Ruby Murray in my drunken past life.

'I used to live here until 1990,' I muse, looking at various vegetables in the organic shop's window. 'In that asbestos-ridden tower block over on the Harrow Road, by the Westway. Back in my day we just had Clash albums and graffiti in the lifts, none of this gentrification you know.'

Inside Planet Organic the customers are much more watchable than in the Elephant and Castle Tesco. There are men with beards and ponytails and women wearing floppy Flowerpot Men beanie hats perusing aisles of flower remedies, comfrey gel, whole leaf Aloe Vera juice and tea tree toothpaste. As I loiter by the leaflets on irritable bowel syndrome, macrobiotics and Feng Shui (is that some form of martial art?) the manager is giving a radio interview mentioning carcinogenic chemicals and depleted topsoil. Meanwhile another assistant called Amos is called over to the aromatic juice bar.

'He's called Amos, did you hear that Flora?' I tell Nicola as she returns with a basket full of pulses, parsley and goat's cheese. 'All very *Cold Comfort Farm*,' I snigger 'Do you think all this organic stuff will ever become mainstream?'

'Of course it will. The supermarkets will have to bow to consumer pressure and they'll be all organic soon, you just wait.'

'I can't see it ever happening. Can we go and have a non-organic curry now?'

'No, we've got lots of lovely organic vegetables here, we can't keep wasting our money on eating out.'

'But I need some carcinogenic chemicals to eat.'

'Now we're living together you're going to be much healthier. Look what that new bloke Arsene Wenger's doing at Arsenal. Even footballers are eating steamed broccoli and pasta now.'

'I know, that's what I'm worried about.'

At least it's warm inside London's temples of consumption. Back at the flat, trying to find places to put our combined possessions raises the temperature. We now have to merge everything – except my West Ham programmes, of course, and also my punk CDs that she hates.

I'm not too keen on jointly owning her library of hefty volumes of eco-babble with even heftier titles. Who reads books like *Mortgaging the Earth: the World Bank, Environmental Impoverishment and the Crisis of Development*? It's not exactly *Fear and Loathing in Las Vegas*, which I've just read because apparently *Loaded* is based on Hunter S Thompson's 'gonzo journalism'. Nor does Nicola's *Global Warming – Can Civilisation Survive?* sound too much like comfort reading before an unsustainable log fire.

Tiring of stacking shelves, I flick through the pages of *The Eco Wars – A Layman's Guide to the Ecology Movement*. Chapter 9 of this tome is entitled Chemical Warfare and has sub-sections entitled Sanctions: Ecological Assassination, A Chronicle of Disasters, Toxic Time Bombs, Poison Food, Poison Air, Gas Warfare, Poison Water, and Gunfights at the Dump.

'You're not going to save the planet unless you can appeal to *Sun* readers and football fans,' I tell her. 'The eco-movement isn't big on jokes is it? It's weighed down by an unbearable heaviness of being.'

'They don't like joking while the planet burns... No, you can't stop for a cup of tea, there are four more boxes of books to unpack.'

Just who edits Green books? Everything is worthy and many of the arguments are probably correct. But the barrage of doom is like listening to an endless tape loop of Private Fraser in *Dad's Army*. Nicola has got hundreds of books that all take thousands of words to say GLOBAL WARMING IS A BAD THING. Not once has a Green writer employed any lightness or humour. They aren't going to pick up many airport readers.

My black-spined Dickens Penguin Classics stand next to her eco-section on the shelves in our living room, the brackets teetering under the weight of so much eco-pessimism. What larks Mr Dickens might have had writing about the messengers of the Green apocalypse. Perhaps I should read some of Nicola's books one day, but when there's a videotape of *Match of the Day* waiting to be watched it's difficult to sacrifice it in favour of *Economics of Natural Resources and the Environment* by David W Pearce and R Kerry Turner.

'OK, name your top five eco-books,' I challenge her, having just read Nick Hornby's *High Fidelity*.

'Well, there's *Silent Spring* by Rachel Carson. And *Pilgrim at Tinker Creek* by Annie Dillard. And... can't I have my top three? Anyway, I don't have all my books up yet, you've nicked all the space for your stupid football books.'

'Do you want to hear my top five *Doctor Who* stories?'

'No.'

There are further changes yet to come in the living room. Despite my refusal to sacrifice our TV, Nicola still insists on changing my viewing habits. That nice red light indicating the TV is on stand-by has to go off. She insists that I put down the remote and walk across the room to turn off the TV.

'Leaving it on stand-by uses nearly as much energy as having it turned on. Eighty per cent in fact.'

'OK, even I have to agree that makes sense. You do realise I'm in danger of getting fit if I have keep leaving the sofa... it could be bad for my career.'

But one area that is not negotiable is her demand to unplug the video.

'Do you know how long it takes to set the timer?' I rave. 'You're just envious of my mastery of a digital clock. And because like all women, you can't set the video timer!'

She has to compromise when I agree to video *Northern Exposure* for her one night while she's at a Friends of Gillespie Park meeting. Loaded Lad one, Green, nil.

It's Year Zero in our flat. My coffee-table reading is changing too. It's no longer *EastEnders* on the box, but earnest reading of alternative newspaper *East Ender*, 'a journal for regeneration by conservation – not redevelopment'. Instead of Pat Butcher, it's 'tree butchers' threatening Epping Forest. Everyone is getting very excited about the M11 link road. *East Ender* tells me that men called 'John the cook' and 'Old Mick' have scaled the roof of Westminster Hall in protest.

It lovingly chronicles the siege of Claremont Road, London, E11 – a Victorian terrace threatened with demolition to make way for the link road. Except it's now called it the free state of 'Claremonte'. Riot police besiege climbers with monikers like 'Aquarius the water carrier' – suggesting that whatever the eco-warriors are on, I'd like some too. Aquarius is photographed clambering over nets stretching from corrugated tree houses to rooftops and up home-made scaffolding erected to defy the road builders in hydraulic cherry pickers. Photos of police are captioned 'The ugly face of the new British Reich', although anyone imagining John Major running a British Reich, is I think, a little overstating their case.

East Ender is addictive reading. Banners read 'Defy the criminal injustice act' and 'M11 Link, You Must Be Choking'. It makes a change from birds in lad mags – although I note that some rather attractive babes in shapeless dresses have chained themselves to wooden scaffolds on top of the threatened homes in defiance of 'the forces of unspeakable evil'.

Another feature details the 'Sacking of Euphoria' and begins 'Traitors to the biosphere, government forces loyal to Mammon attacked the independent free state of Euphoria'.

Euphoria is, like Wanstonia and Leytonstonia, an 'independent free state declared last year due to worsening incidents of diktat by the Conservative yob culture cabinet'.

Demolishing homes for roads is wrong and new roads create more traffic. But I can't help noting that the good citizens of Euphoria appear to be irredeemably middle class. One of their main complaints in *East Ender* is that the police have destroyed a 'minstrel gallery and sculpture garden'. Is this really what we'll have after Major's Reich goes – minstrel galleries? In a few years they'll probably all be web designers.

'Nicola, I'd love to be a Green, but I can't climb and I'm scared of heights,' I explain. 'So I'll just have to watch Euro '96 instead this summer...'

Sometimes it's a relief to go out to work. Subbing shifts at *Loaded* are gratefully received because at IPC magazines the radiators are on full all day, regardless of their carbon allowance. My pale pallor impresses *Loaded*'s editorial team. They assume it's all due to drug and body abuse rather than hypothermia.

At *Time Out* it's days of hot-desking, shuffled from work station to work station, attempting to write the diary page. A bulging file full of press releases from Mark Borkowski PR sits on my desk, then I'm ringing my mate Big Joe at Off The Kerb agency for funny stories from his comics, and then Neil Sean, who seems to spend his life in the green room at TV and radio stations, and now Peter Noble from Noble PR is on the phone sounding ridiculously enthusiastic with his Canadian accent saying 'Hey buddy, have I got a story for you...'. I'm a one-man trivia mountain that should be scrapped by the EU, but hey, the *Time Out* office is so hot I can sit in just my Ben Sherman shirt and still feel warm.

Back at home there are many other lifestyle adjustments underway. Nicola insists we remove all the existing light bulbs and replace them with huge great clunking 15 centimetre-long, long-life monsters. They cost vast amounts, but she claims they last twelve times longer and use 80 per cent less energy than a normal light bulb.

And then she starts to Green the one room she hasn't touched as yet – the bathroom. When the water in the loo turns a rusty red I tell Nicola I fear I'm suffering from some horrific form of anal bleeding.

'No, you idiot, I put a brick in the cistern, it means we use less water with each flush.'

'We can't have red loo water. We're literally shitting bricks!'

She ditches the brick and instead places a plastic mineral water bottle filled with tap water in the cistern. (We're no longer allowed to buy mineral water because the bottles go straight to landfill.) This is more effective and less medically alarming than the brick.

Finally we obtain a 'hippo' from our water company. This is an inflatable blue bag used to save water. I remove the cistern cover and stuff it in. Am I the only man in Britain with wildlife down his cistern?

'Do you know every flush uses nine litres of water?' Nicola declares, gazing lovingly at the hippo now swimming by our ballcock.

'Water is going to become an increasingly scarce resource with climate change. There are going to be wars over water in 30 years.'

'So we'd better tell Madonna to stop jogging with mineral water then…'

'Taking a bath uses 80 litres of water, brushing your teeth with the tap running uses six litres of water per minute…' continues water woman. 'In Ghana they have to collect their well water by the bucket…'

'Well, I don't know where the nearest well is in Highbury!'

Then there's her policy of not flushing the loo if you do a wee. 'If it's yellow let it mellow, if it's brown flush it down, that's what it says in *The Green Guide*,' she tells me cheerfully.

If I'd been living on my own this might have been feasible;

but if you're living with your partner then the least romantic thing you can do is gaze at their urine accompanied by sodden toilet tissue. Even the compost loo is better than this.

All this orifice politics seems unnecessary in London in 1996. The predicted water shortages, arising from a Mediterranean-style climate for Britain, have not as yet materialised, have they? So when Nicola is upstairs, I rush into the loo, turn my back to the basin, and furtively flush before going myself.

Even when the loo is fully flushed there's an expanding brown stain at the bottom of the bowl. Nicola has banned all detergents as they pollute our water supply. Apparently vinegar and Coca Cola are quite good for removing limescale – except we're not allowed to buy Coke because it's produced by a multinational and has too much sugar in it.

We both come with plenty of baggage. The flat struggles to contain our joint possessions. We use the second bedroom as Nicola's office. It's a minimalist room, containing her phone/ fax machine, computer, filing cabinets, numerous loose Lever Arch files on sustainable forestry and lots of useful things such as a Solomon Islands phone directory. The rest of her papers, press and correspondence are on the stairs, each step representing a different category of her mind.

Half of the living room is now my office, containing my Amstrad computer, printer and fax machine. My desk is covered in West Ham programmes, *On A Mission From God* fanzines, press releases and computer print-outs. The shelves in the alcove contain books, CDs, LPs, my hi-fi and speakers. A new book shelf has been created, with skip wood and several loose bricks, in the far corner of the room to house yet more books.

A sofa and armchair compete for space in front of the giant TV someone gave us, and my knackered old video recorder. On the wall hangs a giant wedding kimono. Nicola was given it several years ago, and has for some reason mounted it on wobbly bamboo canes. In the twilight it can easily be mistaken for a suicidal person, despairing of the internal clutter, who is about to leap through one of the rattling windows and crash on to the pavement three storeys below.

After Greening the flat, Nicola sets about Greening my transport habits. Do I need or want to be Ethical Man? No, but she is a born organiser; a combination of Mrs Jellaby, Madonna and a District Commissioner of the Pony Club. And perhaps, like most men, secretly I quite enjoy being organised. Although there are days when it's tempting to tell her where to recycle her ethical lifestyle. Like when she takes me to the communal landing, on the floor below our flat, and shows me an ancient black bicycle.

'That's an old bike.'

'This is my old bike, you can use this to go shopping with now. You'll love it – and you won't waste any more money on tube and bus fares.'

I haven't ridden a bike since the age of 13. Now she's holding something that looks like a bright yellow luminous bondage harness from some iffy San Francisco sex club.

'What's that?'

'It's a Sam Browne sash.'

'Won't Sam Browne want it back?'

'Oh for goodness sake! You'll thank me when you lose your jelly belly!'

'It's not a jelly belly, it's a lad mag writer's tribute to heavy beer drinking, created in a purely ironic spirit, you understand.'

'It'll stop you getting run over.'

And so I don my Sam Browne sash. Later I use an encyclopedia to discover that Sam Browne was in fact General Sir Samuel James Browne VC, GCB, KCSI, (1849-1901) of the British Army in India. He was probably an ancestor of one of the Oxford Greens and designed the strap to help carry the weight of a pistol or sword.

You can't somehow imagine General Sir Sam Browne VC, GCB, KCSI on a pushbike on Holloway Road, but in the 1990s the reflective Sam Browne belt has become essential wear for the urban cyclist beset by juggernauts.

In Norman Tebbit-pleasing fashion I get on my bike and look for work. Well, shopping at least, when I take it to Waitrose. Nicola's old bike is so black and unhip that initially I feel a little like Margaret Hamilton as Miss Gulch/the Wicked

Witch of the West, who rode a similar vehicle when she cycled past Dorothy's farm in *The Wizard of Oz*.

On my early cycling forays I pedal along behind Nicola on her new mountain bike. She heads towards juggernauts with the recklessness of the rider who knows she's on the Sustrans cycle route to righteousness. But soon my confidence has increased enough to allow solo trips to the pub, although on hugely busy junctions like Highbury Corner roundabout I always prefer to wheel my bike over the pedestrian crossings rather than pedal towards a premature death beneath the wheels of a *Top Gear* fan.

The bike is also handy for trips to our local shops, as Nicola insists we shop locally whenever we can. She quotes George Monbiot articles at me, about supermarkets being beastly to farmers and encouraging over-packaging and using excess air miles by importing out-of-season produce. Highbury Barn contains more delis per square foot than the whole of northern England, so it isn't too much of a hardship.

The other main use for my bike is for trips to the recycling bins at Highbury Pool. The limited floor space in our tiny kitchen is covered by plastic bags containing empty wine bottles and teetering mounds of old *Guardians*, *Observers*, *Mirrors* and *News of the Worlds*. (This being Highbury, if anyone spots you with a tabloid in your recycling, you feel as guilty as if it's *Penthouse*.)

Bags of bottles hang from my handlebars; a sports bag full

of papers is fastened to my bicycle rack with elastic straps. Slowly, my overladen bike perambulates up Highbury Hill and across Highbury Fields to the recycling bins. As middle-class mums in hatchbacks deposit shattering bags of glass I exhaustedly drag my papers to the bins, heave them up and away into recycling nirvana.

My personal Green policewoman is ever vigilant, but at least I can claim that I need to watch videos as part of my job – I'm reviewing the latest *Doctor Who* video release, 'The Green Death'.

'It's research, Nicola, I get 25 quid from *Time Out* every time I review a *Doctor Who* video, plus a free video... And it might even come back one day if we Whovians keep campaigning!' I add.

'It finished in 1989, they're never going to bring it back now!' answers Nicola.

'How did you know it finished in 1989? Hey, you're learning, babe.'

I'm now on the BBC mailing list and received every new *Doctor Who* release, including audio CDs of missing episodes from the sixties. It's not going to make me rich, but my chronologically-ordered *Who* video collection now looks fantastic.

'Look, you'll like this, the Doctor is visiting the Nuthutch, a community of hippies camping outside Global Chemicals in Wales,' I enthuse to Nicola, who's making a cup of green tea and honey. 'Global Chemicals is pouring green toxic waste into the mines which has created giant maggots, made from condoms by the BBC Special Effects department... and this is Professor Cliff Jones, he's just like George Monbiot! 'The Green Death' was written in 1971 and is way ahead of its time on Green issues.'

To my surprise Nicola sits down for ten minutes and watches Professor Jones shouting about serendipity to the lovestruck Jo Grant. He discovers that the H_2O she spilt over his experiment can destroy the killer condoms. But then Brigadier Lethbridge-Stewart and his UNIT chaps start being menaced by giant maggots.

'I remember this, I can't watch any more. *Doctor Who* was always too scary!' declares Nicola, rushing upstairs to save more trees. Ah, so that's why she can't watch TV. It's too frightening for her.

Early in the year Nicola entices me on a trip to Newbury to support the road protestors. At least there are coaches to take us there and we don't have to camp up any trees, as far as I'm aware.

We arrive amid a throng of alternative types in army greens and baggy jumpers. Inside the protestors' camp is a place called vertigo. The tree houses teeter amid the trees. It must be bloody cold up there. Even worse than our flat. Think I'll stick to being an armchair Green.

To my relief, Nicola's been scared of direct action ever since a policeman caught her in a painful wrist-lock at a student grants protest while she was at university. She doesn't really like breaking the law, so at least we're united in our woolly liberalness.

We're handed numerous leaflets and flyers for the Socialist Workers' Party. The bypass will rip up 10,000 trees and destroy three sites of Special Scientific Interest, all for the sake of nine miles of bypass that will allegedly relieve congestion in Newbury – although as the protestors repeatedly point out, new roads simply breed more cars.

But never mind the road. The real issue is whether we'll get to see Swampy. His real name is Daniel Hooper, but as Swampy he's now achieved national fame. Swampy was one of the last road protestors to emerge from the tunnels dug under the site of the A30 road extension in Fairmile, Devon.

Now he's involved in the 'Third Battle of Newbury' (the other two were during the English Civil War). Swampy is a national star, having appeared on *Have I Got News For You*. The *Daily Mail* loves him too, as it discovers that he comes from Newbury and has middle-class parents. It must have been a bit of a shock that, finding a middle-class Green.

There's no sign of Mr Swampy, sadly, but it is a laugh here. A pantomime cow is being arrested as it attempts to break through the police cordon to save the trees. And a bloke in a mac who calls himself Columbo says he's with the herbicide squad seeking to track down the suspects who have been murdering trees.

Various protestors have chained themselves to individual trees, looking uncannily like they're in the 'Always Look On The Bright Side Of Life' final scene from Monty Python's *Life of Brian*. And sure enough, one of them shouts catchphrases from the film. The protestors now refer to the security guards as 'Romans'.

The protest takes the form of a long slog through mud accompanied by pixie types. But we run into my mates, football authors Mark Perryman and Anne Coddington, and at lunchtime escape to a nearby country pub. *Loaded*'s Martin Deeson and his photographer are at Newbury too, having collared a couple of security guards and placed pints in front of them. The guards are soon complaining about 4.30 am starts, twelve-hour shifts without a break, sleeping in an old army barracks and the fact that the protesters 'have all the best birds'.

Deeson later writes: 'The best thing about the Battle of the Bypass is that the footsoldiers – on both sides – are young enough to be part of the E generation, and they've spent long hours consuming comedy, sci-fi and drugs. Protest has never sounded so good.'

What have the Romans done for us, eh? Deeson's piece is the finest article ever written about Newbury, better than a thousand worthy pieces in the quality press, because he gets over the humour and absurdity of it all, coming up with the eminently sensible conclusion of: 'Even the Department of Transport admits that by 2006 the traffic will be as bad as it was when the bypass was completed a couple of years before. Is there any point in building a road if it's so unpopular that the only way you can do it is by dragging guys off the dole queues, treating them like shit, and sticking them in hard hats to beat up people who two weeks ago they'd have been sharing a spliff with?'

I brandish the article at Nicola. 'See, I told you *Loaded* was Green! Give that man a place in George Monbiot's first Cabinet.'

In May we set out on another piece of direct-ish action with the Oxford Greens.

'We must go to Wandsworth, The Land Is Ours is occupying the Guinness site!' enthuses my eco-partner one morning after a phone tip-off. An hour later, after a tube ride to Gloucester Road and a walk across the river to Wandsworth, we're standing by a Mongolian yurt on the edge of the Thames. And a man called Twig is blowing into a conch shell by the river.

We're on a derelict piece of industrial wasteground surrounded by Greens walking around among an urban tundra of bombsite bushes and concrete. The 13-acre site once housed a demolished Guinness distillery and has been empty since 1990. Three coaches have arrived from Oxford, full of activists with gardening and carpentry tools. It looks like a New Age camp already; parked buses and lots of eco-clutter.

George Monbiot is standing at the centre of a crowd of earnest men in various types of chunky sweaters. Some have beards, several have Monbiot-esque steel-rimmed glasses. There's a man in a checked shirt, a woman with green hair, a chap who looks like an elderly farmer wearing a cap with a sunflower in it.

Had the Soviet empire won the Cold War this is how a British gulag might have looked; earnest Oxford dons and students in a forced labour camp, busy shifting rocks and stones, pallets, tarpaulins and scaffolding.

Not that they seem to be necessarily winning over the residents of the nearby council estate. 'If I broke into places like that I'd get nicked!' a disgruntled local resident is telling one of the many hacks present. A couple of crop-haired boys from the estate jump up and down on the pallet boards.

'It's quite interesting in an anthropological sense,' I tell Nicola, as I try to distinguish the Donga tribe members from the dons and ecologists.

George Monbiot is running the revolution from a brown pouch (what is it with Greens and pouches?) worn around his waist, in which he keeps his mobile phone.

'What we're doing here is constructive and peaceful, we want to make development work for us, not against us... what we're saying is that we urgently need to use the wasted land in our cities to house the homeless, to relieve urban bleakness and to reduce the pressure on the countryside,' he's telling someone from a broadsheet newspaper.

'These derelict sites reduce people's sense of community: we want to turn this bit of Wandsworth into an asset. We've got the energy here, and the enthusiasm, just look at these people working around us' he says to a TV crew. That's the thing with George. He speaks eloquently and can charm anyone from Murdoch's minions to the police and the Establishment.

Then GM stops to give a morale-rocketing fillip to his troops. 'I've just phoned the police. They said "You're going to build gardens? That sounds interesting!" [cheers] I've met the police and they've agreed this is a civil, not a criminal matter. The land is ours!'

George then somehow inspires an army of intellectuals and crusties into action. A woman in dreadlocks is erecting a bender by lashing together branches. A brick path is being laid out to the compost loo. Oh yes, there's a compost loo. There's always a compost loo. Tepees and tents emerge. A timber structure becomes the village hall. Soya is being boiled into mush over a cauldron. People are building geodesic domes as if it's all a giant set from first-generation *Star Trek*. Captain Kirk might do a theatrical roll while firing a phaser at any moment.

And now George is explaining to the *Independent on Sunday* that he's not a leader, just someone with the office and

PR skills to communicate the arguments of those who prefer to lie down in front of bulldozers.

Which makes me wish that sometimes he'd just admit that he is natural leader among a supposedly leaderless organisation. Just as James Brown is the leader of the *Loaded* revolution, so George Monbiot is the leader of the counterculture. He is the Ernest Shackleton of the environmental movement. If our party is ever marooned in the Antarctic, George will keep up morale with storytelling and feed his crew on soundbites.

By evening the camp looks like a small medieval city, complete with jesters in multi-coloured hats. Monbiot has managed to stave off a request for a rave. Vegan stew is being brewed. We have occupied the moral high ground. But it seems to me the Oxford ecologists don't really get what Jarvis's common people do. Is it really circus stunts, acoustic music and painting? Thankfully, Nicola, while fully behind the occupation, is starting to miss her home and has no plans to spend the night under a bender.

'Have they got Sky installed yet?' asks a shaven-headed teenager from across the road.

A good point, well made. There's a must-see match on tonight. Maybe it's time to go to the pub.

Slowly the summer of '96 arrives and the flat loses its chill. Sunlight illuminates forest certification faxes, heat warms the flesh of Jo Guest on the front cover of an old copy of *Loaded*. Nicola goes away to Mexico for a week-long conference of the Forest Stewardship Council, while I save carbon watching football at home.

Football is coming home for everyone but the Greens. Euro '96 is a near triumph for England. Gazza scores against Scotland and then lies down on the turf to have imaginary cocktails poured down his throat. Inspired by Gazza, Shearer and Sheringham we thrash Holland 4-1 and only lose to the Germans in the semi-final on penalties (again). David Baddiel and Frank Skinner are at number one with 'Three Lions', the unofficial England anthem that contains the memorable chorus of 'Football's coming home...'. A proper football song that sounds as if it was written by real fans. It all merges seamlessly with Britpop, and with a hooliganism-free tournament, the country is overtaken by a mood of optimism. And soon the Tories will be gone too...

My two lives are as diverse as ever. Numerous party invites arrive through my work at *Time Out*. It might be off to Gloucester Road for the launch party of David Baddiel's novel *Time for Bed*. with Frank Skinner, Stephen Fry, Mariella Frostrup, Jonathan Ross, Harry Hill, Jenny Eclair and numerous other comedy luminaries. I'm loitering behind celebs, Chardonnay in hand, hoping to overhear some comments that might make a diary item. Meanwhile Nicola's doing far worthier journalism, reviewing *Green Backlash* by Andrew Rowell for *New Scientist*. Looking at her copy by the bed, I notice it has the pithy subtitle of 'Global Subversion of the Environmental Movement'.

Or it's off to see Will Self read at Filthy McNasty's in Islington followed by a trip to James Brown's birthday party at the Cross Bar where a wide-eyed Liam Gallagher is looking mad for it. Oh, and who's this at the *Time Out* bash – there's Damon Albarn from Blur chatting to Miranda Sawyer on the stairs. Everyone's grown sideburns and is wearing retro Adidas tops and trainers while the Greens are still in waistcoats.

Nicola likes to be in bed by ten. She likes to get up early and go to sleep with a hot water bottle; I prefer to get up late, not talk to anyone until after 10am and then stay up late at night loitering with celebrity intent. She never seems to worry that I'll get off with any babes; either this mean she thinks no-one else would want to get off with me or that actually I'm more loyal supporter than lad.

She does take me to some eco-parties though. We visit the Design Museum where there's a bash to celebrate the fifth anniversary of the NPI Global Care Unit Trust. Afterwards, everyone's invited to continue the celebrations at the flat of Tessa Tennant, some sort of Green financial guru. 'She's chair of the UK Social Investment Forum,' explains Nicola, expecting me to know what this is. Her gaff is a plush penthouse in Bankside overlooking the Thames and I note with some surprise that there's a mounted stag's head on the wall. We leave with our party bags full of press releases on sustainable unit trusts.

Amid all the relentless hedonism and consumption Nicola's eco-pal George Marshall often comes over to kip on our sofa bed before heading off to some climate forum. He's always amusing company and, unlike many of the more earnest environmentalists, even possesses a sense of humour, pretending to be our landlord and demanding his rent and regaling us with tales of pursuing eco-babes. But one night, in one of his more pessimistic moods, he declares that in forty years, civilisation might be unsustainable. To my surprise, he means it too.

Is it really that bad? As a boy I'd been worried about fossil fuels running out. I remember telling my parents about this and their utter certainty that 'they'll think of something else'. Oil and petrol would disappear in around thirty years and there was nothing wrong in trying to conserve it.

Even if global warming was a myth created by people justifying their academic posts, as my dad seemed to believe, the precautionary principle could do no harm. Saving energy would reduce the running costs of businesses and individual households. But the end of civilisation? The thing about humanity, as Tom Baker once put it, is that we are 'indomitable'. A race renowned for its inventiveness and adaptability.

Soon there will be big money to be made from alternative energy. Ideas that were once seen as crankish will became mainstream a decade on. Surely faced with the panic of declining oil reserves we can invent new forms of wind, wave and solar power and thwart global warming? Adapt and survive and all that.

If even the Sex Pistols can get into recycling themselves then there must be some hope. In the middle of Euro '96, the Sex Pistols are reforming to play at Finsbury Park. My thoughts turn from diminishing oil to getting well-oiled in the Plimsoll pub with my old mate from school, Paul Garrett. We enter Finsbury Park to catch a bare-chested Iggy Pop on stage and then it's the big one. Euro '96 heroes Stuart Pearce and Gareth Southgate come on to introduce the Pistols.

And here they are. 'We're fat, 40 and back!' hollers Johnny Rotten, going into his distinctive warble-cum-sneer as the band open with 'Bodies'. At least they hide their love of filthy lucre with self-deprecation. 'You fat bastard!' chant the loving crowd.

We cheer as Steve 'Fatty' Jones proves he could still give it some bollocks on guitar. And he still looks like he should be fitting your swimming pool rather than owning one. Here is the soundtrack for a generation of middle-class university kids in leather jackets and narrow ties.

'Holidays in the Sun', a searing cover of the Stooges' 'No Fun', 'Pretty Vacant'... one classic after another reverberates over N4. And then of course, Steve Jones' power chords herald the epic 'God Save The Queen', as Johnny Rotten sneers his way through all that stuff about fascist regimes and H-bombs and Paul and myself are acting like lagered-up thirty- something idiots jumping up and down before that final epic chorus about no future for any of us.

Does Johnny Rotten still mean it, man? The Greens certainly do. Perhaps the Sex Pistols were actually early environmentalists. It strikes me that what was once punk nihilism of no future in 1977 has now become environmental orthodoxy – only without the catchy tunes.

CHAPTER 5

That's Yer Allotment

'What's that?' I ask as Nicola appears in our doorway carrying various Hardy-esque agricultural implements.

'It's a fork 'n' shovel!'

'There's no need to swear!'

'No, it's a fork and shovel! I've got an allotment from Islington Council! It's great, isn't it? We can grow our own vegetables...'

'But we're already in an organic box scheme! We've got more Jerusalem artichokes than our bowels can take... we're inundated with Taylor's turnips, parsnips and bleeding beetroots!'

'Pete, this is wonderful. We never need to buy over-packaged vegetables from supermarkets again!'

'I suppose you've said yes to the allotment.'

'Of course.'

'Well as long as I don't have to do all the work. My ancestors worked really hard to escape a life of labour on the land. And now we're going back to feudalism... We don't have to pay any tithes do we?'

'Only to the council. Come on, you'll love it. What's that song you like by Peter Gabriel?'

'Digging in the Dirt.'

'Yes, it'll be like that.'

Vegetables are taking over our lives. Having pared down our energy consumption, Nicola is now reforming our dietary habits. We do occasionally eat fish, but our diet is mainly vegetarian because of something called protein economics (it takes a huge amount of feed to fatten an animal) and the fact that cows' methane is a major contributor to greenhouse gases.

But we're not allowed to eat any old vegetables. They have to be organic. Nicola insists I read *Silent Spring* by Rachel Carson, a Green classic written in 1962.

'It's brilliant, it's the book that started it all. It's so readable and poetic,' enthuses my Green partner. 'She discovers how the US agricultural industry is spraying cancer-causing pesticides on farmland, she exposes the disinformation tactics of the chemical industry and her work led to a ban on the use of DDT in 1972! It made us environmentalists realise what we're up against. The chemical industry didn't care that she was trying to make things better for humanity and the eco-system.'

'OK, it's well written. And even I don't want to eat DDT,' I admit, 'although I know some Britpop stars who'd probably like to score some DDT if you offered it to them in a Camden boozer. You don't want to be Rachel Carson, do you?'

'Of course I do!'

'Oh God. You probably will be, and I'll be the equivalent of the US chemical industry...'

Stoke Newington appears to be full of women who want to be Rachel Carson too. Nicola has already enrolled us in a 'box scheme' for organic vegetables, perhaps realising that growing them ourselves might be hard work. It's called Growing Communities and is run by Nicola's friend Julie Brown, a former campaigner for Friends of the Earth. Julie is a sort of Anita Roddick of vegetables. She's set up the whole Growing Communities scheme from her front room, gaining organic certification from the Soil Association.

Julie and a small group of vegetable evangelists had started growing vegetables on reclaimed waste ground at Clissold Park and were also paying a farm in Kent to grow organic vegetables.

The name 'box scheme' is something of a misnomer, as the vegetables come in recycled plastic bags that people have found in their 'bag bag' under the kitchen sink. Each area of north London has a designated pick-up point, or safe house, known only to the vegetable elite. In 1996 it all feels a bit like being a member of a terrorist cell.

Strangely enough, Nicola is always too tired to collect our plastic bags of earthy vegetables most Wednesdays. So I'm dispatched on my bike, clad in Sam Browne sash, towards the uncharted territory of Julie's house in Stoke Newington.

If you arrive early you have to wait for a man called Brian to deliver the bags from the old fire station that is the Growing Communities HQ. He rides a bike with a three-wheeled trailer full of vegetables and fruit attached to it; at the back of the trailer is a flag with feathers attached to it. He's clearly the Jeremy Clarkson of customised eco-bikes.

Several enthusiastic volunteers join Julie, often earnest women with dreadlocks wearing hooped tights or men with Zapata moustaches. We pick up the vegetables from Julie's back garden by her pottery studio – only now she's throwing potatoes not pots, presumably in an attempt to win artichokes and minds.

We go on a Growing Communities planting day to the organic farm in Buckinghamshire. On a rainy Sunday the farm has turned into a quagmire, and we witness a grower drop his sandwich on his muddy boot. He picks it up and eats it, telling Nicola that organic soil is a good deal better for you than washed vegetables drenched in pesticides.

There's a Saturday morning digging day at Clissold Park, which I reluctantly attend before a pressing engagement at West Ham's Boleyn Stadium. The council has finally lent Growing Communities a piece of land near the park's aviary.

The plan is to plant veg here and return to Stoke Newington's glory days as a market garden.

All that forking is therapeutic after a week spent grafting at the typeface. But it's not the sort of thing they're used to in Stoke Newington. As I sneak over the fence for a pre-match drink of lager from the can concealed in my bag, a woman from the estate opposite comes up to me and looks at the gang of donkey-jacketed toilers.

'What have they done?' she asks. 'And shouldn't they have more warders with them?'

Even Nicola has to laugh.

But sometimes I wonder if I'm in vegetable denial. Everyone takes organics very seriously indeed. Do the vegetable crowd ever snigger at parsnips that have knobbly bits in just the right places to form a penis? Or begin meetings with 'lettuce pray'?

Will organic vegetables soon be a mass movement lobbying Parliament? 'What do we want! Loads of manure! When do we want it! Well, it depends on the growing season...'

I'm sure Nicola's right, eating a higher percentage of organic food will do you some good. But is it worth Greens spending all their lives worrying about diet in the hope they might live a year longer? If you live in the developing world or under Saddam Hussein in Iraq your life can end pretty easily, whatever you eat.

Despite my occasional wavering, I dutifully take the long

nocturnal bike ride to Stokey each week to pick up our bags of veg and fruit. Luckily the ride home goes past the Shakespeare, the only pub in N16 still to have the Clash on its jukebox in the 1990s, so I often stop for a pint. All that organic veg must mean it's safer to drink a bit more, surely?

Inside the Shakespeare it's full of social workers and Greens. There's a mound of some 15 or so bikes. It's clearly too dodgy to leave them outside and the pub now has its own bike mountain. At least a pint of ale and blast of 'White Man In Hammersmith Palais' eases the burden of a ride home with a bike rack laden with root vegetables.

Upon my return to our kitchen I release potatoes, dust, numerous bits of onion skins, onions, cabbages and mud-encrusted carrots on to the kitchen table. Does more mud make the vegetables more authentic? It seems so.

We get every variety. Celeriac, fennel, chard, squash, cavalo nero, they might as well be foreign stars from a World Cup to this errant eater.

Growing Communities practises 'seasonality'; if it isn't in season you don't get it. We have aubergines from polytunnels in July, pumpkins in September and lovely mushrooms in October, but in early spring, during the 'hungry gap' we subsist on parsnips, swedes, turnips and potatoes.

'This is much better than buying vegetables and fruit that's out of season from Waitrose, think of the food miles!' admonishes Nicola as she tempts me to eat another ladle of swede mush. 'No more supermarket vegetables that are suspicious bright colours and covered in layers of plastic and pesticides. We're in touch with the seasons again!'

Each Growing Communities bag contains a leaflet with news and recipes for making cabbage palatable (try it fried with mustard seeds). It's certainly good for my culinary skills; parsnips roasted with rosemary in olive oil and roasted celeriac start to taste quite good.

But swedes and turnips can only be turned into a kind of vegetable mush soup. Jerusalem artichokes create huge amounts of human methane, therefore worsening climate change, and have to be disposed of in the manner of radioactive waste. They probably possess a longer half-life than plutonium. Carrot mountains are a problem too. Some of them can be used in my signature dish of vegetarian sausage with mashed potato, carrots and gravy. But what do you do with excess carrots? Carrot soup? The future is not orange for me.

'I don't want be part of the beetroot generation,' I tell Nicola.

'Why do you always have to pun about our lovely vegetables?'

'Well, it's hard to resist. And I've always thought the pun is mightier than the sword.'

'So it's the thin end of the veg,' she says.

'It is where beetroot is concerned.'

Being forced to eat beetroot ruined many a school dinner

during my childhood. Now they turn up with alarming frequency in our vegetable bags. Nicola gleefully cooks beetroot soup, crimson, pungent and tasting, to me at least, like caustic soda. And she won't go out to a restaurant unless we have eaten our vegetable mountain.

It's a huge relief to escape to West Ham matches and dine in Ken's Café before games. Ken's has proper Formica tables and is run by Carol, a redoubtable East End matriarch. Before eating you're given a numbered ticket to hold and 20 minutes later someone hollers out your number.

Oh, the joy of eggs, chips and beans. Plus white bread, ketchup, salt – all the stuff that's forbidden at home. On other nights I sneak out for a furtive portion of chips or a take-away pizza like some kind of foodie recidivist. While *Loaded* is compiling Top 20s for crisps and biscuits I'm roasting celeriac. What if James Brown ever catches me? It will be more embarrassing than a Conservative MP being found in bed with a rent boy.

Our good life is almost complete. A rotting log has appeared in our front room. Is it for the wood burner we don't as yet have? No, Nicola announces that she's growing shitake mushrooms on it.

'Can't you just grow them in my sock drawer?'

Our flat soon has fungi sprouting from the rotten wood. They taste, well, woody.

In eco-audit terms we must be doing well. We have perfected the art of recycling bottles and papers at the bins by

Highbury Pool and now Islington Ecology Centre has a public access compost bin where anyone can place their kitchen refuse. So we collect all our waste vegetable matter, tea bags and coffee in a black bucket, line it with a plastic bag and when it's full Nicola's bag carrier has to take it to the ecology centre.

My mind retreats to when I was washing up at Hutton Masonic Hall during my sixth-form days. We called this sort of food waste 'the pig bin'. Apparently this sloppy mass has now gone upmarket and is helping to save the biosphere.

It's heavy, but each week I carry our slops down the road, remove the plastic bag and deposit the contents in the ecology centre's compost area. It smells pungent, but makes a satisfying slurp. I'm then left with a plastic bag covered in brown gloop, which Nicola says I should bring home and wash, but is so horrifying that it's time to say sod recycling and throw it in the nearest bin.

Nicola's new passion for allotments awakens when she interviews Bob Gilbert, author of *The Green London Way*. Bob is London's version of Alfred Wainwright, having invented a circular walk around London. He's also the only Green I've ever met who's working class. You can tell that because he's called Bob; anyone middle-class would refer to themselves as Rob.

Bob comes from Bermondsey, is one of life's great enthusiasts, and is an expert in natural history. We all become mates, even though he keeps a pet tarantula in the flat he shares with his son Joel. Bob works for the council and has revealed to Nicola details of an upcoming new batch of allotments.

And thus Nicola finds our allotment. It's a quarter of a mile from our flat, on some reclaimed railway land, round the back of the Quill Street estate. Personally, I thought my free time was for relaxing in, not heavy labour with spades.

We're too Green to have a car. To reach the allotment we have to march along Elfort Road, Drayton Park, St Thomas's Road and Quill Street carrying shovels, forks, rakes, buckets and sometimes bricks. There's no shed at the allotment, just an overgrown strip of ground with an alarming gradient, so everything we need has to be carried there and back. It's a bit like being in an eco-chain gang.

Nicola insists we take a scythe to several hectares of virgin plant life. 'It's all about preparation,' she says. Indeed, the way to sustainable living is paved with recycled house bricks. We spend days laying a spiral path of reclaimed bricks, using old wood to create raised permaculture beds and eventually plant some borage seeds to cleanse the quite-possibly toxic old railway siding. 'The flowers will look lovely,' she says.

Jack, a man with a beard and holey jumper, is clearing another allotment. He assumes I'm a gardener too and tells us long incomprehensible anecdotes about his Jerusalem artichokes and leeks. As always when she's fired up over a new project, Nicola devotes all her time to it; she visits her mother in Hertfordshire, borrowing her brother's car and returns with several bags of horse manure. She then informs her private pack horse that he's going to distribute it over our land.

The project reaches its zenith when the new allotments are officially opened and blessed by Stephen, our local vicar. He's always referred to in the local paper as a 'maverick vicar', mainly because he does outrageous things like support gay clergy and women priests and thinks the church should side with the poor.

Stephen arrives at the allotments in dog collar and white robes, says a prayer or two, swings a silver container of holy water and than proceeds to scatter the water over the upturned sods (and Nicola's horse manure) with ostentatious flicks, watched by an assortment of men with beards in holey jumpers. The whole picture looks like a scene from a British movie, as Stephen intones 'God bless this land and Dave who shall cultivate it... God bless this land and Jack who shall cultivate it...God bless this land and Nicola who shall cultivate it...'.

Then a naked man comes to the window of one of the Quill Street estate houses and shouts 'Is the church going to steal this land too?'

Stephen carries on gamely, leading the allotment holders in a chorus of 'We plough the fields and scatter'. Clearly the naked unbeliever in his bathroom doesn't realise that each man shall have his allotment time on Earth.

The success of comedians Newman and Baddiel has the media calling comedy the new rock 'n' roll. While sitting in the pub with my mate John, we joke about whether allotments are the new rock 'n' roll.

'I bet that in ten years' time rock-star wives will be writing books on growing runner beans and making your own butter,' says John.

'No, it'll never happen,' I counter, 'allotments will never be trendy.'

Towards the end of 1996 Nicola's dad's cancer becomes much worse. Angus has been in hospital and then returns home, now bedridden. Nicola says it's the end. She spends time at home with her mother and proves to be a good nurse.

It's a busy time. My book *The Lad Done Bad* is coming out at the end of the year ready for the Christmas market. There's a launch at Terry Venables' Scribes club in Kensington High Street. Before the launch Angus insists that Nicola sends me a fax wishing me luck. It's a moving gesture. Could he possibly think that Football Man might be good for his daughter?

The launch is a success, my parents are there and Nicola too. El Tel is spotted around the club and we attract a good few journalists. During the launch my pal Neil Sean, the gay gossip hound who supplies stories for *Time Out*, tells me 'That girl really admires you Pete, you want to get her up the aisle'.

Three days after my book launch Angus dies. Nicola is there, then there's a funeral to plan and much more. She deals with his death stoically, and I admire her strength.

After the funeral and a muted Christmas at her mum's she returns to London. She needs me now, and I feel that I must go along with her environmental ambitions. Even if it means labouring on the allotment. I have to tread softly, for I am treading on her greens.

While living in Highbury we become mates with Robbie Kellman, an Australian working for Greenpeace. He lives nearby with his girlfriend Angela, who's training to be an actress. Unusually for a Green, Robbie likes football. He says I remind him of his friend 'who's just like Hugh Grant'. Not in terms of looks (obviously Hugh couldn't compete with a ruffled hack in Gap classic-fit chinos), more my English diffidence when confronted with a karabiner and instruction to scale the nearest crane.

Robbie invites us to the odd Greenpeace party where blokes with beards discuss boarding oil rigs and whaling ships. He's a good source of amusing tales from the world of eco-warriors with ropes, and has a great story for my column in *Time Out*. In the summer of 1997 three Greenpeace activists fly in by helicopter to occupy Rockall, a remote piece of rock 200 miles off the Hebrides. It's famous for being mentioned in

Radio 4's shipping forecast. They strap a survival capsule to the sheer rock surface and declare Rockall to be the sovereign state of Waveland, in order to prevent oil drilling in the area.

Only Greenpeace doesn't allow for the arrival of the Royal Navy's HMS *Monmouth*, hoping to break a tea-drinking record on the island. The sailors opt to hold their tea-drinking session on deck instead of Rockall as, paraphrasing their spokesman, 'the sight of Royal Naval personnel leaping from a helicopter might have led to some misunderstanding'.

Robbie also reveals that the *Daily Mirror*'s rock journalist was sick all day when he visited Waveland. Whether that has anything to do with the fact that the protestors' 'bucket and shove it' loo can't be emptied during bad weather, I don't know, but it does make me wonder whether there is any Green activity that doesn't require tortuous toilet difficulties.

Robbie is also the source of other interesting information. 'I was in the dunnie next to Lord Melchett the other day,' he reveals. Lord Peter Melchett is the head of Greenpeace. He'd recently made the national news for donning a white boiler suit and getting arrested for trashing Genetically Modified crops. He's seriously posh, being the fourth Baron Melchett. Melchett was educated at Eton and is the son of the former chairman of the British Steel Corporation. Not the sort of bloke you'd expect to find in the nick.

Everywhere you look in the Green movement there are toffs and/or children of billionaires. Prince Charles is now an organic farmer. Britain's second best-known Green, Jonathan Porritt, is Eton educated and the son of Lord Porritt. The Marchioness of Worcester, Tracy to her mates, is a trustee of Friends of the Earth. Zac Goldsmith, yet another old Etonian and son of the billionaire financier James Goldsmith, is set to take over the *Ecologist* magazine in a year's time.

Maybe in the New Britain that Tony Blair wants to build this shouldn't matter. The upper middle classes have every right to be concerned about the environment. When a title is flourished, the media certainly takes notice of their opinions. The landed gentry are also more familiar with the concept of stewardship of the land than most of us.

It might be due to the Ted and Ralph factor: the spoof baronet in *The Fast Show* who's constantly talking to Ted about the problem of the drainage in the lower field. Perhaps posh Greens have no problem envisaging the effects of global warming. It will turn much of the world into a gigantic, badly-drained lower field.

It's just that you never meet old Etonians seeking employment at *Loaded* (unless James Brown is a master of downward mobility), *Time Out* or *Midweek*. Even the last two Conservative prime ministers, Margaret Thatcher and John Major, are lower middle-class made good. But here in the eco-world there are more titles than even Prince could give himself.

Is it all some subconscious horror of industrialisation, or a yearning for the time when there was a clear divide between the city and the countryside (most of which they owned)? Can people with mansions lecture the rest of the country on reducing their consumption?

And here I am, sleeping with someone who never uses the words 'lounge' or 'toilet'. I've only ever dated working-class or middle-class women before, people who drive cars and eat at McDonald's without fear. Can my life with Nicola continue or will I soon run away with someone blonde who loves shopping for shoes?

Away from the allotment, Nicola is busy applying for a National Lottery grant for the Forest Management Foundation. Her application appears to be as large as a small book. She's still attending numerous meetings. While officially a freelance environmental writer, she seems to have a post on more acronyms than you can throw a series of jumbled letters at.

'Face it Nicola, there are only seven Greens in the world and they all have posts on each other's committees,' I tell her.

'No, that's not fair. There's at least twelve.'

She might be at a meeting of the WWF (World Wildlife Fund) in Fitzroy Square one night, or an FSC (Forest Stewardship Council) dinner with Prince Philip attending the next. Or at a meeting of Transport 2000 where Michael Palin is speaking, or maybe the FMF (Forest Management Foundation) or FoG (the Friends of Gillespie Park).

The most unfortunate acronym is PIS, which stands for the Pacific Island Society. Nicola joined after her sojourn in the Solomons, but as the membership seems to be mainly old anthropologists and vicars, they seem to have missed the lavatorial connotations of their acronym. She has me ferrying my TV and video in a taxi to New Zealand House for a PIS meeting, in order for her to show a video about the Solomon Islands.

Nicola attends some of my meetings too. She manages to sit through a couple of West Ham games (though she still calls the kits uniforms and now we're a couple doesn't seem half as interested in football) and even attends my talk to the Fulham Referee's Association.

The refs are admirers of my work writing about Sunday league football in *FC* magazine. At the end of my talk they present me with a Fulham Referee's Association tie.

'See, I told you I was respected,' I tell her. 'Was it very boring for you?'

'No, I'm used to men obsessed with areas of grass and interpretations of obscure laws.'

Yes, it can't be too dissimilar to the environmental movement.

We attend a recording of the TV show *Dating The Enemy*, along with Robbie and Angela. On one side of the studio are lads, rugby players, people who organise all-night bus parties, and myself. On the other side of the studio sit the ladettes, a university netball team, two women who like to have a laugh while out-drinking men, and Nicola and Angela.

Nicola sits at the end of the row, desperately trying to keep out of camera shot and dreaming of green tea, not lager.

'Ladettes' like Zoe Ball and Ulrika Jonsson have been snapped supping pints and enjoying footie and now the media is obsessed with ladettes and lads. I'm introduced as author of *The Lad Done Bad* and a 'lad historian'. In my soundbites I manage to describe a few incidents of footballers behaving badly, such as Gazza and his fellow England players at a Hong Kong nightclub lying back in the famous dentist's chair and having Flaming Lamborghini cocktails poured down their throats. My suggestion is that the current fad of lads is a reaction to the preposterous idea of the 'new man' a few years before. It sounds vaguely academic compared to the baying netball and rugby players around me.

'Lad historian, pretty impressive, eh?' I say to Nicola as we decline the offer of a taxi from the TV company and take the tube home instead.

'The only lad history you know about is when you chronologically arrange your videos of *Whatever Happened to the Likely Lads*,' she replies.

'Wow, I never realised you secretly peruse my video collection.'

'You can't avoid it when you're dating the enemy.'

But vegetables and a boyfriend aren't enough for Nicola. Our home is complete when Nicola adopts a recycled cat. Or more accurately a cat whose owner has been murdered.

The previous week the police had questioned everyone in our street about a murder in a squat ten doors down the road. 'We didn't hear a thing, there was an Arsenal game on,' I protested. The dead man was stabbed inside the squat, which was rumoured to be a home for various people with drug addictions. His girlfriend, billed as a 'hostess' in the local paper, was arrested and charged with murder, but found not guilty.

A few days after our visit from the police, I arrive home after a hefty post-*Time Out* session to find a note from Nicola on the landing. I read it before opening the door.

'Dearest Pete, Whoops, I've adopted a cat! She belonged to the murder man and I found her in the garden outside. She's homeless so I've said we'll adopt her. I've named her Honey. Make sure you don't let her out when you come in, Hope you don't mind, love, Nicola.'

Oh God. As I enter our flat I'm accosted by a ginger cat. It immediately sits on me, places its paws on my shoulder and purrs dementedly.

'Isn't she lovely?' beams Nicola. 'She wouldn't come when the fireman tried to rescue her, but she saw me and immediately came over. She wants us to be her owner. She'll have to go to a cat home and be put down if we don't have her.'

I'm not a lad at all. I can't control my home life or my girlfriend. One day I'm going to say no to her. It's just that she's a very difficult woman to say no to. And the cat does seem quite friendly.

'Isn't she supposed to be traumatised if her owner's been stabbed in front of her?' I ask in disbelief, wondering if I'm drunker than I thought. Page proofs, pints, pussies, what is happening to my day?

The cat looks remarkably well balanced for a homicide witness. It's enjoying our armchair and is now using my stomach as a treadmill and clawing my jumper.

'Look, I've got a litter tray for her, it can go in the hallway. And she'll keep us company while we're writing.'

'Well, I suppose it's better than putting the cat into land-fill,' I mutter, knowing Nicola will never relent now. 'But you can clean up the litter tray!'

And so the cat joins our household and Nicola carries on with her allotment preparations. We even manage to plant some potatoes, although Nicola's aberrant borage is smoth-ering everything else. Then she plants an apple tree. 'Are you allowed to do that?' I ask. But Nicola tends to ignore rules that don't suit her. She's delighted with her apple tree – although everyone else seems to be sticking to onions.

But just because we're a couple, we don't have do every-thing together. In late spring I arrange to visit my friends Jackie and Reno in San Francisco, stopping off in New York on the way home. Nicola doesn't seem that interested in the trip and anyway, there's a cat to look after.

Not having flown until my twenties, the idea of loitering around airports is still exciting to me, though after such prolonged exposure to Nicola's views, I feel vaguely guilty about the carbon emissions. But there's no other way of getting there quickly. It's not like flying to Glasgow or some ridiculous short-haul trip that can easily be done by train.

Nicola says she won't go, because 'I'm terrified of flying, there's turbulence over the Atlantic, and it's bad for our carbon footprint.'

'Isn't Carbon Footprint a band?' I quip.

Being a man from Mars I assume that Nicola means what she says. But she's a woman from Venus, so there's a subtext. Her refusal to fly is actually a cue for me to insist she accompanies me. I discover this a few days before I'm set to leave. An offer to pay for Nicola's fare or meet her in New York is too late; she's not coming now.

Jackie and Reno are part of my misspent carbon-guzzling past. I got to know Jackie, a mate of Vicky Mayer, my old pal from *Midweek/Ms London* days, while visiting Australia on my grand backpacking tour of 1992. Jackie met her husband Reno while staying in San Francisco that year.

After my arrival we chill in San Francisco bars and restaurants, spot hippies in Haight-Ashbury, meet uber geeks from *Wired* magazine, cross the Golden Gate Bridge and generally enjoy what seems to be one gigantic film set. They even have trams in SF, which makes it vaguely Green.

It's permanently hot and there are no arguments about central heating. Maybe that's why I had to get away.

Towards the end of my stay Reno suggests that I take an internal flight to Las Vegas. 'You've just got to see it, man, it's just so gross!'

A day later I'm flying in to Vegas over a light-encrusted desert. My room for the night is in the Luxor Hotel, a giant imitation pyramid. In my room the free magazines from reception have numerous numbers for 'escorts'. This should be nirvana for *Loaded* Man. I walk down the Strip looking at casinos, 'Eat All You Can!' offers, huge artificial waterfall displays, giant pirate ships and endless neon. Lights everywhere, in what was once a desert. A few years ago I would have thought this was brilliant, it was all very Hunter S Thompson to explore Vegas as a gonzo journalist. Now all I can think about is the awful waste of electricity. I think my status as a gonzo geezer might be in danger.

On the way home I've arranged to stay with former Oxford Green George Marshall in New York. He's now working for the Rainforest Foundation, founded by Sting and his missus Trudie Styler. George gives me an architectural tour of New York. We visit bars with US Greens from the Foundation, who appear much more open to hedonism than their UK counterparts, and I enjoy the bizarre feeling of visiting the supermarket at 2 am. George's flat is the sort of dilapidated place that Dustin Hoffman would have had in *Midnight Cowboy*. George is saving money, as he plans to return to Oxford, buy a house and convert it into an eco-home.

Honey and Nicola are at the flat when I return. 'You should see the energy that's wasted in Las Vegas!' I tell them.

Our divisions over the San Francisco trip appear to be forgotten by 1 May. It's the day of the general election and surely this time Tony Blair's Labour will win. I've blagged some tickets to see Billy Bragg at the Mean Fiddler. He has a screen on stage listing the results as he plays. There's a huge cheer when the pivotal seat of Basildon goes Labour. Billy punches the air and unleashes much Essex invective.

Sixteen years of Tory rule is ending. We're just looking for a New England. And Tony Blair is different. He promises to put global warming at the top of the political agenda.

People are celebrating in the Harlesden streets and in the taxi office where we order a cab to Barnsbury. Bob Gilbert has invited us to his flat to look at the results.

In the small hours Michael Portillo loses his seat and we all smirk. I'm worried Bob might celebrate by releasing one of his tarantulas. Things can only get better. Tony Blair has undoubted charisma; under him we'll surely see action taken to tackle global warming and get people out of cars and onto public transport.

Nicola celebrates by setting off for talks with Paula and Stuart from Forest Monitor in Ely, leaving me to water the allotment. When she returns we dig a compost pit at the allotment for her garden waste. But the allotment, with its reclaimed brick paths, is not large enough to contain her ambition. She needs a grander project. We have to reduce our carbon footprint by holidaying in Britain and, it seems, her partner must make penance for flying to San Francisco.

'You like Wainwright, we'll do his Coast to Coast walk' she announces excitedly, handing me a guide book. All she's forgotten to mention is the fact that it's 190 miles long.

CHAPTER 6

Walking Class Hero

It's hailing. In early summer. This is what you get when you take a holiday in England. Surely a walk in a park shouldn't be like this? Admittedly it's a national park, but we're being buffeted by 70 mph winds that threaten to throw us off huge precipices.

'We're spending 70 quid a night on B&Bs for two weeks? But we could go anywhere with that money.' I tell Nicola as we plan the Coast to Coast Walk. 'The world is our lobster. In Prague, the beer only costs about ten pence a pint or something ridiculous.'

'Yes, but we won't be flying like everyone else. When climate change hits we're all going to have to learn to holiday close to home. And the Lake District will be lovely. Think of the streams and the wild flowers in the meadows...' she says enticingly. 'And you like mountains.'

'Well, one at a time. Not 190 miles of yomping all at once...'

My holidays used to be so different. Hedonism rather than hardcore walking. A few summers ago on the Greek island of Kos, Yorkshire folk were singing 'On Ilkley Moor Baht 'at', and hordes of drunken English people in lager-lout shorts were mouthing along to 'American Pie' on the juke box. It was a time of 2 am flights, ouzo, languid mornings, cheap holidays and sod the climate.

After that it was internal flights across Australia, scuba diving on the Great Barrier Reef, jet boating in New Zealand and beach huts in Thailand. No, I didn't count my air miles, or wonder about carbon emissions or whether my holiday travel had any effect on the ozone layer. I was a lad-about-Oz with beaches, babes and beers to explore and enjoy. And now, in the early summer of '97, I'm in a blizzard up a mountain with a fresh air evangelist. A man about tarns, looking for a windbreak.

Training on beer and five-a-side hasn't quite prepared me for Wainwright's Coast to Coast Walk. But by the time we set out I've almost adjusted to no mini-breaks abroad. The Lake District mountains do look beautiful as we walk from St Bee's to Ennerdale, although my thighs and calves are wracked with pain the next morning.

Nicola spots numerous wild flowers and effortlessly names them. I wonder why she doesn't use her mastery of

detail for something constructive, like groundhopping or programme collecting.

We climb Haystacks, head down Honister Pass to Borrow-
dale and then cross the mountains to Grasmere. Walking
along glorious Lakeland valleys in the sun, holidaying in
England doesn't seem so bad. At least until the thunderstorm
on top of Helm Crag. Nicola believes we're going to be incin-
erated and demands to know what we should do.

'Sorry, darling, they missed that one when I was training
to be in the SAS,' I explain.

Should you lie down or stand up to avoid attracting a bolt
through the head? Buggered if I know. She doesn't either.

We're now on day five of our expedition and I'm trying to
prevent blisters with special padded plasters. In the morning
we complete a drizzly ten miles from Grasmere, passing a
misty Grisedale Tarn and down to the village of Patterdale,
where we stop for a late pub lunch.

Inside the boozer was one of the ubiquitous Coast to
Coast bores. A Harry Enfield-esque man who spots our OS
map and declares: 'So you're with Mr Wainwright, You're
going up Kidsty Pike are you? You want to go down the
Kirkstone Pass Road, turn away from the bridge, left then
right, up the path to Boredale Hause...'

But the weather worsens. We're on top of Angle Tarn with
winds of 70 mph lashing stinging hail into our faces. We've
just paced up the mountain path from Patterdale, my legs
already feeling overstretched from the morning's trek.

It all starts to go drumlin-shaped. On the other side of Satura Crag we arrive at what seems to be a giant washing machine, set on full wind and rain cycle followed by typhoon spin. The wind is surging across the mountain tops and is so strong it feels like it could blow us off our feet and down any number of horrible crevasses.

The Lake District receives millions of tourists a year, but up here it's surprising how quickly you feel lost and under threat. The mist moves in. We know there are huge cliffs around us but we can't see them, or any of the valleys beneath us. Then it starts hailing again. Pebble-size globules of white hail lash our matching red Gore-Tex coats. Yes, we have matching coats like a sad TV sitcom couple. I'd bought a red Gore-Tex coat for a press trip years ago, long before I met Nicola, only it's not as exhaust-stained as hers. I can see the headlines when our bodies are found: 'Couple from *Ever Decreasing Circles* found dead on mountain.'

Visibility is poor to appalling. We can just see another Gore-Tex clad couple ahead of us. We follow them across the brow of a hill because they look like they know what they're doing. Wainwright's guidebook is in my raindrop-smeared plastic map case but my hands have gone pink and are too cold to open it. I look at the OS Map and think that maybe we should be heading right, but wall and path signs merge into spots and broken lines. It's a mass of immaculately-drawn gobbledygook. Am I on drugs? No, sadly this is misty reality. This is a British summer-time holiday.

How we need one of Mr Wainwright's 'habitations'. If a pub appeared offering non-chilled real ale, I'd even buy him his favourite fish and chips in Kirkby Stephen, if he wasn't dead. And we might be too, soon. What would they say on *Loaded*? Aren't lads meant to die in an F1 racing car, free climbing in Patagonia or snorting cocaine with a groupie in an LA hotel room?

We can see the other couple negotiating peat holes. For an instant the sky clears and we see water in the valley far below. I ask the couple ahead if it's Haweswater. The man says hurriedly that he thinks it's Hayeswater. Then moves on, slurping through a peaty dip. Facing death in the afternoon and they don't want to talk to us. English reserve at nearly a thousand metres in a storm.

At least Nicola is taking it really well. 'Get me off here!' she shouts. Her glasses are covered in rain and her face is pink with cold. 'It'll be dark and we'll be stuck up here all night. We need to walk faster!'

I think of Wainwright's words: 'If you must have a companion, make sure you take one who is silent.'

'Well, we shouldn't have tried to walk 20 miles in a day!'

She's tired, cold, wet and frightened. And I am too. You don't get like this in Ibiza. I halt again. Pull Wainwright out of my zip pocket. And there it is. Of course, on the Coast to Coast you're too knackered to read up the next day's route each night. But my eyes scan the sentence: 'In clear weather the High Street crossing is without difficulties and an exhilarating march. If there is rain or mist it is advisable to avoid it (unless the route is remembered from previous visits) and take the lakeside path...'.

Bloody hell. You should always read the small print in guide books. There's a definite possibility of hypothermia if we're stuck here all night. And the fear that our relationship might not survive this, even if our bodies do. It's seven o'clock. Night is coming. We're in trouble. As an example of teamwork this must rank with the recent spat between Alan Sugar and Terry Venables at Tottenham Hotspur.

We're not unprepared. In my backpack is an orange plastic survival bag, compass, whistle and torch. None of which you need on a package tour. If we were in Europe we'd be setting out for a bar now. Maybe we'll be rescued by a helicopter and appear in the local press with embarrassing quotes about soft Londoners going unprepared into such conditions. Or we'll be found dead in six months' time by Brian Blessed and his camera crew, rehearsing for an Everest documentary.

Then I remember the Kendal Mint Cake in my jacket pocket. Top of any *Loaded* sugar Top 10. I break it in two. This chocolate-covered sugary delight tastes wonderful.

'Try this,' I tell Nicola, 'we need sugar.'

Getting to civilisation requires tenacity. Think of West

Ham and Julian Dicks. Comebacks from 2-0 down. The Kendal Mint Cake kicks in. After five minutes I feel some energy coming back.

Suddenly the clouds clear for an instant. We're looking down into the vast deserted valley of Riggindale Straits, scree scattered sublimely around its walls. Even after our buffeting by the elements and nearly 15 miles of walking it looks stunning.

'It's amazing when the clouds open up,' says Nicola. It's a reassuringly normal comment, a sign we might yet live and even talk to each other again.

After a long scramble we reach the bottom of the path by Haweswater and turn left. It's eight o'clock and almost dusk. This would be a natural spot for a village and a friendly pub where you could take off your sodden boots. And indeed, the village of Mardale did lie here until it was flooded to make the Haweswater Reservoir in the 1930s, much to the annoyance of Mr Wainwright.

There's now only one building on the lake and that's the hotel, its lights gleaming tantalisingly on the far shore. We walk for half an hour. The rain starts heavily again. It's incredible that there's nothing here. The currents are too dangerous for swimming and boating, so no tourists come here. We stop and look at the map.

'Oh no, we've come the wrong way, we should have turned right!' wails Nicola.

'It's miles away. Look at this lake, it's huge.'

Never has a reservoir looked so massive. Nicola's knees hurt, I'm exhausted. We have some four miles along a deserted track to the lake's end. Darkness is closing in. We walk on and on for another hour and then Nicola bursts into tears. Oh no. I can cope with exhaustion and possible death by exposure, but not women crying. Everything is wet, trousers, boots, jacket. It's nearly dark. We must do this again some day. I love non-polluting holidays in Britain.

We walk on through rain and shadows. At ten o'clock it's completely dark as we pass the dam and reach Burnbanks. It's meant to be a village, but it's just a few bungalows built for reservoir workers. Should we knock on a door and ask for a phone? Then, miraculously, we see a red phone box at the side of one of the cottages.

Amazingly, it works. My hands are so cold it's difficult to get my ten pence in the slot.

We get through to the hotel and feel like punching the air and cheering.

'I think it's over, ' I mumble, like a returning Vietnam war veteran. Someone from the hotel is coming to pick us up. And the phone box is dry. Let's stay in here. Anywhere out of this perpetual rain. We've been walking for 12 hours and covered 20 miles.

Jane from the hotel arrives in an estate car. 'We saw you coming down off Kidsty Pike and I knew you'd be a couple of hours when I saw you turn the wrong way. We could have been waiting for you at the car park otherwise,' she says cheerily.

It feels odd to be talking to someone else after our two-person struggle for survival. But will our shared ordeal create Andy McNab-style bonding after a near-death experience? Or will it just mean we never, ever holiday together again?

Ten minutes later we're in the bar at the Haweswater Hotel. Our boots are off, pools of water have been wrung out of our sodden socks. I can feel my toes. We're sitting before a log fire and being offered hot punch by proprietors Ken and Jane. It tastes delightful.

'I hope you're not neglecting your other guests,' I say.

'You are the guests,' says Jane.

We're offered a bath upstairs. The hotel is a 1930s municipal vision of nirvana. 'The locals said it used to be a knocking shop for the directors of the water board,' explains Jane.

Proprietor Ken is full of gritty northern aphorisms: 'You're from London are you? You should see it when they all come here and their mobile phones don't work because of the mountains. They're desperate to be wanted. I always tell them the cemeteries are full of people who thought they were indispensable.'

He asks us whether the hotel should be on e-mail. 'Mind you, whenever I see a computer there's always someone sitting at it who could be working.'

The sound of a saxophone playing comes from the hotel's

boathouse. 'That's Steve, our odd job man, practising on his sax,' explains Jane.

A bath soothes our aching bodies. We drag ourselves downstairs. Safe and warm and dry. I've got a pint of bitter in my hand, Jane arrives with a huge pan of vegetarian moussaka and we eat under the pictures of Mardale village re-emerging from the reservoir during the 1986 drought. And then we collapse into bed. Twenty miles in one bloody day. Less a holiday and more of a carbon-saving marathon.

'I'm sorry if I got cross, I thought I was going to die,' explains Nicola, in what I guess is an apology.

'I'm sorry too. We're down now, that's all that matters. Quite bracing really. Wonder what it's like when it's really windy?'

The truth is we're too tired and relieved to argue about our day.

'I don't think being a journalist prepared me for this somehow...' I sigh to my exhausted, UK-holiday loving partner. We collapse into blissfully warm sheets.

'Tell you what. Next year, shall we cut out the middle man and go on the Great North Run instead?'

My bird has finally made it on to page five of the *Sun*. Only we never expected it to be like this. Nicola is now a national talking point. She has just suffered a sensationalist exposé from the 'super soaraway' paper. Although the *Sun* has used quite a flattering picture of her.

We're back in London for the summer now. Arguments about heating can be forgotten, although apparently an electric fan uses far too much power so on hot days we roast in Nicola's garrett. Somehow we survived the Kidsty Pike debacle, resting up at the Haweswater Hotel as the summer heat returned. Maybe that hellish day in the hail was cathartic in some way. The Coast to Coast Walk even started to be quite enjoyable, sandwiches by the ruined abbey at Shap and then across the limestone pavements of the Yorkshire Dales and on to Reeth, where in my head the lyrics of the Proclaimers suddenly became corrupted to 'While the Chief puts sunshine on Reeth...'.

We plan to return to complete the walk in autumn, but for the moment we need to work. There's a 'Sidelines' column to do, my *Midweek* column to write and a Greatest Living Englishman piece on the astronomer Patrick Moore. Reformed drug smuggler Howard Marks is appearing at the Do Tongues art club in Brighton, which I'm covering for *Time Out*. We both have books to write too, like a proper media couple. Virgin publishing has accepted my idea for a book about Sunday league football, while Indigo has commissioned Nicola to write *The Estate We're In*, a book on 'who's driving car culture'. I'm certainly not driving it, as she won't let me.

But that was all before Nicola becomes the *Sun*'s most odious woman in Britain. It's all to do with her tree-hugging charity the Forest Management Foundation and its successful application for a National Lottery grant. Nicola's always known how to fill in application forms and mention the correct buzzwords like 'sustainability'. We both thought she'd done brilliantly to get £20,000 for the FMF from the National Lottery. But that was before the *Sun* started looking for 'loony Lottery grants'.

When someone from the *Sun* phones, Nicola insists she meet them in person, as 'no comment' means they could print what they liked. 'For God's sake, don't show them our flat!' I plead, terrified at the thought of the untidiest, most-cluttered home in the UK causing building site workers in cafés all over Britain to splutter into their over-sugared tea. Thankfully, she does the interview at the Islington Ecology Centre, which their hack would hate too. It doesn't come out great.

'SCANDAL OF NATIONAL LOTTO-TREE' shouts the headline on page five, above bullet points exclaiming:

'£20,000 for trees on coconut isle'

'Nearly half goes to charity 'director''

'Even locals say it's a waste of cash'.

The *Sun*'s hack, writing under the pseudonym of Sir Lenny Lottery had already 'exposed' several Lottery grants. Mainly for outrageous crimes like the fact they're going to iffy foreigners, 'despite desperate pleas for cash here from cancer charities and groups caring for the terminally ill'.

'The Solomons money is aimed at teaching 20 land-owning families which trees to fell and which to save, in order to sustain forests on the 900-island group,' says the *Sun*, which seems accurate enough.

But then comes the loaded accusation that Nicola, 'admitted she will pocket nearly £6,000 out of the grant as a retainer over the two year project – even though she will work on it only three days a month. Another £200 will vanish in running costs like phone calls and faxes.'

We're journalists so we know what they're doing. Easy target, bit of innuendo. Three thousand quid a year doesn't sound too much to 'pocket' to me. She certainly doesn't blow it on frivolous luxuries like heating. If they knew the austerity of our flat, or the puritanical zeal of the Greens...

Sir Lenny and the subs make patronising comments about 'coconut isles'. The *Sun* has even flown out its own investigator to the Solomons – who probably pocketed a lot more in flight and hotel expenses than Nicola ever has. Still it's quite flattering that she's worth all this trouble. Maybe I'm dating Britain's version of Petra Kelly, the famous leader of the German Green Party. Or a latter-day Rachel Carson. She might even get an invitation to appear on *Newsnight* like Swampy did.

The *Sun*'s man has visited various Solomon Islanders involved in the logging industry. Unsurprisingly, they all say that logging is a great thing because they're making loads of money out of it. 'Poor farmers are paid £12 for each tree chopped down – a fortune in local terms. And they are more than happy for the logging to continue,' writes the *Sun*. One islander 'had never heard of our Lottery and thought its project did not amount to a pile of sawdust'. It's a bit like asking workers at Sellafield what they think of wind turbines. Or butchers their views on vegetarians.

The *Sun* doesn't say what will happen when the last tree had been felled and there's nothing left to sell except a denuded island leeching its soil into the sea, I think to myself. Hang on, that's a bit Green. I'm sounding like a true Green. Maybe you can't live with a woman like Nicola and not assimilate some of her arguments.

'Now you know how Princess Diana felt,' I tell her, attempting to lighten her mood.

The thing is she's the most sincere tree lover I've ever known. The only thing she likes more than trees is the Solomon Islands. And organising things. And chocolate with her porridge. She's the Greenest person in the world. Maybe the National Lottery want a personal affidavit detailing her environmental credentials, the compulsive turning-down of central heating, the cycling, the skip diving, the recycling, the huge tomes on global warming.

It's surprising how indignant I feel on her behalf. My thoughts are focusing on placing a carbon boot print on Sir Lenny Lottery's posterior. Perhaps I'm even proud of what she does.

Still, the article does make her sound very important. And

there's a really nice picture of her next to a Solomon *ngzu-ngzu* (a wooden head inlaid with mother of pearl) with her title of 'director' in the obligatory inverted commas alongside the headline 'I'm worth all my £6,000 cut'.

The *Sun* continues: 'The journalist who dreamed up the tree scheme after working in the Solomons, describes herself as the charity's director even though she has no staff. And she said: 'The payment to myself can be justified as a retainer, I suppose, because I am a director. I get £240 a month.'

'She admitted the money will be on top of fees she earns as a freelance environmental writer. But she said: "If you are running a charity you need someone who knows just what to do. It is a question of networking, contacting people and filling in all the wretched forms the Charity Commission expect you to." Nicola, 33, called the grant "just a small amount compared to what other charities and arts organisations get".'

Maybe we should call Max Clifford. Buried at the end of the article are claims of ministers taking bribes from logging companies and the admission that 'some reforestation programmes are in place funded by foreign aid from Britain and Australia'.

The *Sun* had even penned an editorial on the subject reading 'END THIS LOTTERY LUNACY'.

Oh dear. Nicola is a national cause célèb just because she's good at getting grants and wants to save trees. But she makes a reasonably good job of defending herself, and Roy

Greenslade writes a fine piece in the *Guardian* pointing out what an unjustified attack it was.

The night of the exposé we decide to go out to dinner and spend some of the six grand she is 'pocketing'. She needs my support and I'm determined to be sensitive. 'We'd better look out for paparazzi,' I caution, as we enter the Italian restaurant.

'I'll be laughed at and it's not fair,' she says. 'How will any-one ever take saving the rainforest seriously when there are people like those at the *Sun* around?'

'They're bastards, you don't deserve it and I'm right behind you,' I say, as the waiter fusses over wine menus and candles. 'But I did rather like the way they kept describing you as "Nicola, 33". It made you sound just like a glamour model.'

She kicks me. 'And your eyebrows looked really good too, just like Liz Hurley when she had proper eyebrows. Bit over-dressed for the *Sun* though. Still, I feel almost like a footballer. Imagine what James Brown would say. I'm dating a posh page five Lotto-tree-babe from the *Sun*, supported by what the *Sun* would call a collection of politically-correct elitists... You'll laugh about it one day. We could always make a T-shirt of it,' I continue. 'Ah, but it would have to be on unbleached organic Fairtrade cotton' she replies.

'Yes, but apart from that, I still think "Scandal of National Lotto-tree" could be up there with Che Guevara as an iconic T-shirt. Let's have another glass of Chardonnay...'

*

Nicola's woken up in her usual manner, full of energy and ideas, in one of her Flora from *Cold Comfort Farm* moods.

'Why don't we have a baby?' she says, as if she's suggesting a cappuccino.

'We can't there's a Solomon Islander downstairs!'

'No, you durr-brain! Not now, but soon.'

'Yes, and maybe for the rest of our lives.'

'I'm serious. All my friends are having children... and I love you.'

She can always disarm me with a bit of flattery. 'I love you too...' I mumble. 'Although it's a bit early in the morning for me, and maybe you could make us a coffee first...'

Blimey. I was too nice to her after the *Sun* trouble. I should never have tried to make her laugh. Do I love her? Well, sometimes, when she's not making me eat vegetable mush soup or turning off Radiohead's new album *OK Computer* and saying they should play proper songs. But a baby? The cat! The cat was a sign. Is that my radio alarm by the bed, emitting dangerous electro-magnetic rays, or is it a red, winking, biological alarm clock?

'God, I can't deal with big questions at 7.30 am,' I bluster, 'You know I'm terrified of fatherhood, and commitment. I'm a man! And my parents would make a fuss, and it would be really embarrassing.'

'But you do want to have children, don't you?'

'Well, yes, I'm pretty sure, some day, 70 per cent sure,

30 per cent terrified, I guess. But according to you sperm counts are going down anyway because of oestrogen-mimicking something or other.'

'But you're still fertile… and we're getting older. And you'd be a great dad.'

'Would I? Well, I hope so. I guess it's really flattering you want to have babies with someone who can't use a compost loo. Are you sure this isn't all to do with Diana and Dodi?'

'Of course I am.'

'Well, the whole country's gone a bit weird…'

'I'm sure.'

'Or the fact that *This Life* has just finished?'

'Of course not.'

'OK. I'll think about it. But meanwhile we've got to look after Arthur.'

I am indeed getting old. In a few years I'll be 40. Maybe a child would be a good idea, an invitation to the grown-up world. But it would mean commitment. Maybe never writing for *Loaded* again. And it would mean a lifetime with a Green. Maybe she'd mellow and become a born-again mother, less obsessed with saving the world. But knowing Nicola, maybe not. Life with her is sometimes excruciating, but always, erm, interesting. And it does make good copy. She wants me, too, which counts for a lot.

Perhaps it's best to stall for a time. Anyway, it'll take ages to conceive a child. Plus Arthur is staying in our living room.

He's a photographer and journalist from the Solomon Islands who has come to Britain for a course. He and I see the West Ham v Wimbledon match, where he takes lots of pictures of East End geezers in the Queen's pub and sees John Hartson score twice. Then comes the unbelievable news that Princess Diana and Dodi Fayed have been killed in a car crash in Paris. We take Arthur to photograph the wreaths and mourners around Kensington Palace and he sends reports back to the *Solomon Star*.

I find myself telling Nicola that, in all the coverage of the accident, no one seems to mention that if Diana had worn a seat belt she might have survived. I'm obviously already assimilating some of the arguments about the dangers of car culture from her planned book.

Arthur returns to the Solomons, but our social life is as bizarre as ever after his departure.

One night it might be dinner with Ben Burt the anthropologist in Brixton, the next a public meeting on composting at Islington Ecology Centre. This provides more lavatory humour than an entire set by Ben Elton. They're extracting the urine – literally.

Several gardeners announce that they regularly urinate on their compost heaps to promote plant growth. One tiller of the soil says he mixes his urine with comfrey and horse manure to make organic fertiliser. Another man reveals that he puts his urine in a bottle, dilutes it and then sprays his plants.

Urine is also useful on your garden to mark your territory and ward off cats he adds. Apparently men's urine is better, as it contains less hormones.

'It's the only thing men are useful for,' chuckles Nicola.

'So does this mean all those football fans who used to urinate in people's gardens every Saturday in the 1980s were not hooligans at all, just misunderstood Green pioneers of organic composting?' I ask.

'Yes, it probably does.'

When we get home Nicola proudly shows me *The Humanure Book*, a self-published book on composting human manure by J C Jenkins. 'You'll like this. It's on recycling human waste.'

I glance through it and find one reader suggesting that 'Taking urine internally has been going on for thousands of years and is considered by many to be a wonderful medicine. Also urine is used today in ear wax removal and hand creams.' According to the author, the ideal compost comes from China, an equal mix of human faeces and urine, livestock manure, organic refuse and soil. What is it with Greens and weeing in the wind?

Another night we use my *Time Out* persona to crash a black-tie do at Hatchards book shop with John Major, Princess Margaret, Salman Rushdie, Michael Palin, Melvyn Bragg in attendance and Nicola as my Miss Moneypenny substitute.

Some evenings Tom and Katie, founders of the New Luddite movement, stay. Nobody else I know has Luddites to stay. When they leave, much to my relief, the TV is still intact and the hi-fi hasn't been attacked with a crowbar.

The Luddites are Green pals of Nicola's, campaigning 'for the environment and against the dehumanising use of technology' and, of course, the reclamation of the word Luddite: 'Rather than letting it remain a term of abuse we can restore "Luddite" as the proud battle cry for a new direction of non-violent direct action.' At a fringe meeting of the Green Party, the New Luddites led a discussion on whether concrete, computers and television are intrinsically bad technologies, although, as they have an e-mail address on green.net, they seem to have followed Radiohead's example and said OK computer (subject to a conference resolution).

Maybe I'm a reproductive Luddite. Nicola wants a baby and it's terrifying. Can I do responsibility? It's a strange time. The country is in some kind of gloom fest over Diana. Nicola and myself are just too old to be of the *This Life*, Anna, Miles and Egg generation. The series has become a north London institution in our gaff, preferable even to storytelling. The New Luddites probably watch it too. Would Anna want a baby? Or Miles? Can I cope with being a dad? Can I cope with being a Green dad?

What Nicola needs, as always, is a project that might take

her mind off my likely role as a progenitor. And our immediate aim is to finish Wainwright's Coast to Coast Walk.

The hail we encountered on our earlier walk seems typical of the chaotic weather conditions of the summer. Glastonbury festival-goers slurp their way through seas of mud, Wimbledon is washed out and the cricket is rained off. Every month now seems to be the wettest or driest since records began. It all appears to be positive evidence of global warning. What's climate change going do to the traditional English preoccupation with talking about the weather? Maybe in the next millennium we'll be walking into the newsagents saying, 'You can tell it's the cricket season, eh, a 50-foot tidal wave has just swept away the Greenwich Millennium Experience.'

So we decide to complete the Coast to Coast Walk before it's washed away, and here we are in September, back at Ingleby Arncliffe for the final four days of the walk across the North Yorks moors. Whereas Haweswater in the hail was hellish, it's all an enjoyable autumn romp now. We have amazing views across a quilt of fields towards the monsters that are Middlesbrough's chemical works and power stations. The Wainstone crags are bathed in the golden sunlight of early evening. The light sets off rather nicely my Green Philosophy Football T-shirt bearing Albert Camus's aphorism 'All that I know most sincerely about morality and obligations I owe to football.'

We move on through places with quintessentially northern names like Cringle Moor, Cold Moor and Hasty Bank, over the sinuous curves of the disused Rosedale ironstone railway. Staying in a Tudor farmhouse, eating in pubs, meeting an elderly man at Egton Bridge who enthuses about Wainwright's Walk, telling us 'Do it while you still can!' Even the fact that West Ham lose 4-0 at Arsenal on our penultimate day can't erase the satisfaction of having nearly completed the route. Our final day sees blistered feet head triumphantly downhill into Robin Hood's Bay. We're even greeted by a cat that's Honey's double. And there's a free half pint of beer offered by the Robin Hood's Bay Hotel for completing the Coast to Coast Walk. We walk on the beach and dip our sweaty feet into the sea. As Wainwright might have said: 'Yippee!' One hundred and ninety miles completed. Phew.

We stay at the Shepherd's Purse in Whitby. It's a homely place, with a shop selling veggie sausages, beans, pulses and generally right-on foods, a coffee bar and courtyard, then on to dinner at the best restaurant in town, local monkfish and Sancerre wine.

'Do it while you still can!' repeats the voice of the old walker we met on route. Flushed with fresh air, Wainwright-like exuberance and wine we return to our room and have unprotected sex.

We are elemental creatures of the wild moors. Having read all Nicola's press cuttings about diminishing male sperm counts due to chemicals, fertilisers and just about everything else, I'm convinced it will be six months to a year before we conceive. Or we'll have to visit the UVF for treatment, although why Protestant paramilitaries would be of any use I don't know. Yes, live for the moment. We are Coast to Coasters and from now on we'll never walk alone.

The next month we're lying in bed when Nicola announces the news. Set phasers on stun, Captain. There's a jolt of terror, a knotting of the stomach, mingled with macho pride.

'Are you sure?' I gasp.

Nicola flourishes an object that looks like a thermometer crossed with the fluid link from the Tardis, before putting it down on top of her copy of *McLibel* by John Vidal.

'It doesn't lie. You're not firing blanks, as they might say on *Loaded*.'

'Bloody hell, I'm fertile!'

'It means we'll have a baby in June.'

'Great.'

Thankfully I manage to hide from her my horrified realisation that the baby is due in the middle of the 1998 World Cup finals. How could a football fan have overlooked this? It's probably best not to ask if there's a TV in delivery rooms right now.

I drink strong coffee and recoil at more terrors. I'm going to be a parent. One of Bridget Jones' Smug Marrieds, except that we are not. One of those people who exist to annoy non-parents. A horrible baby supremacist who pretends to have discovered a new inner meaning to their life and acts like they're the only person in the world ever to have a child. Maybe I'd become the sort of parent who announced that they were the 'blissed out, wonder-stunned, beauty-struck' parents of a new daughter. Or, even worse, transmit pictures of our new baby over the internet, and hell, I'm not even on e-mail yet.

I think of the Green couple in Oxford who announced 'We're pregnant!' on their card. I don't want to be the sort of man who announces 'We're pregnant!'. No, Nicola is pregnant, and Pete is the father.

We've been sexual bungee jumping and this is the result. A nappy and me? How can it ever work out? And then there's the birth. Modern men are expected to witness everything and what if Nicola follows the example of some mad earth mother I read about in *Resurgence* who made her placenta into a paté? Although if I can get through polenta, then maybe anything's possible.

Are we supposed to get married now? Nicola's always insisted that it's a deeply patriarchal institution and she'd never change her name or subsume herself to a man. So that seems to be a no. And nobody we know gets married any more. The stress of organising a wedding and a birth would be too terrifying.

But then pride begins to overcome terror. Parenting is no doubt a nightmare, but I'll love the child and hopefully that will be enough. And then there's the clatter of the post coming through the letterbox.

Nicola goes downstairs to fetch it. She tears open a letter from the council. Only why doesn't she slit open letters with a knife like I do? We Greens we have to reuse our envelopes and a nice clean cut makes them so much easier to reseal.

'Bloody bastards!' she shouts.

'What's the matter?'

'The council has repossessed my allotment! The other allotment holders have complained that it's overgrown. And they say that I've illegally planted an apple tree!'

I begin to laugh. She smiles too. Instead of nurturing organic vegetables we're now growing an organic baby.

Soon we're off stay with Tom and Katie, her New Luddite mates in the Lake District. Tom's mum owns a boathouse on Lake Ullswater. First we meet in Lancaster, then Tom drives his Land Rover up to the Lakes, past Pooley Bridge and along the shore of Ullswater. He parks at the top of a lakeside track. Then he clambers down to the boathouse and returns with a scythe and various agricultural instruments.

'So scythe does matter,' I tell the unimpressed trees.

We take a scythe each and hack a path through a wilderness of overgrown foliage. It feels like being Levin in Tolstoy's *Anna Karenina*. I'm experiencing a cathartic vision of the dignity of labour. Eventually we reach the boathouse and a small patch of ground around the lake. Tom is an academic like his parents, but also frighteningly practical. He's the sort of Green who knows how to erect a teepee by the lake, and does so in a few seconds. We camp overnight, making a bonfire in a stone firepit, baking potatoes and barbecuing veggie sausages.

The next morning we bathe in the lake and then comes the rowing. We're attempting to reach the yacht club across the lake where Tom's dad has a boat moored. I rapidly prove myself to be the world's most inept oarsman as the boat circles wildly. As I grapple with a reluctant oar I reflect that if Nicola wasn't pregnant and trapped in a boat she'd definitely leave me for ever at this moment.

We eventually reach the yacht club and, powered by eco-friendly winds, Tom takes the helm and races the yacht down Ullswater. The contrast with *Loaded* man is humiliating. But the speed and scenery are invigorating, even if I don't know a boom (at least until it nearly hits me) from a jib or a cleat.

We return for another night's camping at the boathouse. Only without any water facilities, going to the loo involves being handed a trowel. Tom points in the general direction of the woods.

'Don't be so pathetic, get on with it!' chides Nicola.

Please God, just for once let me be involved in some form of activity with her that doesn't involve a compost loo, a drop loo or no loo. Bowel movements by Ullswater involve un-speakable activities with trowels and paper, burying the evidence among the trees, bracken, thistles, nettles and flies. Often during a deluge. Soon I become expert at restraining nature and holding on until the café at the perhaps aptly-named Pooley Bridge (outside loo with cold water and a mirror) or the National Trust toilets at Aira Force (smelly but effective).

Soon we'll have a baby and we won't be able to camp so easily. I won't mind. The Lake District is a brilliant place; but it's still a joy to return home to London where no skills are required in sickle-wielding, rowing or outdoor defecation, just the ability to find the record button on the video.

We're celebrating our fourth anniversary together at the end of October. Four years. Is that long enough to know someone before you have a baby? We'll be linked for the rest of our lives now. I'll never be able to lead a non-Green life again. But then, I'm beginning to wonder whether I'd ever want to. I'm already a long way from *Loaded* lad, but now I'm on a one-way gyra-tory system to parenthood.

Knowing my partner doesn't approve of out-of-season

flowers (too many miles spent on planes and boats) or the card industry, I take the back of a cereal packet and glue on a spoof front page of the *Sun* beginning 'Defiant charity boss Nicola, 33, today claimed she was worth all her 25 pence cut of Lottery funding towards the previously unknown charity the Pete May Foundation (PMF)'.

We're having a baby and the planet has been saved, it seems. It's 11 December 1997. At last the world's governments are acting together to stop climate change. Or at least slow it down very slightly. The Kyoto Protocol is opening for signature in Kyoto, Japan. The signatories will cut their combined emissions of acronyms to 5 per cent below 1990 levels by 2008-12. European Union countries are expected to cut their emissions by 8 per cent and Japan by 5 per cent. The targeted acronyms are carbon dioxide (CO_2), methane (CH_4), hydrofluorocarbons (HFCs), perfluorocarbons (PFCs) and sulphur hexafluoride (SF_6).

'Will it work?' I ask Nicola.

'It's making some progress. But it's no good unless the US signs up,' she says, 'It's just scratching at the surface really, George Monbiot says we have to cut our emissions by more than 50 per cent... And there's no obligation beyond promising to monitor and report emissions.'

'So it's a bit like hoping our sleep levels will only be reduced by 5 per cent below the 1990 levels when we have a baby.'

'Guess so.'

Is reducing emissions impossible? Not yet. The big pol-luters like the US will find some way of procrastinating, it seems. Climate change appears to be real. Is my child going to live in some kind of version of Kevin Costner's *Waterworld* after the Thames Barrier is breached? Maybe the future mat-ters. Although the major question in my immediate future is: Will I be able to I survive the delivery room without fainting?

CHAPTER 7

Green Baby

'Of course we'll be needing a car once we have a baby,' I suggest.

We're in Nicola's brother's car, driving down the A13. It's research for Nicola's new book on car culture, *The Estate We're In*.

'Of course we won't need a car, you durr brain! We're not going to fall into the baby consumerism trap. People had babies before cars were invented... Climate change won't stop just because we have a child.'

'But you look very comfortable behind the wheel. Slow down. You're over the speed limit. Now this is real car country. There's Dagenham Motors, and we're coming up to Lakeside, you've got to have a car to get there. Twelve thousand free car parking spaces...'

'Come on! Doesn't that stupid git know how to drive!'

'Well done, I can see you're really getting into car culture.'

We park the motor at Lakeside shopping centre and look around the giant, American-style mall. Teenage girls wearing Sporty Spice tracksuits are queuing for makeovers at *Sugar* magazine's Face of 1998 competition. A Vauxhall Corsa Breeze is in the concourse and up for raffle.

'Look, that's very Essex,' I say, pointing to a pastry shop called Jeff de Bruges. 'That's our idea of continental sophistication.'

We find a café and sit down for a cappuccino.

'Are you sure about the car?' I continue, thinking that the Essex driving ambience might soften her hard Green edges. 'I thought real dads had to discuss routes and A roads whenever they arrive anywhere. My dad does. And what about all those mother and baby magazines you've made me read? They all say you need a car. And one of those removable car seats that you carry your baby out in and then put them down upstairs, while you get drunk at afternoon parties... and most couples buy a second car when they have a baby, not a first.'

'Have you ever heard of a buggy? Or a BabyBjörn?'

'Isn't he the son of a tennis player?'

'Oh for goodness sake! Cars are destroying our future, and our child's. The wretched M25 went through your dad's farm.'

'Yes, and he was really grateful for the compensation from the council.'

'It costs £3,000 a year to run a car, that's enough for an awful lot of taxis,' she says coaxingly, 'and it's horrible driving on these roads in endless jams,'

'I know, you're probably right. It's just a dream. It's just that sometimes I want to be part of the problem and not part of the solution.'

'You can have a buggy.'

'A beach buggy?'

'No, a baby buggy. *Junior* magazine says the Maclaren Techno is very good... That's if we can't pick up a recycled one.'

'Thanks.'

I know she's right, really. Driving around London is madness. My mate Steve the fanzine editor left the country because he became so angry driving to West Ham. Struggling to park, getting clamped or finding his side window had been smashed and his cassette player had been nicked. The M25 hasn't solved any problems; it's now a circular traffic jam and there's talk of widening it.

We leave Lakeside and drive on down the A13 trunk road to the sea, listening to the traffic updates on Radio Essex. As we near Shoeburyness we pass Ford showrooms, the American Car Company, Kwik Fit, Elite Motors, London Road Motors and a very Essex-sounding garage called Lookers.

'This is great material for your book,' I enthuse.

'And Essex is the Detroit of Britain?'

'Yeah, absolutely right. Bruce Springsteen would be writing songs about working at Ford Dagenham and buying a new Vauxhall Corsa if he lived here. Everyone from Essex has a car – apart from me, it seems.'

Back at home the cracks in our wall are widening, the men from the insurance company monitor them, and nothing else happens. Nicola wants to sell the place and get a place with a garden, but no one will buy while there's ongoing subsidence, so we're stuck here for now.

But our preparations for becoming parents continue. Soon Nicola has a whole shelf devoted to books on parenting. Lots of stuff by literary women saying stuff like 'I've had a baby and it hurts!' My own contribution is to read *So You're Going To Be A Dad* by Peter Downey, an Australian bloke who tackles the real issues of fatherhood – such as how you change a nappy.

'We'll have to join the NCT,' she declares.

'Is that another Green acronym?'

'No, it's the National Childbirth Trust. We'll meet loads of other couple with babies the same age as ours and we can all share babysitting.'

And so we go to the NCT. Every Tuesday night, eight middle-class couples gather in our NCT instructor Erica's house. The curtains are drawn and everyone is looking nervous. Will we be asked to throw our keys into a hat in the centre of the room, just like Sigourney Weaver does at that seventies swingers party in *The Ice Storm*?

Everyone has to give a short speech about their pregnancy hopes and fears. 'I am Pete May and I'm scared I'll never go to another football match again!' I declare. Erica looks a little puzzled.

The drugs don't work for the Verve and it seems they don't work for Erica either. Everyone in the group is against any form of chemical intervention and they all enthuse about the organic process of natural birth. If Erica realised that once her class is over I'm returning home to write a piece on Danny the Drug Dealer from *Withnail and I* for *Loaded*, I'd be expelled from the NCT for ever. Doesn't she know that hairs are the aerials of your brain?

We perform strangely sexual exercises. The women lean on cushions and point their ample buttocks in the air. Us men stand behind them, kneading their backs and bums.

'Do whatever makes her feel good, listen to her body!' coos Erica, as I knead Nicola's posterior and try not to look at the other women's raised bottoms around me.

Erica takes us through breathing exercises designed to help with the hours of painful contractions. She insists we all, supportive men included, intone some kind of yoga chant during these deep breaths. 'Ommmmmmm...' she chants, as if we're in a Tibetan monastery. I feel a bit like Jon Pertwee's Doctor, helpless as Devil worshippers and the Master summon up Azal the Dæmon. Only we're being initiated into a far more sinister sect – the Parenthood.

We do these breathing exercises every week, plus group activities such as listing the reasons pregnancy is painful and the pros and cons of parenthood.

Erica teaches us how to exercise our pelvic floor muscles. 'Just imagine you have a pencil up the rectum,' she explains casually. 'Now imagine you're in an elevator going down a couple of floors. Release and ease the pressure a bit. Now I want you to write your name with the pencil.'

'You could make a hell of a full stop!' I mutter to another prospective dad. The mothers might not need drugs, but right now I do.

There's more technical data than in a Haynes car manual.

At first the baby's head will 'engage'. I imagine a tiny Captain Picard announcing 'Engage!' somewhere in the womb. Then there's the arrival of something called a 'mucus plug', which is part of a 'show'. After the first lot of contractions there's 'transition'. It's worse than trying to understand software.

Apparently there's an awful lot of pushing, which Erica excels at imitating. We sit there aghast, as she makes a huge groaning, teeth-clenching wail. Her breathing chants then change to a strange 'Whooooooooooah!', a sound more appropriate to the reading of a ghost story.

We do contraction exercises; a weird stomping, sitting on buckets and a kind of slow dancing movement that involves all the couples gyrating in unison.

The technical details and the sharing of worries are useful. But I do wonder if Erica, well meaning as she is, quite understands new lads in 1998. She tells us to say affirmative things to our partners, like: 'I'm here for you. That's another contraction closer towards our baby.'

Perhaps she needs to read a year's supply of *FHM*.

'If you dare say anything like that to me I'll punch you,' confirms Nicola.

Then come the birth videos. A wobbly picture reveals a serene Erica holding a woman who looks like she's run several marathons. Nothing quite prepares me for a placenta delivered in blurred, but bloody, full colour. Even Nicola looks a little shocked.

The water birth video features a woman wearing a snorkel in a bloody pool surrounded by her partner, children and extended family. This is clearly where all those new men from the early 1990s ended up; immersed in blood in birthing pools.

'Right,' I tell Nicola. 'You got your own way on the car. But I'm not deviating on this. No video camera is going anywhere near your privates. Particularly if there's an NCT evangelist at the end of it.'

Because we're endlessly reciting all our post-parent fears at the NCT classes, we fret that we'll never spend any time alone again after the baby is born in June. So we decide to take our last-ever holiday in Montpelier, France. Dutifully I travel to the French tourist office to book trains all the way through to southern France.

Unfortunately Honey, our recycled cat, starts having breathing problems two days before we leave. We take her to the vet and the diagnosis is liver cancer. Is it a consequence of her life in a squat? Or a malaise of 20th-century living?

We have to leave Honey at the vet while we take the Eurostar train. On the concourse of Waterloo station Nicola phones the vet from a payphone, She returns with teardrops cascading from beneath her glasses.

'She's been put down,' she sobs uncontrollably. And then she begins to throw up into a plastic bag. Aha. Morning sickness. Except during Nicola's pregnancy it seems to strike at all times of day.

There are two things likely to inspire the flight response in an unreconstructed man. One is a woman's tears; the second is public chundering. Despite feeling a little squeamish myself, I attempt to sound sympathetic, and whisper words of consolation towards the sobbing, vomiting woman some metres away. The passing commuters think it's just another dispute among homeless problem drinkers.

Somehow we make it on to the train and beneath the Channel. In Paris we enjoy a kind of terminal romance, knowing parenthood is about to intervene. We admire the Louvre in the spring sunshine, eat croissants on the South Bank, dodge dog poo on the pavements and light a candle for Honey in the Sacré-Cœur.

As we travel on a high-speed train to Montpelier Nicola notices how much better the French trains are than ours. 'The government has to subsidise rail if it wants to get people out of cars,' she mutters. I think she's recovering from the shock of feline mortality. We relax into days of wandering the walled city of Carcassonne and the restaurants of Montpelier before returning to impending parenthood dans Angleterre.

And still there's so much to prepare. While the other NCT-ers are off to Mothercare and Hamley's, Nicola's determined to use as much recycled baby gear as possible. This Green principle certainly appeals to my pocket. One survey in some awful parenting magazine claims it costs £80,000 to bring up a child for 18 years. That's the price of around 160 West Ham season tickets.

Fleur and Richard in Yorkshire send emergency-aid parcels of baby and toddler clothes. Friends and relatives with kids give us a second-hand baby bath, a cot, a pack of reusable nappies, mobiles and old toys. We're going to use an armchair pushed in front of the stairs instead of a forty quid stair gate.

'Cotton wool is much cheaper and healthier than using chemically-impregnated baby wipes, and babies only need to be bathed in water rather than covered in expensive soaps, oils and shampoos,' she tells me. Where does she find out this stuff?

Nicola is virulently pro breast-feeding and against bottles, having read much NCT literature and spoken to her mate in the Maternity Alliance.

'If natural selection favours breast-feeding in the animal world, it's good enough for humans too,' she announces, coming over all Desmond Morris.

Great. No formula milk, bottles or sterilising. Another bonus of breast-feeding is that I possess no breasts. Therefore it's impossible for me to do it. It'll have to be Nicola who gets out of bed at some Tom Waits-like hour to feed the crying baby. Result.

She starts thinking about a home birth. All I can think of is the NCT video of that woman in a snorkel flopping around a bloody birthing pool. Thankfully, Nicola eventually agrees with medical advice that it's safer to have a first child in hospital. There's also less chance of her partner hyperventilating beneath a hot towel.

Nicola being Nicola, she agrees to stand as a Green Party candidate in the council elections. She's seven months pregnant.

'It's only as a paper candidate, I won't have to do any campaigning. The Greens want to field a candidate in every ward,' she tells me.

I'm terrified she'll get elected by mistake. I'll be a sort of Green Denis Thatcher and she'll be a very loose cannon in the council chamber telling the mayor his dog should be shot or some other gaffe.

Her surname is near the top of the polling paper, another bad sign. At the election count in our local sports hall I'm appalled, but also rather proud, when she beats the Conservative candidate. A woman who's done no campaigning has trounced the one-time party of Margaret Thatcher. But thankfully the Labour candidate comes in first and we're spared a life as party animals.

Five weeks before the baby is due we visit the Haweswater Hotel again, the scene of our Coast to Coast debacle. No car of course. We both ride rented mountain bikes and cycle around the lake and lanes. Nicola is intensely irritated by her mum's suggestions to take it easy.

'The key to a healthy Green baby is exercising right up until the birth,' she maintains with all the authority of a lifestyle guru on *This Morning with Richard and Judy*.

Ken, the hotel manager, marvels at Nicola and her protruding stomach as she mounts her bicycle. 'That's the sort of woman they'll be writing books about in ten years time!' he declares admiringly. No mate, can't see that happening.

Finally the moment arrives. Nicola is in the bath back at our flat when her waters break. Then she's sitting on the stairs groaning rhythmically, as the contractions arrive with horrible regularity. I'm ordering a taxi to take us to the Whittington Hospital. Next I grab our hospital bag including the cassette player on which we're going to play relaxing music, at least that's what the NCT class advises. In our case, it's the Cornershop album, though I'm not too sure she'd want a 'Brimful of Asha on the 45' while being poked and prodded by midwives.

Luckily the taxi driver doesn't realise just how pregnant Nicola is. Then we're at the hospital, rushing down *Doctor Who*-length corridors.

'She's fully dilated,' says the midwife.

'I'm feeling fully dilated myself.'

What if she dies in childbirth like a character in some Ernest Hemingway novel? All I'll have left to mourn over will be her red exhaust-stained Gore-Tex and a pile of recycling.

Then I'm standing at the top end of a bed patting her shoulder. Passing her cups of water. Uttering pathetic cries like 'You're doing really well. Keep breathing now, deep breaths.'

Stretch. A head is emerging. With dark hair. And then a baby arrives, connected by what appears to be an organic telephone lead, all curls and reels. The sort of thing you'd get in Comet.

The midwife cuts the cord, because I'm not taking the scissors to my partner's body.

Holding our daughter, who we know will be called Lola. Or, as The Kinks might put it, 'L-o-l-a-Lola'. Her blue eyes look into mine. She's the ultimate babe.

Suddenly I realise Nicola hasn't used any drugs. Never mind the birth, I'm filled with an all pervading glow of happiness; we can be insufferably pompous at the NCT post-birth reunion.

Nicola has given birth with the same alacrity as she does everything else in her eco-life. It's taken just four hours from start to finish. As a competitive dad I'm proud. We've heard numerous nightmare tales of 36-hour labours from other NCT couples. But clearly, *Loaded*'s agony uncle was right and you simply went for a woman with good child-bearing hips.

For Nicola there's no time to be wasted. She has a planet to save and a magazine called *FSC News* to edit and a meeting of acronyms to attend. Our cassette player lies unused in my birth bag. In the excitement I'd forgotten all about it.

'I'm here for you and I empathise with your pain,' I tell her, mimicking NCT dad-speak. 'I know what you've been through. It looked almost as bad as watching your team get relegated.'

Somehow she manages to smile. I feel a massive sense of emotional release. Not just at the birth of our baby daughter Lola, but because, as it's all happened so quickly, I've escaped having to do those awful NCT breathing chants.

We're allowed to spend the day together until eight o'clock when visitors must leave. Lola's hands are tiny but can grasp my fingers, full of life. There's another service Lola has performed for me too. Her prompt arrival means that after bussing it down the Holloway Road there's still time to watch the second half of England versus Romania in the 1998 World Cup, while drinking some celebratory cans of Stella. We lose in the final minute to a Dan Petrescu goal, but for once it doesn't matter too much compared to the day's other result.

*

For two weeks our baby is sleepy. She watches several World Cup games on my knee. Then she gets very noisy. And the amount of nappies she uses is astounding. Nappy changing is quite easy. Baby poos don't smell too much yet.

Nicola thinks she can edit an issue of *FSC News* a week after Lola's birth. She does it somehow, but even she realises she might need to slow down.

We venture into the streets with our child. Initially I carry Lola in a BabyBjörn. This is a Scandinavian baby harness with so many straps it reminds me of some of the outfits in *Fetish Times*. I seem to be on the mailing list for *Fetish Times* since interviewing editor Nikki Wolf for *Midweek*. Probably enough to have my child taken into care, should the child health visitor spot it.

I wear the baby harness on my front, like an inverse backpack. First I clip myself in and then the baby is placed inside and fastened in. She can face inwards or outwards. I now have my arms free and a babe strapped to my chest.

Maybe being a Green dad isn't so bad. Wherever I walk strange women smile at me. Attractive young women come up to me and make conversation. On Highbury Fields, in the café, at the bank. Carrying a baby on my chest makes me somehow non-threatening. I'm taking a walk on the mild side. And being a baby-handling dad elevates me above barrister husbands who work 12-hour days and hardly see their children. It's now clear how Nick Hornby thought of the plot for *About A Boy*, his new novel where Will pretends to be a single parent in order to meet more women.

Cultivating an air of male helplessness helps. Whenever Lola removes her sock and starts chewing it, a woman smiles and informs me of the missing clothing.

'That never happens to me,' growls Nicola, who hates losing baby clothing.

On Highbury Hill groups of previously swearing and smoking 15-year-old schoolgirls queue up to coo and ask 'are you the dad?'. A man could feel as permissive as Blur's Alex James, until he remembers that all these admiring women are only impressed by his progeny. But I fear my *Loaded* days have gone. New dads are too knackered from abject failures at sleep training to act upon the realisation that they've become role models of enlightened manhood.

Loaded want me to write a piece on the three promoted clubs coming into the Premiership, Middlesbrough, Charlton and Nottingham Forest. Although working from home with a baby can be problematic.

'I can't talk mate, I've got a babe here,' I tell the geezer on the phone hoping he won't guess she's under age.

'Hey, Lola, careful! Yeah, a thousand words on each club, right.'

Lola begins to suckle at my ear. The man on the other end of the line can hear various smacking sounds, but carries on with his conversation.

'I'm sorry mate, she's dribbling down my neck,' I explain. 'Oh shit, she's thrown up over me!'

For once a *Loaded* journalist sounds a little shocked.

For the first few months of parenthood we struggle with lack of sleep. We both become irritable and tetchy, particularly in the early hours while holding a baby over the shoulder watching cars through the window and trying to induce a colic-curing burp. But at least Nicola seems to be taking some time off work to recover. At least I think she is, until she informs me she's speaking at the 1998 Labour Party conference.

And so we travel to Blackpool. Lola is two and a half months old and attending her first Labour Party conference fringe meeting.

Almost unnoticed in the mayhem of parenthood, we've both had books published. My own *Sunday Muddy Sunday* and Nicola's look at car culture, *The Estate We're In*. She's been interviewed by Joan Bakewell on *Heart of the Matter*. Now it's a fringe meeting on transport at the Labour Party Conference.

It's chaired by the *Independent*'s Christian Wolmar, a railway expert, and among the panellists is Steve Norris, the Conservative MP famed for a *Daily Mail* exposé claiming he once had five girlfriends. Don't know how he did it; one's enough work for me.

Meanwhile I've been allocated the Denis Thatcher role, only with nappy changing tasks and less gin. I'm holding the baby as we enter the conference hotel. There's a mass of flash photography and people in suits. Nicola's book must be doing well. Oh, no, there's Tony Blair and Cherie Booth gliding through the doorway accompanied by their acolytes.

Tony sees Lola strapped into her BabyBjörn and gives a cheery grin and matey 'Hi!', perhaps thinking I'm on some New Dads for Labour steering committee. It's Lola's first glimpse of a British Prime Minister. Not bad for two months. Although Blair's spin doctor Alastair Campbell looks worried about possible burp and tell stories the tabloids might pick up.

Once the fringe meeting starts Nicola appears to be making a fine speech in front of 60 or so politicos. Her BBC accent always sounds impressive on the stage. But midway through some figures on car growth, Lola starts to wail and I have to take her outside into the corridor. She needs a nappy change. Not much of a response to meeting Tony Blair, the JFK of British politics.

We enter the gents and discover there are no nappy-changing facilities. So I get out the portable changing mat, place Lola on the floor and get to work. At least Nicola lets her wear disposable nappies for the Blackpool trip.

Nappy changing is best treated like a surgical procedure. First get out all the kit: changing mat, cotton wool, water in which to dab the cotton wool, nappy rash creams, Vaseline, muslin towels to dab your baby's bottom dry with, bin for the dirty nappies.

Wet nappies are easy. Just wipe the baby's bottom, dab

dry and put on a replacement nappy. Nappy changing is the only job in the world where you welcome urine. The big problem is the other stuff. Which is what I'm faced with, on the floor of the gents at the Labour Party conference full of pissed-up triumphant MPs.

To raise my morale during nappy changing I've introduced football chants into my routine. Just as I'm singing 'She's done a poo, she's done a poo, she's done one...' to the tune of Baddiel and Skinner's *Three Lions*, a Labour delegate walks in.

'I remember that. They're wonderful when they're that age. Don't worry it gets easier!' he says cheerily. I mutter something appreciative, forgetting to look at the well-wisher. Maybe it was Tony himself.

We retreat back into the meeting just in time to find Nicola chatting to Christian Wolmar and Steve Norris. Norris has that politician's knack of appearing to agree with whatever you say, and seems to be virulently pro-rail and anti Beeching Report (this closed numerous stations in the 1950s). Then he admires our baby. She's already networking, just like her mum. Soon I'll be living with two eco-bunnies.

After returning to London our bin soon fills up with nappies.

'So now we can stop using disposables,' Nicola says.

'Erm, why? They're really easy to fold up and put in the bin. And we're knackered.'

'If King James I had been put into disposable nappies they'd only just be rotting today.'

'Well, I'm sure that'll be very interesting for *Time Team*. "Tonee, Oi've got a pelvis in a disposable nappy 'ere in trench one!" Royalty can be a bit odd though. Was it a kind of *Madness of King George* situation?'

'No, you idiot. I hope Lola hasn't inherited your environmental ignorance gene. They can last for 500 years! And they contain a cocktail of chemical super-absorbers and plastics too. They go into landfill where they release methane into the atmosphere. We dump 800,000 tonnes of nappies in landfill every year.'

'But aren't reusable nappies just towels and pins?'

'No. They're really modern now. They have Velcro straps, look at these...'

'And that's your bottom line...'

We decide to try and keep my daughter's methane out of landfill. The reusable nappies are not as bad as I feared. What I like best about them is that they require some colourful plastic pants to be worn over them. This allows another football chant to enter my nappy changing repertoire. It goes: 'On with the plastic pants. On with the plastic pants, on with, on with, on with, on with, on with the plastic pants!' to the tune of *Knees Up Mother Brown*.

Soon Lola is too heavy for the BabyBjörn and it's time to get a buggy. I choose a lightweight black Maclaren Techno. It even sounds like a Formula One competitor. This is my BMW substitute.

The Techno is certainly preferable to the current mania for ATP buggies. ATP stands for the All-Terrain Pram, those big three-wheeler buggies with chunky tyres that look like something from the pod of Thunderbird 2 and are far too big for buses. They cost 300 quid or more and are the buggy equivalent of having a four-wheel drive.

My Maclaren has all the accessories. There's a splendid Velcro pocket on the back and a military-style black mesh luggage basket underneath for keeping copies of the *Guardian* in. My buggy pockets now hold pots of home-made solid baby food. No shop-bought jars of organic baby food for us. Nicola insists on pureeing her own mush of potatoes and spinach. Fewer additives and no wastage of glass, you see.

On the paths around Highbury Fields I perfect the art of buggy racing. That's where I run as quickly as possible pushing the buggy with my excited child strapped inside.

'Pete what are you doing? That's dangerous!' exclaims Nicola, when she spots me doing this.

'I'm playing silly buggies,' I answer.

Lola chuckles at my racing techniques and survives without injury too. Sometimes I take my hands off the buggy and run in front of it while it's still moving and wave at my surprised daughter. One-handed steering is also an essential requirement for the nonchalant dad and is good for developing my wrist muscles.

My buggy is so lightweight you can lift it and the baby up the steps on the Underground without suffering a double hernia. And it folds up easily, with a reassuring click, so it can fit on buses or under train seats.

There's even an answer to worn tyres: a buggy repair shop in Wood Green where you can get a service and reconditioned wheels. When I visit, a bloke in overalls stands before trays full of straps, tyres and swivel pins, muttering 'You've got problems there mate, your support cross has gone...'

Maybe Nicola's right and walking is better than driving. There are always plenty of mums to meet on my childcare days. We have a complicated childcare rota involving me taking Lola on some mornings, some afternoons and every complete Wednesday. Being a dad is cool. Everyone watches a new series called *Cold Feet* about three couples in Manchester and we all laugh knowingly when new dad Pete falls asleep on the bus to work because he's so tired.

Once I attended press launches at the Groucho Club and Soho House; now my clubs of choice are the 2 O'clock Club and The Hippo Club at a local church.

I'm the John Travolta (circa *Saturday Night Fever*) of the knackered dad generation. For the first time in my life I can impress a room full of 60 women – by the simple expedient of wheeling my daughter to the local church playgroup.

I've always been crap at dancing in nightclubs, but now I'm admired for my ability to change a nappy, chase a toddler along a church pew or sing 'The wheels on the bus go round and round'. It's Wednesday morning fever. I am the white-suited maestro of The Hippo Club.

Organised singing is more problematic at the weekly singing group. Being the only male among 20 women and their under-fives, all performing the hand and feet actions to 'Row Row Row Your Boat' feels a little like being initiated into some bizarre sect of female masonry.

It's strange how women do everything they're told by a nursery school Joan Baez with an acoustic guitar. While 'Lola's Dad' is being told to clap along, I reflect that a bunch of blokes would surely guffaw a little more when singing 'What Shall We Do With The Drunken Sailor?' while marching in a circle. Or turn some of the songs into football chants.

At the church playgroup and the 2 O'clock Club I'm offered biscuits and coffee by the organisers, eager to encourage changing male roles. If any other dad turns up we're instantly introduced, even if the only thing we have in common is that we happen to be from the male half of the human race. (I meet the son of Brighton FC's chairman this way.)

Out pushing my buggy, I've cracked the mysterious mothers' network of two o'clock clubs, playgroups, softplay mornings and dancing classes. Although being the only man had some disadvantages too. One mum sees her friend talking to me and exclaims: 'I didn't realise you knew the vicar!', which ditches the sex bomb theory. Obviously my playgroup persona is more Father Ted than John Travolta.

In all the mayhem of parenthood I almost miss one piece of precious news about the Green Party – it owes its origins to *Playboy* magazine. It's all revealed in Nicola's bumper 25th anniversary edition of *Green World*, the Green Party's magazine that is in a chaotic pile of books and newspapers and tomes on motherhood sitting by her side of the bed. The Green Party was founded in 1973 by 13 activists, full of anxiety after reading Rachel Carson's *Silent Spring* and Teddy Goldsmith's *Blueprint for Survival*. No surprises there. But then comes the unexpected confession: 'It was an article on world population growth by Paul Erlich in the summer 1972 edition of *Playboy* that provided the catalyst.'

'Who'd have thought it, eh? It's the Greens that read *Playboy* for its articles?' I tell Nicola.

It seems that pornography has played its part in saving the environment, and for once the Greens have claimed the low moral ground. They can never criticise *Loaded* again.

Somehow we make it through a year of parenthood. Lola's first birthday in June 1999 is a cause for reflection and satisfaction. All those Neurotic Parent magazines that Nicola buys claim that your relationship is most at risk during the first year of your child's life. But I've not wavered, despite the odd dubious thought about Cerys Matthews of Catatonia as she sings 'Road Rage' in her enticing Valleys accent.

We hold a baby party in the Ecology Centre. Although Nicola says Lola's too young to have presents she receives numerous new toys, some made of plastic, games, jigsaw puzzles and new clothes.

I'm learning new parenting skills every day. My CD collection has been utilised as a stimulating learning device.

'Can I introduce you please, to a lump of Cheddar cheese?' I sing to Lola as she lies on the living room floor. Playing 'Vindaloo' by Fat Les at loud volume causes her to kick and shake her arms, as does Blur's 'Song 2'. She also likes being bounced to the 'Barmy Army' chorus of the Barmy Army's Cricket World Cup theme 'Come On England', while Ian Dury's 'Mash It Up Harry' is subtly altered to make it a theme of infant empowerment: 'Don't call Lola a human potato/ Don't call Lola a spud/ Don't call Lola a walking King Edward/Lola's made of flesh and blood!'

Football chants can be adapted to just about every childcare need. Lola's first excursion into the armchair for the European Cup Final results in 'E-i-adio! Lola's in the chair!', while the West Ham theme song 'I'm Forever Blowing Bubbles' lulls her to sleep during teething troubles. Trips home in the buggy are enlivened with 'Three Lions', becoming 'She's coming home, she's coming home, she's coming... Lola's coming home.'

As a slack dad, I begin to resort to TV. While Nicola works upstairs, the highlight of our mornings is watching *Teletubbies*.

At last I have an excuse to watch the flab four and wonder who dreamt up Tinky Winky's little cloud. There's Nu Nu the Hoover, Tubby toast and a chance to sing along to the Teletubbies theme. Nicola shouts at me to turn it off, but I argue it's a useful tool in child development. Lola's now trying to count from one to four.

A man's second childhood doesn't have to wait until old age. Stay-at-home dads can watch kids' TV and claim we're supporting feminism through doing it. Even if some mothers try to undermine our role by claiming we've given the child nappy rash.

Lola probably won't remember her mum trying to halt climate change. But hopefully she'll recall that her dad knew all about the Teletubbies' big hugs. Emotional intelligence, we call it in Green dad circles.

Soon after Lola's first birthday Nicola starts a three-day-a-week job in the publications department at Friends of the Earth. It's perfect for her. She works late a lot and spends a lot of time at Real Food meetings (is that how they describe a long lunch?). So now my childcaring skills are even more vital to the wellbeing of the planet.

Nicola is also working on the Friends of the Earth members' magazines *Earthmatters* and *Change Your World* plus various booklets. She gets to interview TV chef Hugh Fearnley-

Whittingstall, another eco-toff and a man known to eat animal testicles, though even she's a little shocked when he started fingering the sugar on their café table because he liked to feel his food. She's soon writing about why Zac Goldsmith hates supermarkets and Oliver Heath's eco-designs, and lobbying Parliament for a household waste recycling Act and Climate Change Bill. She's a natural editor; in fact she's been editing my life for years.

The only problem is that Nicola is so committed to her job that she seems to work 900 hours a week rather than three days. And she seems to spend a lot of her time dealing with line managers and filing in appraisal forms. And there's more five-year-plans and strategic planning than in Enver Hoxha's Albania.

Unlike Greenpeace, Friends of the Earth tends to lobby MPs rather than board ships. Its staff are more likely to carry bikes than karabiners. Just inside reception there's the biggest pile of bikes I've seen since last drinking in the Shakespeare on the way home from collecting our organic vegetable bags.

Most of the staff dress like Nicola; no make-up in the case of the women, plus utilitarian trousers, bike helmets and Sam Browne sashes. No room for City-style glamour here; they have to be ready to lobby Parliament or negotiate the Old Street roundabout at any given moment.

Sometimes there are Friends of the Earth birthday drinks in trendy Hoxton. One night we go to a bar called the Foundry.

Situated in a former bank, no effort at all has been made to do it up, which seems to have made it remarkably popular with Greens and boho artists We're fighting for seats on old office chairs that look like they've been retrieved from the nearest skip. Dimly-lit *Blade Runner* chic has finally reached Hoxton. The Foundry's cement floors and bare concrete walls are so distressed you can almost hear them trying to phone their therapists. Whoever decided to scrap the expensive refit, sack the interior stylists and just leave the old bank as it was, is clearly a financial genius. I've not seen anything like it since I last stayed with Chris and Jane in Powys. Amid all the dangling wires and ripped armchairs there's even a wood-burning stove to give it a certain post-apocalyptic urban cottage feel. A trip to the ladies' loo finds no sign on the door, just a message in felt tip pen reading 'no cocks in here'. I think I'd rather be at home with the baby watching TV.

But they seem a decent crowd. Friends of the Earth is even home to a couple of Whovians and we exchange news of signings and video releases. Christian in the Web department keeps a cyberman mask at work, presumably in case he needs to disguise himself as an on-message New Labour politician. Nor do they play Ultimate Frisbee like the Oxford Greens. Several Friends of the Earth staff actually play five-a-side football at the Sobell Centre in north London (the local hoodies do tend to target their bikes outside though). Soon I'm joining them.

At Christmas Friends of the Earth has a big party. There's much jubilation when they bag the Union Chapel in Islington ahead of the real enemy – not George Bush or the oil corporations, but those splitters down the road in Greenpeace. Everyone eats organic Indian vegetarian food and drinks Eco Warrior organic lager as the staff stage a revue on stage. I'm even allowed to write a *Doctor Who* sketch staring Nicola as Nikkala, the Doctor's new companion. The Doctor is a Friend of the Earth and my script has several Friends of the Earth in-jokes, plus the regeneration of the Master – all years before Russell T Davies.

Liam Gallagher at the *Loaded* Xmas bash has been superseded by a glimpse of Friends of the Earth director Tony Juniper. Am I succumbing to some kind of Green osmosis?

We spend New Year's Eve at Nicola's mum's place in Hertfordshire and party like it's 1999. Nicola's mum has stocked up on tins and we're wondering if we can live off the apple trees in the garden as society is apparently about to grind to a halt on 1 January 2000 because of something called the Millennium Bug. Old computers can only read dates up to 1999 and the collapse of the financial system is likely, say the techie experts. Only nothing happens.

Nicola insists on taking Lola and myself shopping one Saturday because there's no match on. We enter a small shop with a bright pink facade and a sign reading Green Baby. On the wall some faux handwriting reads 'caring for your baby in an eco-friendly way'. There's a table of nothing but reusable nappies all with names like 'ecobotts'. I point to another display labelled 'Eco Balls'.

'Look, Nicola, at last a sense of self-effacing irony among Greens.'

'Erm, no, Eco Balls are what you put in your washing machine instead of washing powder. They prevent detergents getting into the water system and we're getting some.'

'Oh.'

Around the walls of Green Baby hang various items of baby clothing. They're so ethical it's unbelievable. Each one has a Green label saying 'made of 100 per cent organically cultivated cotton... all made on a community project in India... environmentally friendly production... this garment has not been chemically processed so there may be slight shrinkage'.

Plus a short mission statement, 'The choices we make today will affect not just our children, but our grandchildren too. Whether the threat comes from our ever-increasingly disposable society or from chemically-treated cotton in babies clothing and toys, what we use today can not only harm our environment, but affect our children's health tomorrow.'

'Ten quid for a sleepsuit! Twenty-five quid for a jumper!' I mutter uncharitably.

'You have to pay for quality! That knitwear is handmade by a women's collective in Uruguay.'

'This T-shirt would be quite nice for Lola though. The

one that says "Think healthy think Green organic think environmental think trees think Green baby". Maybe you could wear one too.'

There's just so much to worry about, so many things to avoid. A whole industry in middle-class fears. Is it fair traded, is your cotton organic and pesticide-free, should your child's shampoo be neutral?

The Green Baby mail-order catalogue on display features gels without parabens and phthalates as recommended by the Women's Environmental Network, nickel-free cutlery sets, PVC-free teethers, shoes with chrome-free leather, gel-free nappies, unfragranced washable wipes, a non-PVC potty chair and fire-retardant free mattresses. My parents just gave me Angel Delight and crisps outside the pub.

Various eco-parenting books and magazines are here too. I browse through features on the feminine art of breastfeeding, how to involve children in the changing seasons, raise a vegetarian child, invest ethically in your children, build a treehouse, deal with guilt, have a happy home, and use cranial-osteopathy to relax your precious babe.

Standing in Green Baby I start to feel a little faint. Organic cotton stripey sleepsuits blur into environmentally-friendly nappies and natural nursery products. Lola's buggy and Nicola's Peruvian hat start to move in and out of focus. This is only the beginning. Once I'd thought having a child might mellow some of my partner's deep Green tendencies. Suddenly I realise, in a fair-traded organic epiphany, that I'm in this for life. Now Nicola is a mother she has an ever-expanding set of additional eco-worries. Where once she just wanted to Green my life now she has a family to convert. She's going to turn the heating down in the name of our children's health tomorrow.

'Pete, be careful, you're bumping into the Eco Balls! Are you all right?'

'I'm sorry Nicola, I've just seen the future, and it's deep Green...'

'You're right, it's time we had another Green baby.'

'But we've only just started to get our lives back.'

'Lola needs a sibling, Otherwise she'll grow up spoilt.'

Sales at Green Baby are set to boom. My lapse into contented one-child dadhood has been halted. And now my copy of the *Guardian* predicts that the Apocalypse may arrive some time soon.

George Monbiot says that climate change is happening faster than anyone expected. I'd hoped that global warming might be as over-hyped as the Millennium Bug. Only George reveals that we've learnt that the Arctic ice is melting, wiping out the feeding grounds of cuddly polar bears. Marine biologists are saying that nearly all the world's coral reefs could be dead by the end of the coming century. The Red Cross reports that natural disasters had displaced more people than all the wars on Earth in 1998. It's all leading to 'the greatest calamity our species has ever encountered'.

And then George compares fliers to paedophiles, which doesn't seem likely to win over many non-Greens: 'It makes genocide and ethnic cleansing look like sideshows at the circus of human suffering. A car is now more dangerous than a gun. Flying across the Atlantic is as unacceptable, in terms of its impact on human well-being, as child abuse.'

Even worse, in a radio debate of the Society of Motor Manufacturers and Traders (SMMT), the SMMT staff laughed at him when he mentioned resource use and global warming. His article concludes 'The world is dying and people are killing themselves with laughter.'

It doesn't seem very hopeful for my child. George can appear over-earnest, the right-wing press dismiss his warnings as hyperbole and I still don't feel as bad as a paedophile on the Green sliding scale of moral equivalency for flying to Greenland on a press trip (well, it was free) to promote Smirnoff Ice last December. But the thought occurs: what if George Monbiot is right?

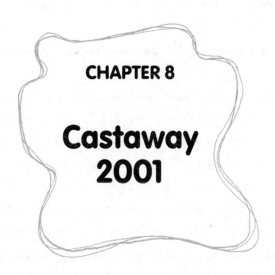

CHAPTER 8

Castaway 2001

'No, I don't want a sodding taxi! I'm delivering a baby!'

The doorbell's just rung as two midwives are fussing around Nicola in the living room. I'm supposed to be getting towels ready. No one has ordered a taxi at all, unless it's for our neighbours downstairs who are trying to escape the sound of labour groans.

But perhaps that mysterious taxi has been delivered by providence. Answering the door means I don't have to do anything practical at the moment of delivery. While I'm dealing with the buzzer, our second daughter, Nell, has just popped into the midwife's arms. It's been a two-hour birth, even quicker than the first.

Nicola's standing up with one hand resting on the TV (thankfully I took it off standby), surrounded by two attentive midwives. She was determined to have a home birth this time, and you get lots of extra attention that way: most of the NHS seem to be round at our flat.

It seems fitting that Nell's birth takes place in Nicola's flat. It was here that the cold war first broke out when I moved in some six years earlier. So much has happened since then. Lola has developed into a lovely two-year-old who has to walk on every garden wall and open every gate as we make the journey to nursery. She picks up anything she finds on the street and places it in her pockets. Stones, buttons, straws, bottle tops, elastic bands, bits of plastic. I think she might take after her mother.

We think Nell was conceived as a result of too much Guinness at our friends' Laura and Wesley's wedding in Northern Ireland.

Luckily we'd missed the May Day 2000 anti-capitalist riots in London while we were away. Once more I was thankful that Nicola wasn't a crusty type of Green. All that lobbying of the World Trade Organisation, IMF and World Bank while battling riot police in Seattle and Washington looked far too dangerous, particularly now we were parents. In London, after a mainly peaceful protest, some protesters had dug up the turf in Parliament Square and given Winston Churchill's statue a turf Mohican. It looked rather stylish.

It was no surprise to me, at least, when an Eton pupil was found trashing McDonald's. The media loved it and in one of the many features on toff agitators, Friends of the Earth's

Charles Secrett revealed that 'among the aristocrats there's a sense of stewardship, of noblesse oblige, of wanting to use your position for the general good'. One amusing postcript of the riots was that a crop of marijuana plants, planted by guerilla gardeners, was later discovered growing by Winston Churchill's statue in Parliament Square.

Nine months after that trip to Northern Ireland we have another child. Nell's home birth is much less clinical than being in a hospital. A couple of hours after her arrival I'm making Nicola a bowl of spaghetti and we drink a champagne toast to our new daughter. Then it's time to fetch Lola from nursery. 'There might be a bit of a surprise for you when you get home,' I explain.

We have more time together these days. Lola is at nursery three days a week and Nicola has taken her standard maternity leave from Friends of the Earth, plus an unpaid six months leave. She's so convinced of the benefits of breast-feeding that she wants to do it for at least a year.

So I'm going to try to be a 1950s man and support my family from the proceeds of my *Midweek* 'London Spy' column, a fortnightly 'Sidelines' column at *Time Out* and a not-very-big advance for writing a book, *Irons In The Soul*, about West Ham in the 2001-02 season. There's less lad mag work. The editorial team at *Loaded* has changed now and with two kids, it feels like I'm slipping away from the laddish oeuvre.

Everything should be fine, only our house is still falling down. I thought Nicola was a woman of substance. Instead it seems I'm living with a woman of subsidence.

It's been three years since the insurance company placed studs around the huge cracks in our walls and began to monitor them. Since then there's been plenty of talk about verticality surveys, but we are heading towards a verticality crisis while they continue to procrastinate. We need more space but Nicola can't sell the place with subsidence and gets tearful about wanting more space and a garden. I want to be able to say I jointly own a house too, as at present I'm still sleeping with my landlady.

As the new baby thrives, the house seems to be collapsing around us. On the landing a ceiling falls in over the utility room, showering our bikes and Sam Browne sashes in wet plaster. The family on the ground floor has already moved out and in the week of Nell's birth John in the flat beneath us goes too, leaving our family alone in the building. When Nell is five days old, we're burgled. We'd been storing our bikes in the empty flat downstairs. Thieves get in through the back garden, smash a rear window, and take the bikes out of the front window. Nicola and the baby are asleep upstairs as our bikes are half-inched. I'm worried about their safety. The only positive spin is that without a bike I can now take the tube or bus without Green censure.

We need to move. And so I dispatch a long Micawber-esque

letter to the chief executive of the insurance company, pointing out the Godot-esque nature of his operation, threatening
exposure in national newspapers and asking who will come
to the aid of Little Nell. His troubleshooter agrees to host an
emergency meeting at our crumbling flat. After much debate,
mainly about strapping versus underpinning, the men in
suits agree that they will pay for us to rent a place until the
subsidence is repaired.

Finally we escape our subsidence-ridden, chaotic top-
storey flat and move into a cottage in Whistler Street, some
300 metres away from our old gaff. Instead of a two-bedroom
flat we now have a house with a garden.

The new house costs £300 a week – and it's all paid for by
the insurance company. We feel like Basil Fawlty when, after
many shenanigans, he finally retrieves the money he won on
the horse Dragonfly, finds there's an extra ten quid, and for
the first time in his life he's ahead.

Our new home is a former railway worker's cottage, two
upstairs bedrooms with one knocked-through living room. A
grown-up house with granite worktops in the kitchen, a gas
hob, fitted carpets and cabinets around the radiators. Only it's
not easy being Green here. To Nicola's dismay, everything is
spotlights and dimmer switches. It looks like Will and Grace's
New York apartment. All the bulbs are screw-in or clip-in and
nothing is suitable for a long-life energy saving light bulb.
There are 20 spotlights in the kitchen ceiling alone. Our car-

bon footprint is now moving from a metaphorical sandal to a high-leg 16-hole Doctor Marten's boot.

'At least it's only temporary,' sighs Nicola, 'If it was ours we'd eco-audit the whole place.' Although I'm quite happy with the carbon-guzzling luxuries. Our cold war is finally at an end too. Because the house is in a middle of a terrace it's much warmer than Nicola's old end-of-terrace garret flat.

As ever we have too much stuff and several crates of paraphernalia have to be put into storage because the new house already comes with furniture. But a major bonus is that it has a converted attic, ideal for use as an office. Finally we find a use for all Nicola's books on global warming. We place boxes of them in the attic, where they make excellent roof insulation.

The TV reception is rubbish, which gives me an opportunity to install cable TV.

'All the houses in this street say terrestrial reception is appalling. It would cost £150 to even install a new aerial. And I've already arranged a date for the installers from Telewest to come.'

'You'll just watch football all the time.'

'I've just got a contract to write a diary of West Ham's season. So we really need Sky, and we are getting our rent paid. And I won't watch any other football apart from West Ham. You might even see your uncle on the Racing Channel. There's some good racing, you'll like that.'

The man and van arrive, connect various bulky leads and leave us with a digital box.

'Can't you turn that box off?' she says, aghast at the green light that stays on even when you switch off the numbered channel display.

'No, it takes ages to download again if you do that.'

'We shouldn't have a television.'

'I write about sport! And it's essential if you're staying up all night with a baby. They repeat *The Clangers*! And Lola can watch *Maggie and the Ferocious Beast* on Nick Junior too... And *Doctor Who* on UK Gold on Sundays.'

The TV is installed and I'm in set-top nirvana. Meanwhile Nicola's excited over something earthier. At the back of our cottage is a tiny L-shaped garden. It's about three metres long with a raised patio area containing just enough room for a table and chairs and some of the landlords' plants in designer urns.

'Now we can compost our household waste! No more trips to the Ecology Centre!' Nicola announces joyously.

'Suits me. No more lugging buckets of slurping decaying vegetable matter to the Ecology Centre. Finally I'm behind one of your ideas,' I reply.

Nicola orders a green plastic compost bin from the council. It looks like a giant pepper pot, or, if you stick an eyepiece on the top, a green Dalek. If you gave it Green Party membership and told it to exterminate frequent fliers, it might even get elected as a councillor in Stoke Newington.

The council's bin comes with lots of handy tips. If your compost bin is too dry then you should add more 'greens', such as grass, nettles and comfrey leaves. If it smells of rotten eggs then it's because your bin is too wet and you need to add more 'browns' to soak up the moisture, things such as egg boxes, toilet rolls and kitchen rolls.

'We're going to fill it up and it's all going to be lovely! Like a chocolate box for our plants,' enthuses my partner, eagerly anticipating adding greens and browns to the mulch.

We're supposed to unscrew the top and insert our vegetable waste (but nothing that's been cooked as this attracts rats). Then, after the worms and bugs have broken it down for a year or so, we'll open the hatch at the bottom and remove nice black loamy compost for our organic vegetables. The bin is placed in our back garden – a decision that is to affect us for the rest of our stay in Whistler Street.

After the trauma of pregnancy, birth and moving, our thoughts turn to a summer break. We're still doing no-flying holidays. The thing is, I'm starting to think Nicola is right. Is this what Johnny Rotten meant by 'cheap holidays at other people's misery'?

We don't actually need to travel abroad. Our parents never did. And to my unscientific mind it does seem that emitting carbon in the sky must be more harmful than releasing it at ground level.

Maybe it's having two children that's suddenly making

me worry about the future. Am I becoming the sort of buggy-pushing Green dad I once wanted to pour lager over?

'Although if it's a free press trip, well, obviously I'll still be tempted,' I add as a caveat to my personal environmental auditor.

Still, I admire the way Nicola is prepared to sacrifice her travelling for the good of humanity. She won't be flying to PNG or the Solomons, at some cost to her kudos in Oxford.

My usual tactic of never organising holidays in advance pays off. News filters through about a Scottish island seeking publicity. It seems like a good chance to go on holiday and maybe sell a few articles about exploring the Highlands. We're going to the Scottish wilderness. As seen by millions of TV viewers.

Taransay was once an obscure island in the Outer Hebrides; now it's the most famous island in Scotland, thanks to the huge primetime success of the BBC's *Castaway 2000*. A group of strangers lived on the island for a year and the BBC filmed the rows and the romances. Now, following the departure of the castaways, owner Angus Mackay is opening up the island to tourists.

Everyone in London says how brave Nicola and I are, taking four-month-old baby Nell and soon-to-be-three Lola to an uninhabited island, accessible only by boat (weather permitting) and a tenuous mobile phone link. This does rather ignore the fact that island people have been raising children in such conditions for thousands of years, and all without Orange or Vodafone.

More worrying is the fact that Nicola is reading a copy of *Downshifting: The guide to happier, simpler living*. Maybe visiting Taransay might give her ideas. She has Scottish ancestry, which might account for her love of cold houses. Other couples from the playgroup are leaving London before they have to select primary schools. Rachel and Tag are going to Bicester and Sarah and Nick are escaping to Brighton. And most of my best mates now inhabit the 2 o'Clock Club.

In *Downshifting* (the term comes from the US and sounds a lot better than 'voluntary poverty') authors Polly Ghazi and Judy Jones evangelise about 'how the dream of 'having it all' has turned sour... As the stress and insecurity of the rat race grow, so more and more people are choosing instead to opt for a better way of life. For some, it has meant switching to a less stressful job or part-time work. For the braver, it means leaving career, house and city to start a new life in the country.'

There's a chapter entitled 'Freedom in freelancing'. A freedom from payment is one freelance problem that still affects me; the accounts sections of many magazines operate with Dickensian alacrity. And downshifting sounds suspiciously like it might involve a compost loo. My inner coward starts imagining the children suddenly developing nut allergies with no way of reaching the mainland or else they end up eating us in a *Lord of the Flies* scenario. Perhaps only our video footage will be found in two years' time, with my tearful, terrified face frantically saying 'sorry' just like in the *Blair Witch Project*.

Maybe I'll wait until my dad sets up a trust fund for me before I consider downshifting. Meantime, forget Spanish hotels with safely-enclosed swimming pools, child minders, day clubs and everything else you need to take a holiday from your kids. Our Scottish island holiday will be where London Man meets Robinson Crusoe and survives without delis. It's my chance to become the Ben Fogle of the knackered dad generation. Albeit minus the woolly jumpers and group conciliation skills.

We board the sleeper train from Euston to Inverness laden with a buggy, four backpacks, two bags of food, a bucket and spade and a not-very-*Castaway*-like sturdy umbrella that Nicola insists we take, claiming it's essential for island life. I didn't even know we owned an umbrella, but bizarrely she's carrying one, complete with *Horse & Hound* logo.

'Well, I used to work there,' she says,

'OK, I suppose it's vaguely credible now Hugh Grant said he worked for *Horse & Hound* in *Notting Hill*. Just as long as no one thinks it belongs to me.'

After 15 minutes Lola asks 'Are we in Scotland yet?'. The kids sleep tucked up in nests on the floor while we take the bunks. From Inverness we travel, via a hired car and ferry to Lewis and then on to Harris by road. At Tarbet we meet

Angus, owner of the island. He shows us the launching point for Taransay, at Horgabost.

'We won't be going today, we'll just have to sit it out,' he declares, looking at the heavy waves.

The beach is a gorgeous white expanse of sand, littered with driftwood timbers and watched over by the Macleod standing stone. There are white horses on the waves. We can see Taransay a mile or so offshore, inviting but inaccessible. Clearly bad weather is the equivalent to tube strikes up here.

After three days gazing at windswept Taransay we make a big decision. We'd been hoping to return to London for Lola's birthday party in the park. We decide instead to postpone her party and give her an emergency set of presents on the island, a toy dog and Jaffa cakes from a store in Tarbert. We're going to get to Taransay whatever it takes.

After four days the sea is calmer and Angus says our trip is on. I wonder what Lola will make of island isolation?

'It'll be just like your Katie Morag books,' we suggest hopefully.

Trying to pass a baby from slippery, seaweed-strewn rocks on to the ramp of a cattle boat bobbing precariously in a choppy sea is not the stuff of a typical family holiday. Or indeed health and safety regulations. But it's one big step off the rocks and at last we're on Angus's small blue boat, more commonly used to shift sheep.

Caledonian MacBrayne it isn't, and that's half the charm

of getting to Taransay. Baby Nell watches from mum's chest while held in the BabyBjörn, gurgling excitedly as the boat cuts through the swell. She's wearing the baby lifejacket that we purchased at great expense back in London. Lola is excited rather than scared. 'Daddy, I love the sound of the waves,' she tells me.

The crossing is only a mile or so over a still-choppy sea, with waves washing over the deck as we stand by the tiny wheelhouse. As the boat edges closer to the beach at Paible the view of the schoolhouse, farmhouse and steading is instantly recognisable from the TV programme.

We step off the boat on to more rocks and then on to a glorious deserted beach with the mountains of the mainland clearly visible across the sound. We walk up a bank of shells and over the dunes to the building known as the Mackay house. 'I'll send the island taxi for your stuff,' quips Angus, as his shepherd Callum arrives on a quad bike to carry our bags.

It's all as stunning as it looked on the box. Lola picks up a winkle ('a snail!'), then a dead crab and a limpet before running up a bank of shells to the farmhouse. It's surprisingly comfortable, with electricity generated by a very Green windmill, a gas cooker and plenty of fuel for the Rayburn in the cosy kitchen and even a cot and baby-changing mat. In the utility room we find a broom marked 'pod four' which may once have been wielded by Tammy Huff – the hot babe who inspired all the interest in the TV gossip mags.

'There's a Teletubby windmill!' says Lola pointing to the island's wind-powered generator. When baby Nell cries, a trip to visit the numerous sheep soon calms her. There's a tame cow too. Angus tells us it was used during the making of the film *The Rocket Post*. The cow now rushes over to any stray human to give them a big lick

We're here on the very island where Ben Fogle paced in his fluffy jumper. There's the school house where Ray the boozy builder waited for his boat to the tabloids, the loch where Roger the doctor built a raft for his kids, and the common room where bearded lecturer Peter had a cup of coffee thrown over him. I'm sure that most Greens would say that there's more to wilderness than images from a TV programme. But then maybe they deserve cups of coffee thrown over them as well.

All food has to be brought over from the mainland. We arrive in the kitchen with bags of stereotypical soft southerner goodies such as real coffee, muesli, sundried tomatoes and fresh pasta. We wouldn't make very good castaways, but then neither did the castaways themselves, to judge by Mark McCrum's book *Castaway* in which he reveals they smuggled champagne, whisky and radios on to the island. A very valid sort of upshifting for the 21st century. And we'll be taking our 21st-century rubbish away with us too, in keeping with our Green holiday ethos. Angus and Callum depart with a promise to fetch us in a few days' time and from now, our only link with the mainland is via a dodgy mobile phone link.

On the night of the summer solstice I take Lola for a late-night walk on Paible beach. The island once had a population of 170 and we discover bleached white bones from the cemetery emerging from the eroded shoreline. Lola treats them with the same acceptance as the numerous sheep bones we've discovered earlier. Watching my three-year-old daughter examining the sad sight of a child's skull protruding from the dunes is not how I imagined our holiday would be.

You can scale Taransay's highest point, the 267-metre Ben Raah, and feel like the lord of your own island, or make a day-long trip circumnavigating the whole isle. We walk up the main valley of the island past its four lochs and the remains of a mill over the burn. Three metres in front of us a startled fawn then bolts for cover.

The children with the TV castaways all thrived at the school. The theory is that imaginative play fosters intelligence, and this island is one giant playground. With Nell in the BabyBjörn and Lola fortified by additive-laden sweets, we walk past the remains of the old black houses and up towards Loch an Duin, which contains a 2,000-year-old dun, a defensive fortification on the loch reached by a submerged causeway.

We see otters scampering into the sea, carnivorous flowers and ten metres ahead of us another fawn runs unsteadily out of the grass. Lola sits down by a burn and we fish with sticks, then float reed boats away along the bubbling waters. No batteries needed for this type of play.

On Lola's third birthday Taransay looks like the Pacific, all indigo sea, burning white sands, and postcard-vivid mountains on the mainland. When she wakes up she's delighted to receive a solitary present, the cuddly toy puppy.

'You see, they don't need endless Barbie dolls, we can make our own birthday presents from now on!' announces Nicola. She duly makes Lola a birthday necklace out of shells and a piece of string.

In the afternoon we walk to the beach at Corran Ra and Lola runs along the huge sand spit, her red shirt tiny beneath the mountains. She admires dead jellyfish, discovers a starfish and leans over the pontoon jetty to find small green fish swimming below. We light three candles on a Jaffa cake, sitting on the sand under a dazzling sun, having presented her with her own island for her birthday.

'Her name is Lola May and she's been to Taransay!' I sing to her, to the tune of the Arsenal fans' 'Vieira' chant.

It's light until nearly midnight and on our final day I take a late-night walk towards the bothy (where the castaways retreated for solitude) at the old village of Uidh. It's an up and down trip as all around the island are lazybanks, curved ridges and ditches where banks of potatoes were once cultivated. Uidh is a remarkable spot, where the north and south parts of the island are joined by a slim stretch of land flanked by golden beaches on either side and with a fine natural arch on the adjoining south island.

The standing stone of Clach an Teampuill guards the spot. It was a sight of reverence to the old islanders and in 750 a brave priest drew a Celtic cross on the stone to reclaim it for Christianity. White cotton grass stands out on the tussocky ground in the dusk. There's a sense of peace looking over the two beaches and watching the sun's rays sink over St Kilda way out in the Atlantic. I feel totally relaxed; our Green holiday experiment has been good for all of us.

The next morning, as the Proclaimers might say, it's Taransay no more, Lewis no more. When Angus picks us up we don't want to leave. We've gained much more from the trip than from being stranded at Palma airport like so many British holidaymakers have been this summer. There's wilderness here, in Britain, and you can get there by train, car and boat.

On the ferry back to Ullapool a tanned but grubby Lola, still wearing her seashell necklace, heads straight for the four dreadlocked crusties sitting cross-legged on deck, who have been celebrating the summer solstice at the Calanais standing stones. 'Hello, I'm three!' she announces, joining them to study a book of wild flowers. Perhaps our Taransay trip has been a little too successful. Our deli-baby has become a New Age hippy. Could her newly-Green dad be in danger of downshifting too?

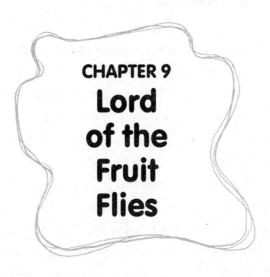

CHAPTER 9
Lord of the Fruit Flies

Our new house is under attack from fruit flies. It feels like some sort of Biblical plague. But in reality it's all to do with the compost bin.

We've dutifully filled our giant green bin with peelings, tea bags and general organic detritus. Nicola often gazes lovingly at it, imagining the contents decaying into a brown, oozing, gelatinous goo. I've rarely seen her look so happy.

When you unscrew the lid it's a fine study in entropy. Cabbages turn yellow and squelchy, ancient coffee grounds sit on broken egg shells, onions turn to mush, potatoes sprout tentacles. And into the mire come wood lice, worms and slugs. But no-one warned us about the fruit flies.

We've returned from Taransay and in the June heat the fruit flies have multiplied like something from an American B-movie. Whenever we open the bin we're engulfed by swarms of them. They form a black moving cloud like some single living entity. The compost bin has slits in each side to aerate the matter inside. These simply serve as launching stations for squadrons of fruit flies. It's like *Day of the Triffids* merged with *The Birds*.

The main problem is that our garden is too small. The composter might have been fine at the end of some 100-foot plot. But in our tiny cottage it's only a metre or so from our kitchen window. And Nicola insists on having the window open all day. Fresh air is a non-negotiable item on her Green agenda. And so in swarm the fruit flies, settling on everything in our designer kitchen.

'This is very Annie Dillard,' I tell Nicola, referring to *Pilgrim at Tinker Creek* by the American writer Annie Dillard, a book that Nicola has recommended to me. 'Ah, the fecundity of nature,' I add, swatting at a fruit fly with my tea towel.

Pilgrim at Tinker Creek is a long meditation on nature, and an eco-bunny classic. Dillard gets very excited by frogs being eaten alive from the inside by horrible parasites. She'd love this – Highbury humans slowly consumed by flies.

Black dots speckle the kitchen's white walls and ceiling. So we thrash at them with tea-towels. Every fruit fly we flick leaves a tiny red bloodstain on the wall. Our landlord's metrosexual designer kitchen has suddenly taken on a pattern of white and red gore. It looks like some obscene meditation on war by the Chapman brothers.

'Nicola, we've got to decommission the compost bin,' I plead.

'Oh nonsense, a few fruit flies never hurt anyone. We can't go back to binning our food waste now. Think of the landfill!' she replies from behind a black cloud.

I'm thankful there's a trap door in the attic office. Every time I close the hatch I feel like Marlon Brando's Colonel Kurtz in *Apocalypse Now*. Soon I'll be sitting up there in darkness wearing ripped Army greens. My house is already covered in blood and fly corpses. This is the end, my friend. Travel far enough down the overgrown jungle track towards the deep Green vision and you confront the seething mess of the compost bin.

We become a collection point for Growing Communities, organic vegetable scheme. Every Wednesday 16 bags of fruit and veg are deposited in our front room to await collection from those who have ordered them in our area. They drive the fruit flies demented with excitement. Even some of the vegetable people look a little shocked to be collecting their bags from a fruit fly-ridden mound of bags by the door.

While Nicola is on extended maternity leave she is working on a new book called *The Toxic Home*, a cheery guide to all the things in your house that can kill you, commissioned by The Women's Press. So we attempt to recruit a child minder for two days a week. The fruit flies are not a great selling point. Nor are the snails.

A huge colony of snails has made its home on our garden wall and the creatures delight in eating the runner beans Nicola has just planted. She refuses to use slug pellets, which poison wildlife, and so we're instead putting old coffee grounds and eggshells on the garden, adding to the third world ambiance of our wildlife reserve. But nothing deters the snails, so Nicola, suddenly sacrificing all Green principles in the name of expediency, starts picking up the snails and depositing them in the compost bin.

'Nicola, that's not very Green, snails are for life, not just for Christmas,' I remonstrate.

'Oh, for goodness sake! The wretched things are eating my runner beans!'

But the snails don't die. They thrive in the oozing slime of decomposing carrots and turnips until their shells are too large to allow them to escape from the compost bin through the air vents. Nicola has created a very effective snail prison.

We're interviewing one unfortunate young woman from Hungary about the child-minding position when it rains. Big summer rain after a week of humidity. When it rains the snails stick their bodies and antenna through the compost bin's vents searching for water, slowly moving as if they're part of some gigantic, half compost-bin half-snail science-fiction monster. Our prospective employee glances through the kitchen window at the wriggling snails oozing out of the compost bin and promptly runs out of the house.

Eventually the plight of the trapped snails moves me to perform a mollusc raid. Reaching into that horrific bin, I pick up the snails by their shells, collect them in a plastic bag and retreat into the street, where I'm accosted by the lager-drinking, chain-smoking mad bloke who walks up and down our street all day muttering about Rodney King. He notices that my plastic bag is moving and sees a snail's head emerge from the top. He looks at me as if I'm the deranged one, and takes another swig of super-strength lager. I've probably set his care-in-the-community treatment back ten years.

My plan is to release the snails, not very ethically, in the street's community garden. Only when carrying a plastic bag of snails there's always the risk of bumping into neighbours who might then want to talk. To save embarrassment, I decide to dump the snails at night, on wasteground and verges, in gardens, anywhere that might give them a slithering chance of life.

Finally, we recruit Sharon, a rugby fan who also likes *Doctor Who*, as our child minder. We can only assume she must be desperate for work. Or perhaps our menagerie is preferable to the demanding City mums she complains about. Sharon is bribed with gifts of old *Doctor Who* videos in return for not reporting our blood-spattered health-and-safety nightmare of a kitchen to social services. She even helps name 'Charlotte the Spider', Lola's new kitchen pet. Charlotte is a happy spider, sitting on our ceiling eating fruit flies. One morning Nicola is delighted to find that a frog has colonised a bucket full of rainwater in our garden. I feel like Ray Mears every time I open the French windows.

'Just one thing, Sharon,' I whisper to her one week, feeling like the Herman Munster of employers. 'Don't ever drink from the beer bottles here...'

The flies in the kitchen have inspired me to fiendish new depths of ingenuity. This ain't rock'n'roll, this is fly genocide. Called upstairs one night for some baby emergency, I'd left the dregs of my Bishop's Finger in the bottle overnight.

Serendipity! In the morning the bottle of beer is full of drowned fruit flies. Their bodies float like hoppy sediment at the bottom of the bottle. It looks like the sort of brew you could happily flog to bearded blokes at a CAMRA festival, citing high specific gravity, a full-bodied, flyish flavour for the connoisseur.

The fruit flies love Bishop's Finger, Ruddles County, Abbot, Hobgoblin and numerous other fine ales. Altering a lifetime's habit, I start leaving my bottles of beer unfinished. When a dribble of beer is left in the bottom of a bottle, hundreds of the silly buzzers dive into the booze like insect Oliver Reeds. Maybe fruit flies in CAMRA T-shirts will soon be demanding crisps, peanuts and cocktails as well. I start leaving semi-filled bottles of real ale all over the house.

Life here seemed so inviting when we moved in. The compost bin was meant to improve our house, not subsume it. Now it feels like we are living inside one giant piece of decaying real estate, slowly turning into mulch.

*

September 11 2001 seems like any other day. The breaking news alerts start while I'm searching Ceefax for team news about West Ham's trip to Reading in the Worthington Cup. Red letters at the bottom of the screen declare: 'ATTACK ON AMERICA'.

Two hijacked planes have been flown into the skyscrapers of the World Trade Center. A third hijacked aircraft has crashed into the Pentagon and a fourth into a field. There are people trapped in the upper reaches of buildings, facing death by fire or horrendous leaps to the pavements below. This is real life-and-death in close-up. It's live TV coverage with no one to censor anything on the grounds of sensitivity or taste. Ordinary office workers are hanging on to window ledges above impossible drops, the buildings being consumed by fire.

And then the impossible happens; the towers collapse, and huge grey clouds of toxic dust shoot down the narrow streets of New York like some live creature in a disaster movie, chasing panicking pedestrians, shrouding everyone in funereal dust.

Nicola has heard the news while at the playground with Lola and seven-month old Nell and has rushed home.

'Don't you see, it's the end of everything!' she exclaims. 'History will change from this moment!'

As an environmentalist, her world view is hardly optimistic, even without destruction on this scale. Now she has a doomsday scenario where the world financial markets collapse, America will start a nuclear war, the property market collapses, and we'll never be able to sell our flat and move into our own house either.

The early estimates are that around 5,000 people could have died in the World Trade Center today. There's talk of someone named Osama Bin Laden and an organisation called al-Qaeda that I've never heard of. I realise that my partner needs emotional support, and immediately phone my mate Denis to tell him that I won't be attending the West Ham match tonight.

Tony Blair announces that all flights over London have been grounded. We drink Chardonnay while not being sure whether London is facing imminent disaster or not. It's hard to gaze through the window at the autumn sky without looking for planes. At this moment I want to be with Nicola and my children.

There's talk on *Newsnight* of dirty bombs, poisoning the water supply and crop-spraying planes depositing lethal toxins on our cities. Nell is only seven months old. All our Green fears multiply as we discover it's religious fascists, not corporations, who might be doing the polluting now. It's like Quentin Tarantino is directing Rachel Carson's *Silent Spring*.

During the next few days the world reels. Many planes remain grounded and airports closed. And, obscene as this act of annihilation is, I start to think that we shouldn't be flying so much anyway.

There was very little security on the internal US flights that were hijacked because every American regards it as their right to jump on a plane as if it were a bus. I'm worried about terrorism but I'm worried about climate change too – a threat people don't see coming because it's not carrying a knife or hijacking planes with murderous intent.

Ultimately, climate change is going to kill a lot more people than al-Qaeda. It's hard not to bring an environmental perspective to the disaster. Maybe that's the way I think now.

As the US gears up for a 'war on terror' I'm thinking of the waste involved in any war. Manufacturing army vehicles, tanks and airplanes and then blowing them up, vomiting yet more carbon into the atmosphere.

As the weeks pass, the US is shown at its worst. Instead of proving itself better than crazed fundamentalism, the Geneva Convention is ignored and detainees of the 'war on terrorism' are shipped by the US to Guantanamo Bay in orange jump suits. In Britain there's much shock about their treatment there.

At home, we have more domestic issues to contend with. Since we returned from Taransay, baby Nell has been suffering from acute eczema. Nell has had terrible eczema since she was three months old. At first she just seemed itchy, but at night she often scratches herself until her skin bleeds. Eventually we find a mail-order company that sells cotton sleepsuits with built-in gloves. We sleep holding her hands at night.

Nell's skin becomes red, dry and itchy, and sometimes becomes infected, so we have to use steroid creams and give her oral antibiotics. We agonise about her long-term health. Other mums at the 2 O'clock Club won't let their babies play with Nell because they think she's got chicken pox.

We try to research the cause of eczema. Nell has atopic eczema, something now suffered by an astonishing one in five infants, compared to one in 30 half a century ago. She may well go on to develop asthma, we learn. 'It's got to have some connection with modern life,' I tell Nicola.

Dermatologists at Sheffield University claim that increased bathing, with associated increased use of soaps, shampoos and gels, is one of the main reasons for the increase. The detergents break down the fats on the skin's surface and, a bit like my two-decade old Gore-Tex, the skin loses its water-proof quality and allows allergens and irritants to seep in. Yet everything we have is organic.

Some say genetic factors contribute to eczema (Nicola still suffers from mild eczema herself) or that allergy triggers such as dust mite faeces, pollens, animal hairs and dairy products can cause the problem. Others suggest particulates from car exhausts and chemicals in the atmosphere might be a con-tributing factor. Some of Nicola's Green pals think that pollution can attach itself to pollen. When I ask our doctor what causes eczema, he sighs and says, 'If I knew that I'd be a millionaire'.

People suggest remedies – Chinese herbs, homeopathy, that new wonder cream on BBC's *Watchdog*, cranial-sacral therapy, kinesiologists, aloe vera cream, salt from the Dead Sea, sunshine, African tree oil, oatmeal in old tights in the bath, dilithium crystals, Romulan cloaking devices...

Our bathroom contains a battery of creams and lotions. We try everything – dust-mite covers on the mattress, bathing and not bathing, keeping her away from dogs and cats.

Nicola cuts out all dairy and nuts from her own diet in case these travel through her breast milk and trigger another scratching episode. All this does is make a very over-tired mother even more bad-tempered as the comfort of chocolate bars is removed.

Our relationship suffers. We're too tired to make love. No one sleeps. We're both trying to write books. I'm working on a diary of West Ham's season, *Irons In The Soul*. Nicola returns to her three-day a week job at Friends of the Earth, and is still researching her *Toxic Home* book, which arms her with information about how everything in our home is destroying us. When I proofread her chapters it's more scary than al-Qaeda. Old carpet can still contain long-living pesticides such as DDT. Old paint might contain lead, while Volatile Organic Compounds (VOCs) are often present in modern gloss paints. Our air quality is being compromised by VOCs in aerosols, dry-cleaned clothes, disinfectants and cleaning fluids too. Hormone disruptors known as phthalates leak from plastic kitchen utensils.

Furniture made from bonded wood mixtures like MDF and plastics containing formaldehyde all add to the toxic soup. Even our ancient sofa is probably full of brominated flame retardants (BFRs) – chemicals with a long life that can sneak into our bodies, disrupt hormones and cause developmental problems, so that you end up supporting Chelsea. All this and fruit flies too.

Early in 2002 *Time Out* magazine decides to stop using freelances. My 'Sidelines' column, which has been slowly getting smaller and smaller, is finally axed. They want to save money and there are too many other magazines writing about nothing but gossip. Maybe I shouldn't have turned up at that Café de Paris bash covered in baby sick. No more calls from Mark Borkowski PR and his indomitable assistants. We'll miss the money.

Nell makes it to her first birthday but the eczema won't clear up. I take Nicola and Nell to stay in the West Ham Quality Hotel, inside the Doctor Martens Stand, as part of the research for my new book. But we spend all night trying to prevent Nell scratching. Like many a West Ham striker, we fail to score at Upton Park. Although we do get to drink West Ham's own-brand Chardonnay, and think of the eponymous character in the new TV series *Footballers' Wives*.

We're exhausted. Things must be bad, because when one exhausted evening I insist on ordering a take-away pizza, Nicola doesn't object, or even remind me to recycle the cardboard box. Throughout 2002 we drift through parenthood and life.

*

Maybe it was because she was so different that the affair started. Nikki was blonde and wore lots of make-up and didn't worry if it had been tested on animals or not. She wore only hugely expensive unsustainable underwear that hadn't been certified as organic. She drove a 4-wheel drive Jeep Cherokee, and brought back pizzas from the supermarket, using lots of plastic bags which she then threw away without recycling them. She was a hot babe with a hot pad. Nikki's central heating was always on maximum. Which was probably why the lovemaking was so fantastic...

'WAKE UP! WAKE UP PETE! She's scratching again! You've got to hold her...' Nell has just poked me in the eye and her feet are kneading my testicles. Oh my God. I'm in bed at home.

'Daddy, there's a wolf in my bedroom! I'm scared of the wolf!' says Lola, emerging from her bedroom next door. It's going to be a long night's journey into day.

As Nell reaches 18 months her eczema improves. She still wears her gloved suit all day, but her face is clear and there's soft white skin emerging at last. Sharon has left to work for a less insect-prone family. Towards the end of 2002 we sleep a little more. We can almost think of ourselves as sentient beings again, between nappy changes.

But there's disaster for Nicola's book. The Women's Press changes hands, and her title has been cancelled. Nicola is left in tears because she'd worked through exhausted hour after hour on *The Toxic Home* for nothing. I try to make her laugh, as always.

'Look, never mind anthrax in letters, we can post an anonymous container of fruit flies. And anyway, you can use all that material elsewhere,' I reassure her. Friends of the Earth is talking about a new book called *Save Cash and Save The Planet* – and surely she's the ideal author?

Meanwhile we hold the launch party for my own book at Sportspages Bookshop in Charing Cross Road, London, managed by David Luxton, later to become the Don Revie of literary agents. Dress is formal – scarf, Harrington jacket, high-leg Doctor Martens boots, etc. All my West Ham supporting mates are there, Denis, Nigel, Gavin, Matt, Fraser, Big Joe, my old school friend Paul Garrett and his dad, club DJ Jeremy Nicholas, our nanny Sharon and anyone else who turns up. And of course Nicola, whom I thank in my speech for her patience. She even looks quite proud of me. After a year lost in eczema creams and nappies, it feels like I'm still capable of something in the outside world. Still not great on Greenness, but big in Green Street, E13.

In April, the US and Britain invade Iraq. Everyone around us in Highbury seems to have a 'Not in my name' poster in their window. Operation 'Shock and Awe' blitzes Baghdad. We worry about the unneccessary deaths, but also about the plumes of smoke from burning oil wells, the unexploded shells and the tanks on fire. Has anyone ever done a carbon footprint analysis of war?

West Ham are about to fade and die as they head for relegation to the Championship. During a 4-2 defeat at Charlton the fans sing: 'We want a new back four!' Russian billionaire Roman Abramovich has bought Chelsea and is throwing money at it and the fear is no other club will win anything ever again. There's a Scouse medium called Derek Acorah on Living TV's *Most Haunted* and I'm finding it strangely addictive. And for some reason Johnny Rotten has agreed to appear on *I'm A Celebrity Get Me Out of Here!*

But I'm also worried about snails. Nell and Lola keep a menagerie of snails in an old fish tank with some spinach leaves, spending hours watching the creatures try to escape over the sides. Nell brings them in for tea and places her favourite snail on the kitchen table, insisting it stays beside her. Clearly she's her mother's daughter.

Nicola is travelling to Devon to interview Satish Kumar, editor of *Resurgence* and a man admired by Prince Charles for his views. We decide to turn the trip into a family holiday by the coast, so we all travel down by train, then hire a car and Nicola drives us to numerous organic farm shops and enthuses about 'local produce for local people', sounding like a character from *The League of Gentlemen*.

A cat in Totnes sets off Nell's itching, and the wild flowers at Hartland affect her eyes for a time. Downshifting to rural parts might not be the answer. There seem to be just as many things in the country that affect her eczema as in the city.

Back in London Lola, Nell and myself watch *Maggie and the Ferocious Beast* on TV, but it seems that most of the beasts are in our home. I've just accidentally trodden on one; silver trails are on the doormat and chunky shells are suckered to the French windows. And a daddy snail is attached to the back of my computer.

'It seems like we've taken to a life of slime,' I tell Nell.

In the summer of 2003 London, and indeed the whole of Europe, swelters. In France around 15,000 mainly elderly people die as a result of the summer's heatwave. The *Guardian* manages to fry an egg on a London pavement. A haze of polluting smog is hanging over the capital, car stereos are being played at full volume, drivers are shouting abuse at each other at Highbury Corner. The Victoria line smells like Johnny Vegas's three-day old socks, my sandals are oozing sweat and those poor people who work in the City still have to wear jackets, ties, shoes and socks to work. At least their offices are probably air-conditioned, though at what cost to the environment? My attic office is hotter than Baghdad and mosquitoes are rampaging over my skin during my early-evening cold beer in the garden. If global warming continues London will soon be like Rome, where the locals decamp for all of August. Meanwhile in north Yorkshire there's soothing torrential rain, storms and flooding. Oh, to be a northerner.

Sales of lager boom while Marks & Spencer's sales of clothes wilt in the summer heat. You can't travel on the tube without carrying water. This seems far more than some cyclical fluctuation; global warming is here. Give it another ten years and there will be wild camels wandering through the deserts of Bermondsey.

Eventually a welcome downpour arrives to end the heat-wave. Faced with war abroad and the demise of her book project, Nicola boosts her spirits with regular visits to farmers' markets. On Sunday mornings we take the bus to the market at Angel. Nicola loves it here. Farmers' markets are burgeoning all over London she tells me. So this is where all those people in their trendy Robbie Williams-style farmers' caps now hang out.

At Angel we see women with Green Baby bags, gay couples and trendy characters who belong in *Private Eye*'s 'It's Grim Up North' cartoon strip being served by ruddy-faced cheesemen and pie-makers from Somerset. There's almost enough pukka grub on the stalls to make Jamie Oliver remember his glottal stops. We stroll among pigeon breasts, buffalo steaks, Sussex sizzler bacon, goat meat chops, brown oyster mushrooms, mulled spicy cider, real pork pies, Egremont russet crisp and nutty-flavoured organic apples, wholemeal walnut bread and some splendidly strong unpasteurised buffalo cheese. Nicola makes me buy some really rather good onion bread and some buffalo cheese and I find myself muttering 'How much?' as if I'm my dad. And then we spend five quid on a bottle of organic cider.

How Britain has changed. People in the country shop in Spar and Iceland, if their local branch is still open, while we in the city now get more rural fare than Ambridge. If Thomas Hardy was alive today, he'd surely be writing about Islington Green rather than Egdon Heath.

We're now house hunting. The subsidence work on Nicola's flat has finally been completed after a mere two years and we're trying to rent or sell the place, although the property market is unusually slow. My aunt Audrey from Stoke died the previous summer and has left her money to my two sisters and myself. Thanks to her kindness I'll have around 50k to put towards a new house.

We visit a mortgage broker and discover that we can apply for something called a self-certification mortgage. We can include my turnover, not my profit, rental income from Nicola's flat, likely book deals, useful items found in the street, liquidity of compost bins and extent of football programme collections.

But where can we live? Taransay seems a long time ago and the wind reaches 100 mph in winter. We consider other cities such as Oxford and Bath. We house-sit for Richard and Fleur in Yorkshire, looking after various ponies and sheep. While there Nicola decides to look at Snape Castle, on offer at only £330,000, the price of a small house in London. She's taken seriously by the estate agent, which is impressive, while he no doubt assumes that I'm her gardener or loyal retainer. But half the building is a listed ruin, with even worse subsidence problems than our old flat.

Walking through sunny Highbury after returning from Yorkshire we meet several people from the community nursery, the local school and even the vicar. It feels like Frank Capra's Bedford Falls, just with slightly more mobile phone and iPod muggings.

'You know, it was horrible having to drive everywhere in Yorkshire, ' I tell Nicola. 'I quite like not having a car. No parking worries, no permits, no wardens. People talk to you when you walk.'

'That's what I think too,' says Nicola. 'It's actually much easier to be Green in London.'

The Thames might flood one day, but here we have a community. We know lots of parents from Lola and Nell's school and nursery. We don't have to drive anywhere. We're surrounded by tubes, buses and taxis. In the country, Tesco is the only choice for shopping and it's usually eight miles away. We even have pavements here, unlike all those country roads in Yorkshire. The council has introduced green recycling bins. We can leave our recycling on the doorstep and the dustbinmen will take away.

Lola's started school and Nicola tells me before every PTA meeting not to let her volunteer for anything. Nicola then ignores me and ends up as PTA secretary. And I seem to be treasurer. She's prepared to work hard to make an inner-city school better. So for now, we're going to stay.

And somehow, via an eccentric corner property in Finsbury Park, we scramble onto the property ladder. The house is close to Finsbury Park mosque and there are TV crews there filming Abu Hamza whenever we visit, and on Fridays the British National Party turns up to demonstrate against muslims, with the police in between the two sides.

But we don't see any trouble and if it brings the house prices down then that's fine with us.

Our street is quiet enough. It's a Victorian home with a garden at the back, a pond and a large hedge around the front.

'Nicola, do you know what this means?'

'That we finally have a family home at last? That we can feel fulfilled?'

'No, not that. Don't you see? There's enough garden for the compost bin to be placed at a sensible distance from our windows. We might finally have beaten the fruit flies!'

CHAPTER 10

Greener Than Thou

It's January 2004 and finally we own our own home. The subsidence work on Nicola's flat has been completed after two years' work undertaken with the alacrity of lawyers working on the Jarndyce v Jarndyce case. Plus there's been a seven-month wait for all the correct parts of a new fitted kitchen to complete the flat. It didn't sell in the spring; uncertainty over the war, plus a history of subsidence puts off some buyers, so instead Nicola decides to let it to tenants. We're landlords; it makes me feel like coming over all Rigsby-esque, with Nicola playing the part of Miss Jones.

We're sitting in our new home surrounded by hundreds of cardboard boxes with felt-pen writing on them indicating designated areas, including the rather over-grandiose title of 'library'. It's a real house with three bedrooms, two front rooms and a garden. It's even got a cellar, which feels really grown-up.

We've been together for ten years now and have accumu-
lated around 200 years' worth of junk. The so-called library
has boxes from floor to ceiling. 'We've got so many boxes we
could build our own eco-home with them,' I tell Nicola. 'It
would be a bit like a straw bale house, only with Penguin
Classics instead. They'd be much better insulation than
Victorian bricks.'

I'm as bad as Nicola at being unable to throw anything
away. We take a break from unpacking to stroll around the
area. An Arsenal match is about to kick-off and crowds hurry
through the streets, but I still notice a white sofa in someone's
front garden.

'That doesn't look bad,' I say. 'They must have thrown it
out today. It's not even wet.'

'I could re-cover it. We just need some new cushions.
Come on, let's move it,' agrees Nicola.

We carry the sofa back to our new pad past puzzled
Arsenal fans.

'They have seats at the match, you know,' says one.

'It's OK, we're armchair supporters,' replies Nicola.

We deposit the sofa alongside all the other upturned chairs
and tables. As we sit by our boxes, stepladder at the ready,
wondering what to unpack and where, I notice the newspaper's headline. It says, quite starkly, that global warming poses
a greater threat to the world than terrorism. I read on, and discover that this isn't just an over-ambitious headline writer's

claim. This is the startling view of the government's chief scientist, David King. He says quite clearly that global warming is the most serious problem we are facing today, more serious even than the threat of terrorism. He goes on to say that we can no longer delay taking action about this, and he's so convinced that if we don't begin to stop global warming now, then more substantial and even more expensive changes will be needed in the future. Which is presumably coded scientific language for saying we're all up an inundated London creek without a paddle unless we act now.

King predicts that by 2080, flood levels that are now expected once in 100 years could be recurring every three years. As an afterthought, the paper mentions that *Nature* magazine predicts that climate change will cause the extinction of a quarter of land animals and plants. It would be nice to think that the eco doomsters are wrong. But it doesn't seem like the Greens can now be accused of exaggerating.

Yet what can we do? David King states that the UK is only responsible for 2 per cent of the world's emissions. The US is responsible for 20 per cent of the world's greenhouse gases, even though it has only 4 per cent of the world's population. China is catching up in the Champions' League of polluters. King attacks the US for withdrawing from the Kyoto protocol and 'refusing to countenance any remedial action now or in the future'.

So why are we bothering to fit long-life light bulbs in our

new house? If everyone else does the same across the UK then we might reduce a little of our 2 per cent.

But I'm suddenly determined to reduce our own carbon consumption, because individuals can make a difference. If enough individuals act together in the UK, the US, China and everywhere else then we become not individuals but society, and that forces governments and multinationals to take action.

'If we're going to be Green then we might as well make our house as energy efficient as possible,' I find myself telling Nicola.

She looks a little shocked.

'I'm a man and I'm competitive...' I explain. 'Where other blokes may go for a few pale Green changes, ours will be deep green and meaningful.'

What we do will make little difference if everyone continues flying and driving mini-tanks, but is that an excuse not to try? It's going to take more than planting a few trees as carbon offsets to change things.

The future is frightening. And suddenly the thought occurs that maybe I'm morphing into a fully-fledged Green. As my mates at West Ham might chant: 'You're not cynical, you're not cynical, you're not cynical any more!'

A few years ago someone took us to the Holy Trinity Church at Brompton. It was full of the fervour of those who had just completed Alpha courses, interspersed with soul music played by a surprisingly funky Christian band. At one point a working-class taxi driver rose to take the stand, saying how he'd once mocked God, but now he'd completed the holy knowledge and taken a one-way route to redemption.

Maybe one day I'll be like that taxi driver, addressing packed meetings of Green evangelists. 'Comrades, I once scoffed at the *Independent*'s front-page warnings about climate change. Yes, I laughed at the attire of the holy prophet Monbiot. I sniggered at compost loos. My soul was lost to Sky, CDs, DVDs, consumption and emissions. My life was weighed down in carbon. But now, friends, I have seen the glory of the low-energy light bulb! You can not fly to salvation. You can not get there in a 4x4, you can find true Greenness only in your own heart!'

Although presumably there would always be the risk that, like some hypocritical American TV preacher, I'd be caught by the tabloids downloading football highlights, ordering a plasma TV or turning on the central heating in October.

The other immediate appeal of going Green is to my short arms and long pockets. Perhaps we all become our dads. This new mortgage is going to stretch us financially. Children are expensive. Low-energy bills might help save our home from repossession.

Like most Victorian homes, our new gaff is something of a carbon disaster. The walls are only one brick thick, and hence there are no cavities to insulate. The windows are draughty old sash originals, rattling in the wind. In three rooms the sashes have been replaced with louvres, fitted during some mysterious bout of 1970's interior décor madness. The slats are draughty and exceptionally easy for burglars to remove. In fact we're heating the rest of the street.

We decide to work with what we have. Initially we do the simple things, firstly fitting low energy light bulbs in every room, including the cellar and attic. We don't have the ready cash for solar panels and we're not sure if they would necessitate a new boiler. Solar panels cost several thousand quid, but they can come later when we've written a few bestsellers. There's also the problem of council bureaucracy. Although you don't need planning permission, you have to get a letter from the council saying you don't need planning permission, which seems to take forever. As for wind turbines on the roof, people who know about these things tell us that although they look impressive, in a city they'll be of little use.

The bathroom loo is leaking. The previous owner has scarpered with the loo seat, so we hire a local plumber, who moves into expensive action and fits a new loo. Every new lavatory is now required by law to have a dual flush system – no more wasting nine litres of water every visit. Our water consumption will be halved. And finally we can lose the hippo in our cistern. It's travelled from Aubert Park to Whistler Street, but now it sits stranded out of water, deflated and awaiting a new, less sustainable home.

Our next step is to get the loft insulated. Nicola discovers that the government will pay half the cost through a grant, so the whole thing costs us just £200. It takes a couple of blokes an hour to lay a thick carpet of insulating material across our attic floor. This saves us a hundred quid a year in energy bills.

'I guess we're guilty of woolly thinking,' I quip as the men in blue boiler suits depart. It works too. When the snow arrives we stand in the street and observe how the snow takes much longer to thaw on our roof than on the hot roofs of our uninsulated neighbours. We stand there in mittens and bobble hats with self-satisfied grins, finally Greener than thou.

We screw draught excluders to the bottom of the exterior doors and the cellar door. A simple piece of felt stuck to the hinge-side of the front door frame drastically reduces the draught coming in from outside. Nicola makes a curtain to fit in front of the house door and fits thick linings to our existing curtains. I fill in the gaps between the kitchen floorboards.

We remove most of the old sash windows and replace them with double-glazed versions. Nicola vetoes PVC on grounds of taste and iffy chemicals, so we employ a local company that builds double-glazed wooden sash windows in the original style. Each costs several hundred quid. No doubt it's a ridiculously expensive middle-class fad, but it's worth it to remove the louvres and their transport café chic. The glass stops rattling and the house seems immediately warmer. Our security is improved too.

The ancient gas cooker we inherited is leaking and dangerous. We arrange for the council to collect it, along with several old purple carpets. We opt for a relatively low power consumption electric cooker to replace it. But other things we keep. The kitchen is mainly horrible white MDF cupboards, built in the 1980s, but it works and we reason it will last a few more years.

The boiler is old, not one of the flash new condensing models that can cut heating bills but again, it works and we decide to run it until it gives up. It's not as if we use the central heating that much. We turn off the upstairs radiators and let the heat rise from below. The timer is rationed to an hour and a half in the morning and three hours at night. Even more low tech, we wear jumpers and fleeces.

We screw an old-fashioned airing rack to the landing ceiling, one of those which has wooden poles held together by what look like giant metal coat hangers. We can pull it up and down through a pleasing combination of ropes and pulley. To hold it in place we wrap the rope around a hook on the wall. I feel a little like a Roman engineer hoisting it up and down, damp boxer shorts, socks, shirts and jumpers assembled above my head. This means we can dry everything inside without using an energy-guzzling tumble dryer.

In the garden Nicola installs water butts to harvest rainwater and keep us alive come the day of the great warming, She builds raised permaculture beds from bits of reclaimed skip wood.

Now we own a whole house Nicola initiates a strict water-saving routine. It's not as if we're experiencing a drought in the early months of 2004, but just in case there are water wars in north London she starts saving our bathwater and washing-up water.

Even as a new Green convert this seems a little unnecessary to me. She places a bucket by the bath. Every time we finish having a bath we are now supposed to leave the water so it can be ladled into the bucket, all soapy and congealing. When we shower she insists we shower over the black bucket to catch the precious drops.

'We can water the garden with a bucket of water every day,' she suggests. 'Or we can give the privet hedge a drink. It's going to need lots of water and it will stop us getting subsidence and save us cash.'

'But it's going to start smelling and we're not on a water meter.'

'Don't be such a wimp! Think ahead to ten years' time when climate change is really hitting us. We won't have any of the services we have now.'

A similar regime is soon in place in the kitchen. Whenever we wash up Nicola expects us to save the washing-up water in the plastic washing-up bowl, pour it into a bucket by the sink and then when that's full, take it into the garden to water the chard and jasmine she's just planted. I spend my time lugging greasy water outside, trying not to let it slurp on to the hallway floor. Sometimes when she's out, I secretly pour it down the sink and claim that I've dutifully watered the garden. What's the point of collecting water in butts outside if we then have to save the dishwater too?

However, all this water saving does have one unexpected benefit. The children are safely in their room asleep. We're in bed too, although unknown to me, Nicola's going through one of her nights when she can't sleep because she's worrying about the future of the human race, her workload, my parents, her mum, her sister, her brother, what role she should take on the school PTA, who's going to organise the summer fete and a myriad other concerns. Why can't she be more like a man? We drink beer and go to sleep. Still, if Nicola didn't worry so much she'd never have been awake to save the street.

'FIRE!!!! FIRE!!!!! WAKE UP!!!!!'

The curtains are wide open. Nicola is standing at the window, bathed in an orange glow.

Ugh, what? Our house is burning down? Am I awake? Is this *Fawlty Towers*? Oh God, I'm never good in the middle of the night, I need my eight hours. Fire? Bloody hell. I'd better get the children and my West Ham programmes.

'Our house is on fire?' I mutter blearily.

'No, it's the skip across the road. Come on, move, it's going to set their house alight and that horrible four-wheel drive. You ring the fire brigade and I'll try to put it out.'

I stumble towards the window. The house opposite is having building work done and there's a skip full of windows, timber, rubble and carpets in front of it. Orange flames are rising three metres into the night air. They're lapping against the front of their house. It's like a scene from a David Lynch film.

It's the work of our local arsonists. We've already had several skips in the area set on fire by a couple of toe-rags who think it's funny. This week the paper warned that someone could be killed if they're not caught.

I fiddle while the skip burns, searching for my dressing gown and glasses as there's no time to put contact lenses in. Staggering downstairs feeling unsteady at the strange hour of 5 am I find the phone and dial 999.

'Uh, erm, there's a skip on fire across the road and it's about to set fire to the house opposite. My partner's in the street trying to put it out with washing-up water.' It must be one of the more unusual emergency service calls.

Nicola remerges in the kitchen taking another bucket of stale washing-up water. 'Quick, get the bathwater too,' she appeals, before rushing out, with the sarong she's wrapped round her flapping in the wind.

'Be careful Nicola,' I plead, 'I've called the fire brigade they're coming soon.'

The fire engine turns up within three minutes. The children have been woken by the siren and the flashing lights in the street outside.

'Daddy, what's happened?' asks Lola.

'Mummy put out the fire with our old bathwater,' I tell the children trying not to laugh. 'She's a local hero.'

Well, she has made some impression on the flames but it still looks a potentially lethal conflagration. We watch together through the bedroom window as the firemen turn their high-pressure hose on the skip and systematically soak it. It's one mass of charcoal.

'I saw two young guys running off after they started it,' says a breathless Nicola, now returned to the house.

'Well done, you saved our street as well as the planet.'

'Well done Mummy, you should be in the fire brigade,' add Nell and Lola.

The next day a policeman comes to take a statement from Nicola.

'Two male suspects seen running in the direction of St Thomas's Road,' he notes down. Before asking 'And you rushed out with a bucket of water?'

'Yes, we recycle our bath water and the washing-up water. We keep buckets by the sink.'

I look a little embarrassed but then I'm not the have-a-go skip-dousing heroine. The policeman looks a little quizzical too, but dutifully notes it all down in his book.

Nicola's exploits soon become street folklore in our area. 'There was this woman who ran outside with no clothes on and put the fire out,' we hear one dad telling another.

'Well, my sarong probably wasn't done up that well,' confesses Nicola.

'Naked woman hero of skip inferno. Can I ring the local paper?' I ask.

'No.'

'Mummy should be in *The Incredibles*,' adds Lola, referring to her favourite film. Indeed, she's the first Green super hero. Although I can still do without the water recycling.

Nicola seems to tire a little of me spilling the water on the way to the door. And indeed, I think she's fatigued herself from lugging water outside on top of all the other house refurbishing tasks. Thankfully, the rains arrive and we have an excuse to give up on throwing the bathwater out with the dirty dishes water.

The children get a giant Wendy Hut for the back garden. 'It's like another room,' I declare. 'This will add 50 grand to the value of our house!'

It has to be passed over our garden wall in pieces and assembled by sociologists. Our near neighbour Scott, a sociology lecturer and Blackburn fan, arrives with his electric drill to help pin the thing together. Meanwhile Lola and Nell trawl our garden pond looking for newts. How many sociologists does it take to build a garden shed? Probably less than it takes to construct a new paradigm. The shed is finally erected and Nicola draws pictures of the girls and horses on the interior walls.

Yes, we are becoming insufferable eco-home bores, inviting friends round to admire our lovely new double-glazed windows and loft insulation. I have become a Bob Ferris of the Noughties, flourishing electricity bills from Good Energy (all from renewable sources) rather than prawn cocktails and avocado pears.

We even have a car club car we can park outside our new gaff. Nicola becomes one of the first members of the City Car Club and is pictured in the local paper with several councillors. For a monthly fee she gets a swipe card – no keys necessary – and cheap access to a new car whenever she wants to phone up and book it. We just pick the car up at one of the reserved parking spots and when we've finished return it to the same spot. There's no way we need a car in London, but for trips to deepest Hertfordshire to visit Nicola's mum it's useful. No problems with servicing, MOTs, road tax, geezers nicking your stereo or reserving parking spaces. Another unexpected bonus of joining the car club is that in London it's exempt from the congestion charge.

'This is great. We get to be sanctimonious gits while still having a nice new motor,' I say, handing Nicola her swipe card.

Through the early months of 2004 we busy ourselves preparing a sort of Noah's Ark for the eco-generation. We are no longer thinking about ifs, just water butts. It's surprising how satisfying it is to own your house and then to give it an eco-refit. But just as I'm thinking how easy it is to be Green Nicola takes me, as always, way beyond my comfort zone to somewhere 53 miles west of Venus.

'Pete, we're going to get chickens!' she declares, as if such a thing is an entirely natural course of events in inner-city London. I hear the sound of eco-dreams coming home to roost.

CHAPTER 11

Clucking Hell

Normal women just require a dinner date without the kids and some Green & Black's organic chocolates for their birthday. Nicola wants chickens.

'But we live in London!' I declare, aghast at another of her bird-brained schemes.

'Don't be so conservative. Everyone in London had chickens during the war,' replies my fowl-loving partner. 'And we'll have our own fresh eggs. And think how good it will be for the children to have some pets and see where their food comes from. People have lost touch with the land...'

'It all sounds a bit *Good Life* to me...'

'We can buy them from the city farm. Lots of people are doing it, look it's in the *Guardian*...'

'Well, I suppose we can live on eggs when the consumer economy goes into meltdown and the water riots start...'

Nicola produces a cutting about the boom in urban chicken farmers. There's a picture of an Eglu chicken house, a designer creation with stylish curves that's apparently now an essential garden fashion item. If you're a rock star's wife that is. It says more than 2,000 eco-friendly designer Eglu chicken houses have been sold to wannabe urban farmers.

'Well if it's in *The Guardian* it must be worth getting...' I sneer. 'What if G2 wrote about a designer-friendly home for velociraptors? We'd probably get one of those too.'

This is to be my chicken feed for the soul. There's no deterring Nicola, or indeed the children, who think it's a marvellous idea. Resistance is useless in my home.

'Well you and the kids can look after them, I'm having nothing to do with it!'

We're going to transform our garden into a city farm. The Eglu is a little too conventional for Nicola. A carpenter at Freightliners Farm, our local city farm, is given the task of building, at huge expense, a bespoke coop for our back garden.

When this edifice arrives at our house it's more than two metres long, and built of chicken wire and wood. At the bottom is a chicken run; a ramp leads up to a covered sleeping and egg-laying area. With some difficulty this chicken hotel is lifted over our garden wall because it's too wide for the back garden gate. Then Nicola arrives with two squawking Araucana chickens in a cat basket, held on to the back of her bike by elastic straps. All very *Last of the Summer Wine*.

We've agreed that I'll buy them for her birthday. One chicken is christened Kokorako (it means 'chicken' in Solomon Island pidgin) by Nicola. The other one is named Violet by four-year-old Nell.

The chickens cost £12 each, and Nicola is delighted with my gift. The chickens themselves seem less pleased. For the first few hours they make terrible clucking sounds that can be heard all down the street. They have beady eyes and dinosaur claws and look decidedly sinister to me.

'This is London, not Somerset. We'll get chicken vigilantes coming round!' I mutter, while listening to the garden din. It's amazing there are no queues of irate neighbours outside our door already. Can you be given an Anti-Social Behaviour Order for keeping noisy chickens? Yes, surely you can, it's exactly the sort of legislation Jack Straw would encourage.

At our old house someone had once abused me with many swear words for putting my rubbish in the wrong place for the binmen. What will the neighbours do when they can't sleep because of noise pollution from chickens? We will surely become the first victims of chicken rage, shot on our door-steps and then dismembered by a strimmer.

Thankfully, the chickens do quieten down a little after a few hours, once they have become familiar with their new surroundings. On their first afternoon in our garden Violet and Kokorako lay two eggs, both with attractive blue shells.

But the next day an urban fox arrives at dawn. It sits

outside the coop watching the hens in the manner of a *Big Brother* viewer. These asbo foxes are so urban that they dine on food from discarded Kentucky Fried Chicken containers left in the street. And our Islington chicks seem more neurotic than their country cousins. The fox's appearance so traumatises the chickens that they stop laying eggs and Kokorako sits down, apparently unable to use her legs.

The Freightliners farmer pays us a house visit. His diagnosis is that the bird is in shock and 'needs some love'. Chickens, eh? Other animals adopt a flight-or-fight posture when confronted by foxes, but our bird has lost the use of its legs – as an evolutionary survival technique this ranks right up there with getting into a Tyrannosaurus Rex's mouth.

After two weeks of being nursed in a cardboard box Kokorako is still in shock. Green and white chicken poo amasses beneath her prone form, which I make Nicola clear up because it's her bloody bird.

We start keeping Kokorako isolated in the children's Wendy Hut, so that she doesn't get to see Mr Fox. A visit to the vet produces the astonishing verdict that we need to give her physiotherapy on her legs to help her walk. Soon she'll be demanding aromatherapy oils for her mud bath.

After two weeks of intensive therapy on the legless chicken, plus much removal of chicken poo, we give up and return the neurotic bird to the farm, where she's ultimately 'put down' – although we don't reveal this to the children as yet.

Still, at least we have one chicken. But then Violet, healthy and able to use both legs, eats a slug while she's exercising in our garden. She falls ill that evening and dies in the morning. It's so sudden we can only conclude that the slug must have consumed poisonous slug pellets from someone else's garden. Nell cries all the way to nursery and all the way home, shouting, 'I want my Violet!' as her dad tries to calm her and talks about 'chicken heaven'. When she returns that night Nell displays a healthy interest in the bird's rigor-mortis ridden body, now lying in our Wendy Hut-turned-mortuary.

'I guess they're learning about life and death,' I muse.

Nicola is not to be deterred. 'We've just been unlucky,' she says, and buys two new chickens from Freightliners Farm, imaginatively named Violet 2 and Kokorako 2. Both show less intimations of mortality than their predecessors and they even start to lay blue eggs.

The early morning clucking isn't that bad, although crushed chicken poo on the soles of my shoes is a hazard. I now have a dedicated pair of 'chicken shoes'. These are an old pair of black Doctor Martens minus their laces. They can become caked with mud and fowl faeces, and then left in 'the player's tunnel' (our passage into the garden) before I change back into civilian footwear. When I first met Nicola in 1993 I never envisaged owning a pair of chicken shoes. Now here I am in 2004, dressed like Worzel Gummidge. What happened to the lad about town that I was? Has he become the victim of a very British coop?

Strangely, Nicola, as the mover behind the chicken project, seems very happy to delegate all the mundane duties of chicken husbandry to her partner. Each morning I open up the coop and check their water, add feed pellets to their eating bowl and any leftover bits of food from the kids' dinner the previous evening. My next task is to extract the converted coat hanger from the pair of metal rings that holds shut the ramp that leads to their sleeping quarters.

The pesky chickens shoot down their ramp into the coop, scratching around in the straw as they forage for food. I open the door to their sleeping quarters, which is held in place with a combination padlock. The combination lock is of course essential; a sign that we no longer underestimate the intelligence of foxes.

Then it's time to clean up what the birds have left during the night. A waft of malodorous air enters my nostrils as the door is opened. The soiled straw is, of course, stored for recycling into garden compost.

Inside their roosting area we find an egg or sometimes two, each day. At last we were nearly self-sufficient, although a diet of eggs and the chard that Nicola is growing in the front of the garden might not necessarily get us through the years of post-climate change anarchy. Our new harvest of home-laid eggs also provides a use for my talking model Dalek.

When we have home-laid boiled eggs for breakfast my routine is to get out our remote-controlled Dalek (bought nominally for the children but really for me) and point it at the eggs. The Dalek first says 'Seek, locate, exterminate!' as I chip away at the top of the egg with a spoon. Then each daughter takes turns to make the Dalek say 'Exterminate!' at which point I exclaim in a Dalek voice 'Egg-sterminate!' and flip off the top of the egg in one skilful action. This is followed by cries of 'Egg unit damaged! My vision is impaired! Out of control! Out of control! Aaaaargh!!!' Soon my daughters refuse to eat any egg without a spectacular egg-stermination.

Within a few months our garden has been destroyed. Where once there was grass now lies a dust bowl of bare earth. Every blade of grass, every seed, has been eaten by ravenous chickens. The autumn rains arrive and turn it into a quagmire.

A small area of grass remains in the fenced-off area by the garden pond. Lola and Nell use fishing nets to dredge the pond and trap and then release our pet newts. A friend of Nicola's at Friends of the Earth gave the newts to her so that they could be saved from a soon-to-be infilled Hackney pond. Nicola kept them in her Tupperware sandwich container at work all day and they were very nearly eaten in error by her when she mistook them for her hummus sandwich and raw carrot lunch.

The garden is starting to resemble the sort of thing you see in documentaries about buy-to-let landlords leasing out their properties to problem families in the poorer areas of Manchester.

Various decrepit objects litter the mud. A frog sandpit, children's plastic buckets with holes in them, a model tiger, a plastic cooker recycled from outside Clive Anderson's house by Highbury Fields, various plastic compost bags that Nicola thinks might be useful for something, someday. The elements have fatally weathered the ropes holding together the trampoline donated by our neighbours Nicolette and Nick. Its yellow sheet now dangles in the dirt, devoid of all tautness. Nicola has found a series of old paving slabs left by council workmen on the street. She's used them to make an ad hoc path towards the chicken coop in an attempt to prevent me being consumed by garden quicksand.

The children's Wendy Hut, deemed an essential purchase when we first moved in, is relegated to the role of chicken supply shed. Inside it is a bale of straw, the cardboard box Kokorako 1 was nursed in, a space hopper, and a plastic dustbin containing sacks of feed pellets and corn.

Every man needs a shed. The Wendy Hut becomes my refuge. As the autumn rains arrive I retreat into my hut, wearing my chicken shoes and an old Barbour jacket of Nicola's that had now been assigned to me in my new role as gamekeeper to Lady Finsbury. I'm starting to resemble Ted from *The Fast Show*.

Here, I'm undisputedly the master of my own shed. I can pretend that I can control my partner and her eco-whims. The chickens have to be watched whenever we let them out of their coop. They forage in the hedge, bathe in dust, groom themselves and eat any stray seeds of grass left on our lawn.

Here in my shed there's a welcome respite, too, from the turmoil of family breakfast. Lola's book bag has to be found, her PE kit placed at the ready, Nell's steroid has to be administered (her eczema has now developed into asthma) notes written for teachers, forms returned and lost shoes retrieved.

Attending to the chickens provides a welcome excuse for retreating into the garden. Initially it feels like I'm talking to my chickens in the manner of Marlon Brando and his pigeons in *On The Waterfront*. But lately I've begun to imagine myself as Henry David Thoreau in *Walden*.

Nicola insists I read Thoreau's *Walden*. In 1845 Thoreau became the US equivalent to an Oxford Green. Despairing of the commercialism of modern life (even before the Virgin Megastore was invented) he built a wooden shed and opted to live in solitude in the woods by Walden Pond.

He certainly appears to share the Oxford Greens' dress sense. A revealing passage of Walden has him lambasting fashion, commenting that his tailoress tells him what he is asking for is not made any more, and opining 'A man who has at length found something to do will not need to get a new suit to do it in; for him the old will do, that has lain dusty in the garret for an indeterminate period. Old shoes will serve a hero longer than they serve his valet...' The food ingredients he lists (potatoes, peas, rice, molasses, rye meal, flour, pumpkin, lard) suggest he's living off an early version of Newbury road protestors' stew.

The book blurb calls him a Transcendentalist and describes his search for spiritual truth and self-reliance. Maybe my shed in Finsbury Park is an island of Transcendentalism too. I sit listening to the rain pattering on the Wendy Hut roof, drinking hot coffee from my West Ham mug, watching the hens trash my garden and hearing the rhythmic thump of the street kids' football against the garden fence.

Thoreau's famous aphorism states: 'If a man does not keep pace with his companions, perhaps it is because he hears a different drummer.' And sitting in my shed by my own version of Walden Pond, it occurs to me that I too am listening to a different clucking.

Particularly when the fox arrives. It bounds over the garden fence and skulks by their coop. There's a loud agitated squawking followed by the birds entering into complete panic mode, running up and down and around the garden. They have a ridiculous tendency to run or half-fly anywhere but the safety of their coop.

Sitting in my Wendy Hut defending the chickens makes me feel strangely territorial. Soon I am yearning for death to all foxes. It's tempting to form the Islington Hunt.

Our foxy friends visit at least once a day, often more. They are no longer nocturnal creatures and have little fear of humans. Bold urban foxes are happy to hunt by day. They have killed a neighbour's guinea pig and a friend's kitten. I sit by my hut guarding my chickens, broom in hand, stones placed by my side ready to fling at the mangy creatures.

My dad spent years trying to persuade me to be a farmer. And now I'm a proxy chicken farmer. I begin to adopt all the traits of an irascible old farmer, including an irrational hatred of foxes. Had there been a footpath across my land, any walkers demanding working stiles, as they once did with my dad, would be berated as 'not having enough work to do'.

Any attack on my animals is a personal affront.

'Daddy, was God in a bad mood when he made foxes?' asks four-year-old Nell, as I prepared to defend the chicken coop from a skulking urban fox with a rock and a child's plastic sword at 7.30 am.

'Yes, I think he was,' I agree, as the fox slopes off through the hedge. Carnivorous guests remark on how attractively plump our birds are becoming, though we can never contemplate eating them. They have names, after all. That would be far too Hugh Fearnley-Whittingstall. But the foxes are also noticing how succulent our chickens seem.

Most mornings it seems possible to go inside to the kitchen and wash up, knowing it's just a short dash along the players' tunnel to the garden. But then one terrible morning there's a furious clucking and I drop the plate I'm wiping to rush through the door. A fox has Violet in its jaws.

Then it all goes into slow motion. Experiencing hitherto

unknown surges of adrenaline, I bound across the garden. The fox makes for the fence and hesitates as I lunge towards it. Then, incredibly, it drops Violet in order to jump over the fence itself. There are grey feathers everywhere, but I quickly shoo Violet into the coop. Is she injured? It seems not. Her Rod Stewart barnet still looks OK. She stands still, motionless with shock, but is physically unharmed.

It's the most exciting incident that's happened in my road for years. 'We heard the man chase off the fox,' some of the kids playing football tell my daughters. It seems that my sprint towards the hunting fox was accompanied by a primeval roar. Pete May has saved a chicken's life. It's the bravest thing I've ever done.

From that moment we review our situation. We're spending many hours sitting in the garden as chicken sentries. The two small fowl exert a disproportionately large influence on our lives. We can't go away without someone to look after them. Our neighbours Nicolette and Nick often act as chicken minders. They play the Margot and Jerry roles to our Tom and Barbara. Nicolette somehow manages to feed the birds while wearing court shoes and pencil skirts, en route to some literary lunch. One weekend she manages to lock herself out in our back garden, scales the fence and walks through the back door of our startled neighbours. And it seems positively unfair to be asking Nick, a former editor of *The Bookseller* now a cookery writer, to be soiling himself with our bird-poo shovel when he should be doing sophisticated things with aubergines.

On extended trips away we take the chickens back to Freightliners Farm, where they can stay for £5 a night. Most farmers probably just eat their chickens before a holiday; we're paying for ours to stay in the equivalent of a chicken bed-and-breakfast.

But as any football manager can tell you, success can breed complacency. You're only as good as your last man v fox match. I take my eye off the feeding bowl.

Working upstairs in the office it should be possible to hear any fox-related clucking through the bathroom window. But there are roadworks outside and a pneumatic drill is pounding the tarmac. Half an hour later I go outside to check the chickens and find Violet alone. Apparently unflustered, but minus her companion. Oh no.

How do you tell two children that their chicken has been taken by a serial killer? Lola and Nell are distraught on the walk home from school. Then with, touching childish hopefulness, Lola and Nell knock on every neighbour's door asking 'Have you seen a brown-coloured chicken called Kokorako?'

It takes Nicola, returning from a day's work at Friends of the Earth, to reveal the truth. She displays all the perspicacity of Inspector Columbo, making a detour into next-door's garden, finding some freshly disturbed earth, and pointing out the tail feathers emerging from the ground. Mr Fox had partially eaten Kokorako 2 and then buried her body, ready to return later.

'At least the fox will have been able to feed its cubs,' says Nicola, displaying a *Guardian* reader's liberalness towards foxes when really shooting or maiming by hounds is too good for 'em. Gently I suggest to Nicola that as we only have Violet left, perhaps we should return her to the farm and accept that we are never going to be chicken farmers.

'Of course we're not giving up! We're getting another chicken and that's that! It's good for you. You're getting in touch with your hunter-gatherer instincts. And you'd just watch telly otherwise!'

And so Nicola places another new chicken on the back of her bike. She travels home from the farm via a parent-teacher meeting at Lola's school. The new chicken sits in a cat box on the back of Nicola's bike in the corner of the classroom while Nicola chats with the teacher. 'There's only one parent that could possibly belong to!' says headmistress Rosie.

The new chicken is not going to be named Kokorako 3. It's not been a lucky name. Instead, Lola names it Romana, after the *Doctor Who* companion played by Lalla Ward, a distant cousin of Nicola's. Romana settles into the coop.

My fox deterrence techniques become more sophisticated. Someone says that lion poo will frighten them off. Short of raiding London Zoo for some leonine excrement, this seems a little impractical. But apparently male urine is pretty good. So each night I drink a bottle of Abbot Ale then head out into the darkened garden, and urinate around the coop. I pace up and down marking my territory with a ring of wee. The fox responds by leaving poos on my urine. Clearly, this is going to be one long war of ablution.

Our subsequent projects with Violet and Romana include hatching eggs. When Romana becomes broody we buy six fertilised eggs from Freightliners Farm and sit her on them. Eventually three hatch and fluffy chicks emerge, to the delight of the girls. One chick disappears though, and is later discovered dead under the ramp. An even more unpleasant fate awaits another chick, John Smith. We hear a clucking and then find the chick minus a wing in the coop. The fox's jaws have somehow managed to grab a piece of wing through the chicken wire and wrench the whole thing off. John Smith appears oblivious to the wing loss, a bit like *Monty Python*'s Black Knight. But the vet says that terrible infection will set in, so we have him put down. I rapidly nail a secondary layer of chicken wire around the coop. The children are upset, but also take a grim delight in telling their friends of the mutilations going on in our garden. The last chick survives, and is given back to the farm where it's hopefully now leading a fox-free life.

On the positive side, the chickens do bring some security advantages to our house. Any burglar trying to get in via the back garden would have to climb over the back fence, extricate themselves from Nicola's rose bushes and then find themselves falling through a chicken coop into a pile of wet straw and chicken excrement while the birds clucked in demented fashion. They'd also be at risk of fox attack, and would probably run to the nearest police station.

Nicola thinks the chicken experiment has been beneficial for our children. Both girls now have a better understanding of life, death and mutilation in the natural world. They know where eggs came from, unlike many city children who think they're made by Tesco. Each morning they eat freshly-laid eggs and they taste great.

As for their father's sanity, well, who knows? I thought the Oxford Greens were barkingly eccentric when I first encountered them a decade ago. But now here I am, rushing out of the kitchen door brandishing a broom at 7 am, wearing shoeless DM's covered in straw and mud. I'm still in my dressing gown as I lunge at the fox, which is escaping over the fence, only my dressing gown is flapping open in the wind and my privates are exposed. Opposite me is our new neighbour, taking an early morning smoke in his garden. He tries not to look startled.

'Hello,' I say cheerily. 'Bloody foxes, eh?'

I'm holding a broom and exposing myself while chasing a fox. Maybe I've finally made it as a Green.

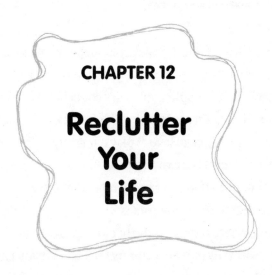

CHAPTER 12

Reclutter Your Life

Nicola is saving the planet. The only problem is that most of it is saved round at our house. Ethically I can't argue with her. Well, she works for Friends of the Earth so she must be right.

We've unpacked most of the numerous boxes from our old homes and all the stuff that's been in storage for several years. We've come a long way in the twelve years since we first met and kept every bit of baggage, including suitcases, trunks and cardboard boxes containing Nicola's life in minute detail.

'Do you really need a Horse of the Year Show ticket from 1989?' I find myself asking her.

'Just as much as you need a 1980 FA Cup Final ticket!' she answers.

The furniture we brought with us is expanding. Our new house is a sort of ecological black hole, sucking in clutter from across the universe. The sofa we found on our first weekend here wasn't enough. Nicola's just deposited a piano in our library.

'I saw in on SwapXchange, the council's swap site. It was free from a trumpet player and it didn't cost much to get it delivered. The children will love to play it one day...' she enthuses.

'But we don't have room for it...'

'Yes we do, there's a spare wall in the library.'

'But that's where the sofa is.'

'Let's put that against the books.'

'But isn't the point of a library the fact that you can see the shelves?'

'Oh for goodness sake! You'll be thankful when Lola and Nell are playing *I'm Forever Blowing Bubbles*!'

She's also acquired a bureau from some shop on Holloway Road. It has glass cabinets on the top, but the delivery men smashed a pane while removing it from their van. They knocked 20 quid off the price and so Nicola is happy to have a one-windowed bureau in the living room. It's next to the leather chair that she found our neighbour Mike depositing in his garden. Admittedly it had a rip in one arm, 'but it's leather and far too good to throw out' she explains, pushing it in front of the sofa that's blocking our bookshelves.

The thing is, we appear morally unable to turn down clutter. Like most Greens, Nicola is ravaged by guilt. And there's so much to feel guilty about, so much to be saved. Everywhere you look in 21st-century society there's waste, over-consumption and built-in obsolescence. Clearly, if people put perfectly useful things in bins and skips then it is Nicola's duty to save them from going into landfill. So our home has become a kind of new millennium rag and bone yard. Minimalist we are not.

In the library our new book shelves made from FSC-certified plywood are now obscured by an abandoned six-foot high poster featuring a Matisse figure of a naked woman. Nicola saw it on a nearby street while she was cycling to work and ordered me to carry it home whatever the difficulties, because 'the girls can draw dots on it'. My Green goddess refuses to get rid of the picture of three rather poorly-drawn horses that she found in a skip outside St Martin's Art College 20 years ago, because 'it's on a nice canvas'.

The library also serves as a bike repository; it holds Nicola's bike, her Sam Browne luminous sash, elastic straps, helmet, gloves and various sustainable hessian bags full of work papers. These are placed on the giant wooden fertility chair that she rescued from her late father's waxworks (yes, he was a bit of a hoarder too).

The bike gear I can just about cope with, but Her Outdoors has also started a British Trust for Conservation Volunteers (BTCV) course/OCN in conservation management. She now works three days at Friends of the Earth and spends the other two being driven around in a transit van to the parks and cemeteries of London.

'What exactly do you do on your CCTV course?' I ask.

'It's BCTV!'

'Oh sorry BCTV, but what do you do?'

'It's really useful. We learn how to lay hedges and use hay rakes, scythes and shoveholers and we learn how to sharpen knives on whetstones.'

'Which come to think of it, might be quite useful the next time we take the 43 bus. People are always getting stabbed on the Holloway Road.'

'Oh for goodness sake!'

The other BCTV volunteers are a friendly bunch united by their love of horticulture. They're a mix of the unemployed seeking to use their time profitably, people signed off work with depression and mental health problems and those recovering from various addictions. So in a way it's not too different from working with her fellow Greens. She speaks highly of 'Paul the Bird Man'.

More and more bits of tree appear in our home, cast into the library alongside her donkey jacket and hobnail boots. Various sawn segments of indigenous hedgerow adorn the marble mantelpiece.

'They'll be useful for teaching the girls about tree types,' she reasons, which is also why we have various catkins and budding twigs around the house. There's also a basket of wood chips, personally chopped by Nicola, that she says will make good kindling for the fire that we won't light again until October.

The living room is overflowing not just with children's toys (one night we thought we were being burgled only to discover that a Teletubby's voice box had been activated by the sheer weight of toys in the wicker basket and the burglar was in fact saying 'Eh oh!') but also with Jiffy bags. Our neighbour Nicolette, who receives hundreds of books each week now gives the delivery bags to Nicola, who plans to take them in to work to recycle (eventually). In the fireplace, the entire lavender harvest from our garden is drying near the sock bag, full of socks with holes in.

'We can't throw them out, I can turn them into glove puppets for the children,' Nicola says. Even my old boxer shorts can't be trashed; she cuts them up and turns them into handkerchiefs.

The kitchen has also succumbed to Green clutter. Next to the 'bag bag' for plastic bags (they're sent to Growing Communities eventually) and the council's brown container for kitchen waste, stands a mountainous edifice of flattened Tetra Paks. They once contained orange juice and rice milk. Nicola knows a factory address in Scotland where they will recycle them just as long as we spend a huge amount on postage sending them there. They stand next to the huge pile of washed hummus and yogurt pots awaiting a sustainable end.

Our dresser is a grey MDF monstrosity that Nicola found in a skip. It's ideal for storing useless felt pens without tops, leaflets from school, ancient conkers, elastic bands, five-year-old diaries, cleaned-out marmalade jars that Nicola says will be ideal for using as home-made jam containers, yogurt pots full of magnetic letters for the fridge, kids' pictures from school and nursery, invitations, scrapbooks, glue, scissors, and much, much more.

On the kitchen table sit numerous flowerpots full of sweet pea, basil and pumpkin seedlings, awaiting transfer to the garden. Two years ago one of my daughters mistakenly referred to soy sauce as 'soil sauce'. Today her mispronunciation sounds eerily accurate.

We've just bought a new basil plant, not for us but for the free-range stick insects (they escaped from their tank earlier this year) that now roam the kitchen and love chomping on green leaves. There's also a four-foot pile of paper, aka Nicola's in-tray full of unopened letters and catalogues. Everything else is filed on the stairs.

To add to the general air of some madly-overstocked Dickensian emporium, the kitchen is now full of cardboard boxes. Nicola has joined the Suma food cooperative.

'It's really good, especially if you live in the countryside, you can order healthy food in bulk and wholesale. I can do a big order and sell any extra to people in the street and some of the other parents at school.'

'But we don't live in the countryside. And we have no room...'

An articulated lorry arrives outside our house. Into our kitchen and living room come the Suma boxes packed with jars of artichoke hearts and pesto, tins of organic chick peas, recycled unbleached loo rolls, soap, spaghetti, pasta, organic baked beans and much more.

'Nicola, why do we have a box of 12 Kingfisher Mint natural toothpaste tubes?'

'I did worry that might be a lifetime's supply of toothpaste, but that's the smallest order Suma does. And you know the speed we get through it...'

Thank goodness we didn't live through World War II. Nicola would have filled every room from floor to ceiling with Spam and nylons in 1938. She's now the Private Walker of Finsbury Park. She'll soon be wearing an overcoat with organic spaghetti and artichokes clipped to the lining.

It's not that I'm innocent of hoarding myself. Football programmes, books, *Doctor Who* videos, several months' worth of newspapers for essential research, are all things I just can't give away. Our shared upstairs office is another clutter mine; on top of the overflowing filing cabinets, football autobiographies and fanzines vie with several boxes of Nicola's that haven't been unpacked since we moved in. They are filled with files, paper clips, pens, hole punchers, staplers and a 14-year-old telephone directory from her VSO assignment in the Solomon Islands that she insists might prove useful.

I fear our attraction to refuse might be genetic. Lola is inheriting all her mum's clutter instincts. I've just washed her extremely grimy coat and found a wax crayon (broken), a twig, 20 pence, a broken bit of bracelet, a Yum-Yum wrapper, a hankie, and the end of a TV lead. During a 15-minute walk down Holloway Road Lola picks up a white plastic pole that she intends to keep because 'I can be a blind person with it' and a broken umbrella frame, which 'will make a great alien'.

Both bedrooms are dominated by book mountains, over-stuffed wardrobes and bags of baby clothes that might one day be recycled or given to our children's cousins, once they arrive.

Our bed is now like something from *Lord of the Rings*. Having accosted a tree surgeon, Nicola extricated several branches before they were put through the chipper and then got our mate Robert to lash the whole thing together into a bucolic four-poster bed. Oh, and she's draped fairy lights over the branches. If any of my football mates ever visit they are kept away from the bedroom.

There is no relief outdoors. To the previous mix of chicken coop, Wendy Hut, frog sand pit, paving stones, hoola-hoops and plastic cooker there are now the scaffolding boards retrieved from skips waiting to make raised permaculture beds and one half of a set of French windows now converted into a cold frame.

There are also the logs turned into garden seats that Nicola reclaimed from another tree surgeon. They're all around the back garden and Nicola is delighted when they start to grow bracket fungus and became a refuge for our napping newts.

The biggest issue in my life is stuff. It's not that we lack space – it's just that our eco-clutter expands to fill it. Somewhere Nicola forgot the first part of the 'reduce, reuse, recycle'.

I like to think our home has character, a bit like the depiction of Iris Murdoch's chaotic but academic-looking home in the movie *Iris*. But I'm starting to believe it's more like Krook's abode in Dickens' *Bleak House*. Can preventing needless landfill compensate for appearing on reality TV series like *Filthy Homes From Hell*? I'd send for a skip only we'd probably be the first people to raid it.

'We've got to do something,' I plead to Nicola. 'Our house is a monument to built-in obsolescence.'

'Why don't you try Freecycle, it's that website I mentioned in *Earthmatters*?' says Nicola. 'You just offer stuff on it and then people come to take it away.'

'Are you sure? There's no catch?'

'None at all. And you can pick up things yourself from other users...'

'I think it's best if I do the Freecycling for both of us from now on...'

And so I join the world of Freecycle, a virtual rag-and-bone market for the 2000s. A kind of freeBay for those who know the value of everything, but not the price. Nicola may have already written about it but I'm the one who plans to use it. It was started in 2003 by Deron Beal, from the US recycling group Rise, in Tucson, Arizona. Beal and like-minded pals wanted to prevent the desert landscape being covered with landfill sites. Their motto is: 'One person's trash can truly be another's treasure.' And now it has millions of users worldwide.

Initially it seems like a good way of clearing our office, starting with getting rid of two ancient Apple Mac computers. I post an 'Offered: Two Macs, one desktop, one laptop' message.

'Look at this!' I shout to Nicola downstairs, 'I've had thirty replies in three hours!'

Suddenly I feel worthier than Bono, providing much-needed Macs for the world's computer-less souls. An altruist dispatching gifts from an office teetering under piles of Nicola's Lever Arch files on solar energy and my own 20-year collection of *Rothmans Football Yearbooks*.

Never have my dusty old Macs seemed so desirable. Lewis is 'a nurse/therapist/artist/reviewer needing more technical support, particularly for live performance, music and photographic work'. Karl e-mails three times to emphasise: 'I didn't really express how much of a Mac fan I am, they are such quality machines. And there is something really nice about the way they've been designed, truly like a toy for adults.'

Freecycle etiquette dictates that you don't necessarily give it to the first e-mailer and must reject anyone who sounds like they might want to sell the goods (eBay are clearly the real enemy and terrible splitters). I opt for friendly-sounding people who can collect immediately; shifting the computers to Andy from Stoke Newington, who'd been on disability benefit for three years, and Ruth, a cash-starved student in Holloway. They're friendly and grateful when they collect them and being fellow Freecyclers it feels like we're part of a virtual clan.

It's much easier being a cyber Green compared to the compost-loo using version; if you get bored with Freecycle there's always BBC Sport online. Although obviously I turn off my computer and modem whenever I leave my office rather than leave it on sleep mode.

In fact Freecycle becomes more interesting than work. Freecycle helps me shift two fax machines (surprisingly in demand), a zip drive, an office desk, a malfunctioning vaccuum cleaner, a children's desk, some kitchen shelves, a washing machine and the local vicar's sofa bed. Our redundant fridge freezer, replaced by a more energy-efficient version, goes to a woman with cancer who's on a special diet and needs it for her store of juices. We offer unlimited Jiffy bags and they end up going to a psychotherapist heading off on a two-year Buddhist retreat who wants to post all her old books to friends.

One thing they don't put on the Freecycle home page is that it also provides a fascinating nose into other people's lives. Simply file your messages by senders, and you can spend gloriously useless hours wondering just why a person with the e-mail moniker of 'nearthemoon' is offering a free-standing gas cooker and collection of *Friends* videos while seeking law books and a record deck. A barrister turned DJ with no mates and a lot of ready meals in the microwave perhaps?

Why is someone giving away a Russian Navy officer's top in SE15. Who will go for the 'Hideous dog, with bowler hat and cane, that sings "New York, New York", SW19'? And what about the 'Black size 36B Agent Provocateur underwired corset with detachable suspender fittings' that one kind woman is offering with the proviso 'Happy to send to chaps or ladies'?

Bras, cars, 8-track tape machines, bin-liners full of yarn, software, bags of sequins, frogspawn, pieces of antler, cognitive behavioural therapy handouts, and yes, kitchen sinks: anything can turn up on Freecycle.

Some of the Freecycle users just seem to need company. 'OFFERED: My brain!' reads one missive. 'Anyone want to play Scrabble with an expert?' it continues. 'I need to exercise my brain again, and I can't think of a nicer way of doing it! Any takers? This is no joke!' Amazingly, the solo Scrabble player receives several offers.

Maybe some of the strange on-line monikers will meet and fall in love. Perhaps 'lazy fairy' from SW2 will marry 'bohemian' from E13 in a moving ceremony by an empty landfill site.

We decide to do something about our kitchen and send a request for unused tiles; the result is I'm lugging weighty holdalls of them back from Kilburn, Holloway and Caledonian Road.

There are other ways of shifting stuff. Websites like Gumtree, the local council's SwapXchange and eBay. But occasionally we have things we can't shift, including our old kitchen sink, left rusting in the garden by the kitchen refitters. Luckily Nicola finds a scrap metal trader in the street taking stuff from skips and she persuades him to remove it.

A man could dedicate his whole life trying to shift the sediment of modern life. In fact it seems I am. But still our property mountain grows. The kids are now avid visitors to car boot sales and jumble sales. Give them two quid and they'll return with a rabbit sitting in a wicker chair, a foot massager, a *Star Wars* video, a Barbie doll, a copy of *Men are From Mars, Women are from Venus* and a cuddly toy.

We watch one of those TV shows on Greening your life that are spreading across the channels. It features a gay couple who regularly throw their T-shirts into the bin because they've gone very slightly out of fashion.

'That's terrible!' exclaims Nicola. I'm pretty shocked too. We look on aghast, probably with the same expressions my parents had when Fleur showed too much cleavage on *The Forsythe Saga* in the 1960s. We never throw anything away, ever.

The most direct way of moving clutter from our house is to wait until Nicola and the kids are out, furtively sort it into a bag and then lug the stuff to the local charity shop. Of course, it's impossible to avoid checking the used video section, because loads of people are now changing to DVDs and sometimes you can find old *Doctor Who* stories like The Ark In Space and Castrovalva, or even *The Young Ones* in a double box. There's also a big selection of books and 10 pence glass tumblers ideal for my whisky-tasting sessions, and a new glass bowl for our coffee filter. I leave with my bag re-filled.

How did it come to this? Now we recycle there's more stuff than when I was a single man living alone among piles of pizza bottles and empty cans. And is it enough, anyway? While we shuffle stuff from house to charity shop to Freecycle members, everyone else keeps on flying, driving and turning their heating up.

Conscience is a terrible thing. What's my Green babe done to my life? I used to be able to not care. Now every aspect of my life has been taken over by environmental angst. When the Christmas of 2004 arrives we celebrate in our new home with Lola and Nell. I discover that there's a secret stash of recycled presents under our bed that Nicola's been hoarding since last January. Nicola wraps all our presents in wrapping paper that she's saved from last year and she's careful to preserve every piece this year too. After our Green Christmas we're careful to take our Christmas tree to the recycling centre to be chipped.

What will 2005 bring? We're home owners, we're just about managing to pay the mortgage, our children will both be going to school in the New Year. There's surely nothing Green left for Nicola to attempt. But there is – and it's the biggest surprise of all.

CHAPTER 13

Indecent Proposal

Maybe there is hope for humanity after all. Nicola's co-written Friends of the Earth book, *Save Cash and Save the Planet*, is now out and appears to be selling like hot home-baked organic cakes. It's in the top 100 on Amazon anyway.

That's good. But someone else is trying to save the planet too, and he's not even endorsed by Friends of the Earth. On 26 March 2005 the Doctor returns.

Much of my life post-1989 has been spent writing about *Doctor Who* and campaigning for the return of the people's Time Lord. It's a moment of utter triumph. People said I was mad, hooked on nostalgia, trying to recapture my youth through VHS videos. As if... But now, thanks to the genius of Russell T Davies, the Doctor is back on air, ready to return as the supreme power in the universe.

Six-year-old Lola is already familiar with my Tom Baker

era videos. But now both she and Nell are watching new *Who* videos and it seems to be working. On children, not just sad middle-aged Whovians like myself.

Don't let the Greens ever tell you that TV doesn't matter. We're staying with Fleur and Richard in Yorkshire and their four boys are watching too. I'm celebrating with a bottle of Black Sheep ale. So much has changed in my life since 1989, when *Doctor Who* went off air. I guess a lot of it is through Nicola.

Shopwindow dummies are coming alive. Everything plastic is potentially lethal, just like Friends of the Earth said. Christopher Eccleston is just right as the Doctor, at times angry, funny, intense, playful and manic. And crucially, he's playing the role seriously. That speech when he asks Rose if she knows what it's like to feel the Earth spinning at a thousand miles an hour is brilliant. The next week the Doctor even suggests that humanity beats climate change when he says, while five billion years in the future, that although we spend all our time worrying about global warming, we never think we might actually survive.

My children are about to become Whovians and they could have no prouder dad. Lola wants to know about the 'Nesting consciousness', by which I think she means the 'Nestene Consciousness' which in the storyline, lives in plastic. Although maybe 'Nesting' is better.

Nicola keeps saying how good Christopher Eccleston is, before eventually confessing that she fancies him.

The year gets better. By May, West Ham are back in the Premiership having won the play-off final against Preston at Cardiff's Millennium Stadium thanks to Bobby Zamora's goal, having sold Rio Ferdinand, Frank Lampard, Joe Cole, Michael Carrick, Jermain Defoe and Glen Johnson – in fact half the England team. We've been through what Alan Pardew terms 'a cycle of misery', suffering relegation, huge debts, play-off final defeat in 2004 and losing away to Rotherham. Never mind the prosaic Liverpool triumph over AC Milan in the European Champions League Final when they came back from being 3-0 down. This is the real football story of the summer. Two years ago it looked like we'd never return to the Premier League. But now thanks to Alan Pardew's claret and blue army, we're a club reborn. I'm being embraced by strangers, my mate Fraser has lit a cigar and *I'm Forever Blowing Bubbles* is reverberating around the Millennium Stadium. We even get our own page back on Ceefax. I'm phoning Nicola who's staying at her mum's. Amazingly she knows the score.

'But you never listen to football on the radio...'

'I know your entire emotional stability depends upon this result...'

It's a good test. At moments of extreme footballing elation you always phone or text the people you care about. If you don't want to phone your partner when your team has just been promoted, then it's time to leave. Maybe that's love...

There's a Green triumph too. In May 2005 Bob Hunter the founder of Greenpeace dies, but it seems the Green movement has a new leader – Bob the Builder. Bob's PR company's been on the phone to Friends of the Earth about Bob's eco-makeover.

'I told you TV was the medium you had to use!' I tell Nicola gleefully. 'Get the CBeebies viewers and you'll have the kids for life.'

'Hmm, I could maybe use this in *Earthmatters*.'

'What you, write about TV? Ha!'

Can he fix the planet? Yes, Bob can. In the *Bob the Builder* DVD that arrives at our house Bob comes over like he's been reading every edition of *Green Futures* ever published. Appalled by architect Mr Adams' plans to build tower blocks in Sunflower Valley, Bob enters the competition to develop the valley himself. Bob decides that the houses must blend in with nature and comes up with houses inside hills built from recycled building materials, with earth roofs and – whisper it gently to Sir Bernard Ingham and readers of *Country Life* – wind turbines.

Nell and Lola are impressed by Bob the Green Builder. Scoop, Muck, Dizzy and Rolly start chanting 'Reduce, Reuse, Recycle!' like the unlikeliest Friends of the Earth members ever. Bob then takes his machines to live in the woods, and brews up tea using solar energy while they build the eco-village. Maybe Bob's possible love interest, Wendy, will start wearing a Peruvian hat like Nicola in the next series.

The downside of 2005 is that our new house is suffering from subsidence. In fact every house in north London seems to be suffering from London clay shrinking in the dry weather. But this time, our new insurance company is remarkably efficient. It sends in builders within six months and agrees to redecorate and replaster every room where there is a crack. Although they do chop down the ground water-guzzling eucalyptus tree in next door's garden, which makes us feel like evil rainforest loggers.

For five weeks the builders arrive just as the girls are having breakfast, resulting in a chaotic mix of white sheets, ghetto blasters, buckets, Harry Potter books and porridge bowls. The work's going well until the outside world intervenes.

There's breaking news on the radio. A power surge is reported on the tube. Only it isn't. Three suicide bombers from some al-Qaeda linked cell have blown themselves up on the London Underground and a fourth bomber has set off his device on a crowded bus. That image of the mangled wreck of a red London bus dominates the day's coverage.

One of the decorators has a son on one of the trains. He's been walked off the train and is OK. But his dad seems shaken and Nicola tries to persuade him to go home. He won't and gets on with papering our kitchen.

'What are we doing living in London, what if they set off a dirty bomb?' asks Nicola, who is trying not to notice the wrong shade of paint being used by our stressed decorator. 'And what if you were on the train? We're not even married.'

'You said marriage was a patriarchal institution, and you didn't want a wedding that was all about inviting your relatives whom you haven't seen for years and not about us,' I counter. 'And anyway, two years ago on Valentine's Day I gave you a wedding voucher to be redeemed whenever you choose.'

'We'll look too old to get married now. When we first met I looked so much younger.'

Nicola never takes disaster well.

'You're still incredibly slim because you work all the time,' I declare. 'And you haven't got any grey hairs at all. And if you brushed your hair, it would look really good... I'll need a vat of Grecian 2000 for the wedding if I'm to look young again. That is, if there's to be a wedding.'

And then there's a call from Nicola's mum checking we're all OK. And another from Jackie in San Francisco. And now Mayor Ken Livingstone is making a speech in his nasal drone and it makes me realise what's great about London.

'Even after your cowardly attack, you will see that people from the rest of Britain, people from around the world will arrive in London to become Londoners and to fulfil their dreams and achieve their potential,' says Ken. 'They choose to come to London, as so many have come before because they come to be free, they come to live the life they choose, they come to be able to be themselves. They flee you because you tell them how they should live. They don't want that and nothing you do, however many of us you kill, will stop that flight to our city where freedom is strong and where people can live in harmony with one another. Whatever you do, however many you kill, you will fail.'

There are people missing from our area. Russell Square, scene of one of the tunnel attacks, is just five stations away. One of the dead people was a regular in The Faltering Full-back, one of my local pubs. A cashier from the Co-operative Bank at Angel, where Nicola banks, is dead too.

But life carries on and by September more sport cheers me up. England have won the Ashes, finally beating Australia after 16 years. It's not that I'm a huge cricket fan but it's great to beat the Aussies because they take sport so seriously. They have none of our English love of glorious failure. Trafalgar Square is full of delirious England fans and Freddie Flintoff is up all night and in danger of being judged legless before wicket.

It's just as well I'm drunk. My column in *Midweek*, now my main source of income, is axed. All the staff are told through a curt e-mail from the publisher. He thanks us for all our contributions, in my case ten years of weekly dispatches, although unfortunately I won't be getting paid for my final column as the magazine is no more. The National Union of Journalists soon helps win one small victory and a cheque for my last column.

We return to Oxford for a long weekend. It's a decade since Nicola lived here and the Greens have sprouted. George

Marshall lives there with his wife Annie and two children. They've turned their house into a model eco-home. The loo is flushed by grey water from the bath and shower and the house is super-insulated. But I'm reassured that they still seem to have almost as much clutter as us.

George is running the Climate Outreach and Information Network (COIN) and writing a book called *Carbon Detox*. Because of their low-impact lifestyle the family dash out of the house whenever the words 'car boot sale' are mentioned. We rush to join the car booters and return with Teletubbies, crockery and kids' clothes.

Oliver is still nearby, with his wife, kids and a newly-built wooden office in the garden among his organic vegetables. He's still listening to Radio 4 and turning up at George's back door to bemoan something preposterous that he's just heard on *Today*. George Monbiot is soon to be a father and may finally discover the positive uses of TV when he's trying to write an article to a deadline with a crying baby at home. There's talk that some of the Greens might decamp to the moral high ground of Wales soon.

We visit Chris and Jane in Powys and the place is now warm and cosy, the solar panels are working and it's not even that cold outside. I can just about handle the compost loo, with new deluxe urine separator, such are the benefits of maturity. Although when Nicola says she wants to put one in our back garden I do threaten to leave.

I've no idea where the *Loaded* lads are now. Most of them are dads, some are divorced according to snippets I read in *Guardian Media*. Time moves on.

Back in London the children are distraught when, on their way to Lola's school, they see council notices threatening to cut down dangerous trees. Apparently branches might fall off them and injure passers-by. So Nicola phones the local paper and our family is pictured by the threatened 'killer trees' with a 'Free the tree' placard, looking just like Clarice Bean's family in the Lauren Child books. The council calls off the tree surgeons and instead calls a meeting. For the moment the trees are safe.

In the autumn I'm at my parents' house with Nell. Lola is in London with Nicola. A year ago my mother's doctor thought she should be tested for Alzheimer's disease. Various medical people have been to visit them, and cognitive tests been performed.

My mum refuses to discuss it and just repeats 'I'm not bonkers!' My dad insists that she's just forgetful and it's the normal dementia that any old person suffers from. But the latest tests seem definite enough and even dad says 'She might have a touch of Alzheimer's' as if it's a common cold.

Mum can't cook any more, my dad has never tried, and so either I help when we visit or we all go out for pub lunches. Most of the time my mum seems normal enough, although she has to repeatedly ask the children's ages. But the Alzheimer's comes in waves. One night she asks if I knew Kaz, who is my sister. Or she says 'It's been nice talking to you' as if I'm a stranger she's just met.

When she's suffering from an unrelated infection she attacks my dad with a stick, saying he's trying to steal her keys and that he isn't her husband. My dad is trying his hardest to cope, but he's never been patient, or a natural carer.

Things can only get worse in Norfolk. Yet my mum remembers her childhood as well as ever. We're walking along the seafront at Hunstanton with Nell, who is demanding to be carried. My mother, hazy about events of a few days ago, remembers a catchphrase from her youth.

'"I can't pick you up, I've got a bone in my leg". That's what my father used to say to me,' she says.

'But daddy, everyone has a bone in their leg!' says Nell after pondering this affliction for a few minutes.

It's always too hot in my parents' house. In the spare room where Nell and myself are sleeping, I turn off the radiator and open the window to reduce the stuffiness.

My parents don't understand my lifestyle with Nicola at all. They come from a different era, an exciting time of supermarkets, motorways and central heating. Technology is always good and there will be cheap energy forever. They run two cars and drive everywhere. My dad drives the car because he's bored, with no thought for the petrol he's using.

After years of living in a draughty old farmhouse in Essex they resolved never to be cold again. My dad still worries about the price of beer and opts for 'two for one' meal deals at the local pub, yet he wastes money turning his thermostat up to 22 degrees centigrade. They come from a time when oil was cheap, the moon was going to be colonised and all technology was good. On *Thunderbirds* a machine called Sidewinder cut roads through the jungle and that was progress.

I've sneaked a couple of long-life light bulbs on to the landing but my dad won't have them anywhere else, because they're not bright enough and they won't work with the timer and he doesn't think the greenhouse effect exists.

Whenever Nicola visits she's shocked at the way bottles and cans are put in the bin, how my mum squirts aerosols of fly killer containing lindane throughout the kitchen, the electronic mole scarer outside on the lawn, their trips to supermarkets that are cheap but not good (and never Sainsbury's, because in their eyes it's Labour) rather than farmers' markets.

Sometimes when we visit we pick blackberries from the nearby common or damsons from the tree in the garden. Nicola turns them into crumble or jam. My parents are retired farmers and think this is odd when there's a Somerfield down the road. Different generations, different values, yet they made me what I am.

Meanwhile climate change seems more real than it used to. Even David Attenborough is now a convert. In his new series *Are We Changing Planet Earth?*, he says he's seen the effect of global warming 'again and again'. Will there soon be wars over water, climate refugees demanding access to Britain, retirement homes in southern Spain overtaken by desert? Much of Norfolk may disappear as the sea levels rise.

We are sleepwalking to disaster while my dad drives for leisure. We're trying to keep our stuff out of landfill, but will there be any land left to fill?

In the US, Hurricane Katrina has just smashed into New Orleans. Hundreds of people have drowned and thousands of people are trapped for days in a football stadium with overflowing loos, an undercurrent of violence and a near-breakdown of our thin veneer of civilisation – sounding a bit like the time I watched West Ham lose 6-0 away to Oldham.

President Bush procrastinates. The US government can organise an invasion of Iraq but doesn't seem able to res-cue thousands of poor black Americans at home. The scientists say that hurricanes are becoming more frequent and the warmer the oceans become, the more devastating they will be.

The only positive thing is that I now know what a levee is, something that's mystified me ever since Don McLean drove his Chevy to the levee in *American Pie*. Plus the fact that the US electorate might soon be offering one used Bush on Freecycle, complete with Kyoto-denial facility.

It's always sad leaving my parents' house. You wonder if

it's the last time. My mum loves her grandchildren and repeats '"Parting is such sweet sorrow, that I shall say good-night till it be morrow". That's from Shakespeare, did you know that?' which is what she always says.

When I get home Nicola is feeling decisive.

'If we're getting married we should do it while your mum still remembers something.'

'But we don't want a big pompous wedding full of relatives...'

'We can have a Green wedding. We'll take control of it ourselves and just invite friends and close family and make sure we leave a low-carbon confetti print.'

Marriage? Maybe my guardian angel will appear just like he does for George Bailey in *It's A Wonderful Life*. He'll show me what my life would have been like if I'd never met Nicola. Nearly all the trees in Highbury will have been cut down without her, the Ecology Centre will have closed without her fund-raising efforts, Friends of the Earth will be in crisis without her editorial skills and the staff toiling under the yoke of a Greenpeace coup. I'll see myself, alone in my bed-sit, weighing 20 stone, with the thermostat on full, still watching DVDs, eating crisps and planning mini-breaks in Patagonia.

'But I said I'd only ever get married if *Doctor Who* came back, West Ham got promoted and England won the Ashes... Oh shit.'

It feels like the right thing to do. After all, we've only waited 12 years.

'I'll call the vicar,' she says.

CHAPTER 14
It's a Nice Day for a Green Wedding

Nicola is happy now she has a project to manage. The date for our Elizabeth Bennett and Mr Darcy moment is set for 10 December 2005. Lola and Nell are very excited. We have two months to arrange the whole thing, so we won't be buying any wedding magazines which probably recommend at least a decade's preparation and a spend of several million.

What we both dislike about weddings are those huge pompous affairs that go on forever and where the seating plan is all-important. We don't want relatives whose names we don't know; we want our friends and close family in a small-scale ceremony. And as my *Midweek* column has gone and the mortgage is still having to be paid, we're skint. So it's going to be a Green wedding.

'We'll tell people we don't want any presents,' announces Nicola.

'What?'

'They can make a donation to charity instead.'

'But I thought the whole point of getting married was to get loads of presents.'

'This is an anti-consumerist wedding! We've lived together for years, we've got everything. It'd be greedy to expect presents.'

'I want my toaster!'

'We could say donate to Asthma UK and Amnesty International...'

'Couldn't they just make a contribution to our mortgage instead?' I plead, fruitlessly.

We may be going to deprive ourselves of lots of gifts, but we'll also be depriving the wedding industry of lots of money. We'll make our own invitations. None of that embossed white card malarkey. Lola and Nell draw pictures of mummy and daddy getting married, we buy a ream of recycled paper and get some colour prints done at KwikPrint.

The DIY spirit of punk didn't die in 1977. This will be a DIY wedding. There won't be a wedding cake, instead Nicola's asking guests to make fairy cakes and bring them along. We're going to get some champagne from France, admittedly, but the wine is going to be English, to reduce air miles. Nicola's godmother makes English wine and we order several crates from the Warden Vineyard in Bedfordshire. We find a local caterer who can do vegetarian food for around £200. There's no need for a professional photographer and all those regimented pictures of first the bride's family and then the groom's.

'And we don't want any photos of us snogging. Remember I'm upper middle-class and we can only show our emotions over pets,' warns Nicola.

Our mate Adam, who works in film, offers to take informal snaps as the day goes on. We'll ask guests to bring their own cameras and snap whatever they choose. Nicola's old university chum, who's coming from Zimbabwe and defying Nicola's order not to fly, has offered to film some of the day on our camcorder.

We're not hiring morning suits or wedding dresses. Nicola is to wear a vintage sixties two-piece she found in a charity shop when she was at university. She has a few alterations done to it, costing all of £6. I'm wearing my best, and indeed only, suit. The kids still have the bridesmaids' dresses that they wore at Uncle Drew's wedding to Kate.

'We can find recycled gold rings at a jewellery shop,' says Nicola.

'Don't people say it's unlucky to have a second-hand ring? It might come from someone who's divorced or dead,' I query.

'But gold has to be mined. And that uses energy and carbon. And gold can be exchanged for weapons in lots of countries.'

'Is that what caused all the problems in Bougainville?'

'No, that was copper. Think of the conflict diamonds in the Congo. They have to be mined and both sides use the money to pay for weapons. Look it up on the Environmental Investigation Agency's website.'

'It's all a mineral minefield. I just want to avoid a conflict marriage. I don't care if our ring's second-hand as long as it's gold. I want some bling!'

And so we buy a pair of used rings from our local jewellers. They might be recycled, but polished gold looks great however old it is.

The wedding won't be in Nicola's home town of Bishop's Stortford, but in London. This will both cut costs and make it easier for guests to arrive by public transport. It's going to be at our local church so we can walk there from our house. On the invites we ask the guests not to bring cars as there's a tube station nearby. From the church the party can then walk to the reception, which we've booked at Islington Ecology Centre in Gillespie Park. It's a lot cheaper than a marquee and right next to the tube. Sorted.

This is certainly easing the financial pressure. And with a bit of luck there won't be any guests at all to bother us, as we're making so many demands of them.

My mum and dad are coming by taxi from King's Lynn as there's maintenance work on the train line that weekend. My dad is very worried the taxi won't wait for them even though the driver stands to gain a £200 fare. But after many phone calls and a list of at least ten people who will put him up in

London should he be stranded, plus the numbers of several hotels, he's almost calm.

Stephen, the 'maverick' vicar who blessed Nicola's allotment all those years ago, will be conducting the ceremony. We learn our vows, but strangely Nicola doesn't want to keep in the bit about 'honour and obey'. As for the honeymoon, we'll take the Eurostar to Lille instead of flying. Our daughters are staying with various friends for three nights.

We both suffer from back pain in the stressful run-up to the wedding. Nicola considers walking down the aisle with a hot-water bottle strapped under her coat to relieve the pain.

On the morning of the wedding a giant organic squash arrives by bike from Growing Communities. Finally we're big in Stoke Newington vegetable circles.

After a *Four Weddings and A Funeral*-style rush, we somehow get our family in costume, find a loo for my mum and dad, and walk 300 metres to the church.

We walk up the aisle together, accompanied by U2's *Beautiful Day* played on the church organ. There's a good gate today. Familiar faces from journalism, football, school, university, Friends of the Earth, vegetable-growing groups, and even George Marshall representing the Oxford Greens. Maybe I haven't been excommunicated from the eco-tribe, as yet. And there's Richard and Fleur from Yorkshire, whose house Nicola retreated to after our first canoodling, looking very country in their tweed suits.

The service begins. There's an introduction by the vicar, a

prayer and then Julie from Growing Communities reads Andrew Motion's Edward Square poem.

Stephen says the first hymn may be familiar to the football fans present. The organ plays 'Abide With Me', the pre-FA Cup Final anthem that made Elton John cry when Watford made it to Wembley. And if West Ham beat Norwich away in the third round, then maybe the lads will also be listening to 'Abide With Me' next May, I reflect dreamily.

Stephen gives a moving and most unusual sermon. 'How can we reconcile West Ham and Friends of the Earth?' he asks. Beats me. As far as I know it's the first time either West Ham or Friends of the Earth have ever been mentioned in the context of a wedding ceremony. Somehow Stephen concludes that West Ham and Friends of the Earth are indeed about to be reconciled today. He even manages to mention the Tardis at one point.

We manage to repeat our vows from memory.

'I Pete take you Nicola
to be my wife,
to have and to hold,
[especially when the heating's off]
from this day forward
for better; for worse,
for richer, for poorer,
[poorer with all this downshifting]
in sickness and in health

[in compost loos and outdoor loos]
to love and to cherish,
till death us do part; according to God's holy laws
In the presence of God I make this vow.'

Nicola repeats her vows, Stephen says a prayer and then I place the recycled ring on Nicola's finger.

Nicola. I give you this ring
as a sign of our marriage
with my body I honour you
all that I am I give to you
and all that I have I share with you
[except the chickens, she can have them]
within the love of God,
Father, Son and Holy Spirit.'

Stephen declares us man and wife. Blimey. We're married. Result.

Nicky from Zimbabwe reads Shakespeare's sonnet 'Let me not to the marriage of true minds admit impediments'. There certainly have been many impediments in the last twelve years. Shakespeare would have needed an extra 14 lines had he been aware of central heating thermostats, TV standby controls, bucket flights and food miles.

As we sign the register a group of children, including Lola and Nell, get up to sing 'With A Little Help From My Friends', the Beatles song they've been learning at school. And then as we walk out of the church we're accompanied by West Ham's theme song 'I'm Forever Blowing Bubbles' – which sounds superb and indeed quite romantic when played on a church organ.

It's one of those fine December days when the sky is blue and the air crisp, despite the fact it's been raining all week. Our party files in a long line through the grounds of Gillespie Park over autumnal leaves and past silver birches into the Ecology Centre itself, which is built on reclaimed railway sidings. It normally hosts school parties but makes a great venue for a wedding. And amazingly there's a huge pile of fairy cakes on the table, brought in by guests. Champagne is served and there's a hubbub of conversation.

Everyone seems to have enjoyed the wacky Greener than thou ceremony. My mum is still forgetful, but enjoying the party. My dad is reassured that his taxi really will wait and is enjoying the free drink and food. And there's my fellow season-ticket holder Matt, wearing his 1950s West Ham shirt, singing, 'You're not single any more!'

We've left out a blank canvas that Nicola found in Gillespie Road. There's a felt pen by it and instructions for the guests to write or draw their own messages on it. It's soon covered in pictures and quips like 'West Hammer meets Green goddess' and 'You touch my wife I kill you!' apparently written by West Ham's Tomas Repka.

After food it's time for the speeches while the children

play in the bower outside. Nicola is up first. Standing before the real-life tree that the Ecology Centre's staff use as a prop, she says that she's more used to making speeches promoting her book *Save Cash and Save The Planet*, but today she's forgotten her lemon, vinegar and bicarb of soda [eco-friendly cleaning materials, you idiots].

She thanks everyone who's brought cakes and notes how many of our friends have said, 'Ooh, I've never made a cake before'. Nicola remembers her dad Angus, who would have liked to be here because he loved parties.

Nicola thanks Julie from Growing Communities for the very large squash and Mary-Louise in the Solomon Islands who's today having a fairy-cake party in our honour in Bellona, scene of the sea snake debacle.

In a parody of the Nobel Peace Prize she presents the economics prize to her mother, for abilities as a seamstress, compost maker, horse minder and tracker down of life-size mechanical elephants that belonged to her dad. Fiona looks slightly embarrassed but pleased. She's probably thinking that it could have been worse; her daughter might have married Swampy from the Newbury Bypass protests and been living in 'teepee valley' in Wales by now.

Nicola also thanks me, and says 'he helps me by making me laugh every day'. Which I've never heard her say before.

Best woman Nicky from Zimbabwe tells the expectant crowd how when she first saw Nicola at York University she was wearing blue suede pixie boots with odd laces. 'She's a

wonderful mix of the practical and the eccentric,' is her rea-
soned conclusion.

Nicola reveals how she 'would certainly like to reduce,
reuse and recycle' some of the stuff in our house and how at
times 'I feel I let her down by liking the more glamorous things
in life like make-up [laughs].'

My old mate John, veteran of many a pub conversation
about how to understand Green women and staying flirty till
forty, warns the audience 'with Pete everything you do could
end up getting published'. As if I'd end up putting his speech
in a book.

It's a bit like Terry Collier in *Whatever Happened to the
Likely Lads*, suddenly giving his surprisingly moving wedding speech as Bob marries Thelma. He starts off with the
anecdote of our first shared flat, where the landlord illegally
changed the locks and we had to break in through the window and moves on to our days in Camberwell together. John
doesn't even mention all the times, cold and chastened,
bemused by the endless guilt of Green life, I'd fantasised over
pints about running away with various *Doctor Who* companions and then turning up the thermostat up to a Spinal
Tap-like 11.

John recalls the time we went camping in Snowdonia and
how every night, 'however tired Pete was, he'd want to ring
Nicola, and all this was in the days before mobile phones'. He
says, 'Nicola was the best thing that ever happened to Pete'
and that 'like Patrick McGoohan in *The Prisoner* Pete and

Nicola won't be stamped, filed, indexed, briefed, debriefed or numbered.'

Then my old school friend Paul sums up the day by thanking us for not having a formal photographer where 'you wait for an hour and lose the will to live'. He tells the story of how I once slept in his kitchen for six weeks when homeless, and then produces a present from his briefcase. 'It's sustainable as I've had it for 25 years and it's environmentally friendly because I'm recycling it. We wanted to give you something that every time you look at it will make you think of today. It's my West Ham mirror, commemorating the 1980 FA Cup Final victory.'

Paul holds the mirror aloft and I'm in danger of feeling moist-eyed. Nicola rolls her eyes. Is it possible she's going off recycling?

And then comes my speech. Standing before an old oak tree that has drawers cut into the trunk. In an Ecology Centre. Who'd ever have thought my wedding day would end up being like this? It's been a great day so far. The audience are on our side, remember that, I say to myself. And there's our friend Paula, formerly of Forest Monitor, in tears. Glasses are full, ties loosened, it's all looking good...

'Well, it's taken a long time for this to happen,' I begin, 'but as those of you who read the invitations might know, today was conditional on several events. The first was seeing a West Ham player lift a trophy. It's taken 24 years since – that's if we discount Inter-Toto Cup – Billy Bonds lifted the second division championship in 1981 and the FA Cup in

1980.' [My mate Matt looks as if he might be about to raise a point of order once he's consulted his *Sky Sports Football Yearbook*.] 'But this summer football genius Christian Dailly and Nigel Reo-Coker held up the Championship Play-off Final winners' trophy on a glorious day at the Millennium Stadium in Cardiff.

'Then, of course, there was England thrashing the Aussies in the Ashes this summer, which has taken a mere 16 years, and as we speak I think I can see Freddie Flintoff at the back of the Ecology Centre drinking our English wine.

'And finally *Doctor Who* returned. It was exterminated by croak-voiced Daleks at the BBC in 1989. They said it would never return, but it did this year and it was brilliant and it beat ITV's *Celebrity Wrestling*. Amazingly all this happened in 2005.

'Now, I'd like to thank Steve Platt who's here today. He was editor of the *New Statesman* where Nicola and I first met. Back in those days the *Statesman*'s offices were in Shoreditch in a converted warehouse called Perseverance Works. Hopefully in our case, perseverance really has worked.'

[Cue laughter and Steve saying 'It's true!']

'When I first met Nicola she was carrying a terrapin across London in a bucket and about to take it on a coach to Oxford, as you do. Life has certainly been eventful ever since. We've found ourselves owning one cat, four goldfish, several hundred stick insects, several million fruit flies from the compost bin, two lovely children and most latterly four chickens, two of which are now deceased.' [More laughter.]

'In the early stages of our relationship I thought I was dating a woman of substance, but as anyone who remembers our time at Aubert Park will remember, she proved to be a woman of subsidence. But we somehow survived that and finally moved to our present house. We've been through many events that have made our relationship stronger. In fact, the biggest tribute I can pay Nicola is that she checked the football fixtures before organising this wedding. West Ham are away today.' [Cheers.]

'Now I know that Nicola is uncomfortable with public displays of emotion, so I shall adopt the language of the environmental movement for my final remarks.

'In terms of our local development framework, over twelve years there has certainly been evidence of both localised and global warming in the Highbury Borders region. The fact that we are here today is evidence of irrevocable climate change. Having completed a full environmental impact assessment of our relationship, I believe that there is clear evidence of sustainability.' [Mass cheers.]

Nicola's mum Fiona has made a cake for us and we cut it together. My mum has enjoyed herself and tells another guest. 'It's been a really good day and we should do this again sometime.' She knows it's been a nice party, but she's not sure what it's for. There's barely time to say a few more thank yous, kiss the children goodbye and make sure that my sister Kaz is ready to escort my mum and dad into their taxi back to Norfolk, before we are leaving the reception.

Ha! Someone else has to do the cleaning up for once. We are in a taxi and on our way to Waterloo. We did it.

We board the Eurostar to Paris and have a candle-lit dinner in the first class diner accompanied by champagne. It's romantic and it feels much better than being on an aircraft. We're buzzing with stories about how the day went and who was there. It's the only time in your life when you and all your friends are in one place at the same time.

In Lille we stay in a hotel that has Impressionist pictures on the wall and, for once in my life, the central heating is on full. The old part of Lille is delightful. We spend two days visiting art galleries, looking at the Christmas markets in the old square, eating croissants, moules marinière and crêpes and drinking Belgian abbey beer. Nicola looks great in a long white coat that used to belong to her stylish friend Fi Forsyth from Condé Nast. She might even have combed her hair. It's been a long journey from 1993 to here. Bloody hell. We're married, with two kids and a mortgage. It seems that all along Elizabeth Bennett was an environmentalist wearing a Peruvian hat.

POSTSCRIPT
The Importance of Being Earnest

We're sitting in a super-insulated house beneath a turf roof on the outskirts of Aberdeen, watching *LiveEarth*, the series of global concerts meant to save the world on 07/07/07.

Our family is travelling around Britain for the summer doing house swaps. David and Natasha's house in Maryculter has an eco-roof made of earth and grass. It's covered in wild flowers and we feel particularly worthy sitting beneath it. Meanwhile Nicola's writing a blog about our travels (http://aroundbritainnoplane.com) on our laptop as she tries to convince people that holidaying in the UK can be both fun and carbon friendly.

Being Green has now become mainstream. You can see that from the pop stars playing today. Even Conservative leader David Cameron ostentatiously applied for planning permission to place a wind turbine on his Notting Hill house. Nicola met

Samantha Cameron at a Friends of the Earth event called The Big Ask. That's like Denis Thatcher turning up at a Greenpeace rally in the 1980s. Nowadays it's actually hip to hang out at Green parties. Thom Yorke was playing live that night in support of The Big Ask campaign for a climate change bill, although thankfully Nicola took my advice and didn't tell him to cheer up and do something singalong.

Sainsbury's is giving out designer cotton bags to replace plastic bags. Even Growing Communities, that was operating out of a back garden when we first joined a decade ago, now packs 680 bags of vegetables and fruit a week and has a turnover of around £200k a year. Our house was used as the headquarters of the Green Party during the council elections and a Green councillor, Katie Dawson, was actually elected in our ward.

Even football's going a bit Green. During the 2006 World Cup in Germany I write a feature on FIFA's Green Goal initiative to create a carbon-neutral tournament. There's free public transport for fans on the day of each game and the Germans have twelve stadiums incorporating eco-design. They even have bike parks.

In my West Ham programme, there's a picture of fat footie fans exposing their beer guts with 'reduce your carbon footyprint' written on their chests. It might not be much, but football fans are the people the Greens need to engage, not *Ecologist* readers.

The world is starting to believe that George Monbiot is right. We were there as Monbiot spoke at the 2005 Climate Change march, admittedly having first purchased a takeaway coffee and not even brought our own mugs. George still sounds like the most intelligent man on the planet and used 'predation' in his first sentence – maybe he's going to have to dumb down a little to get the tabloid readers onside. There's even been a hit TV series *It's Not Easy Being Green*, featuring Dick Strawbridge, a man with a huge moustache that probably houses several eco-systems.

Today there are eight concerts across seven continents. This morning's *Daily Mirror* has a Live Earth supplement called 'Save our Planet... We're In This Together'. Complete with 20 things that will make a difference (not buying bottled water, going veggie for a week, bring your own mug to work etc, but nothing on ditching the flights and car journeys). Catherine Tait's character Lauren is inside quizzing boffin Steve Howard on climate change and concludes there's a lot to be bovvered about.

Even David Attenborough is in there, and that's like having God on board. He's now convinced about climate change. Last summer he broadcast his documentaries *Are We Changing Planet Earth?* and *Can We Save Planet Earth?* on prime-time BBC.

Former US Vice-President Al Gore is also saying that we're in the middle of a planetary emergency. We watched Al

Gore's film *An Inconvenient Truth* at the Leicester Square Odeon in 2006. The film was a surprise box office hit. I didn't think I'd fall for the very American folksy and sentimental approach to climate change, but it's a tremendously powerful film. Our daughters Lola then aged eight and Nell aged five, both managed to sit through it all and now they want to save the polar bears. Al Gore shared the Nobel Peace Prize with the UN's Intergovernmental Panel on Climate Change in 2006.

On the telly, Russell Brand is in the Live Earth studio talking about poo and telling us not to flush in order to disguise your movements. Host Jonathan Ross says that when he sees Madonna at the bottle bank he'll know the message has got through. Alan Carr is bemoaning the fact that he's trying to deliver a serious message with the campest voice imaginable.

While we've been travelling this summer we've been dodging what the papers are calling the worst floods in history. This follows the hottest April ever recorded in Britain. We camped by Tom's boathouse (he's the former New Luddite) at Ullswater in the Lake District. After four days the water was lapping at our tent flaps. In the Yorkshire Dales the downpour was so heavy water was spouting up through holes in the tarmac like fountains. Large parts of Sheffield, including the Hillsborough stadium, are still underwater. Even *Daily Telegraph* readers' second homes are affected. The paper has huge pictures of Gloucestershire homes and sub-stations in a muddy sea.

During pre-season friendlies, Newcastle fans sing '1-0 and you still can't swim!' and 'Where's your wellies gone?' at Hull City supporters. Queen of the South supporters chant 'How's it feel to paddle home?' at Carlisle fans. They might soon be chanting, 'You're not cynical any more!' at me.

On a personal level our youngest daughter has asthma, just like lots of other kids at her school. It's under control through inhaling a steroid in the autumn and inhaling a reliever whenever she has an attack. But what is causing this modern epidemic? She's worse when the mist comes down and pollution hangs over the city. There's something in the air tonight, and it's not Phil Collins.

But here in Aberdeen we're dry and watching pop stars. Nicola enjoys Madonna's set but it's doubtful if concerts will change much, not while China and the US lead the world in carbon emissions. We sign up for texts on our mobiles and receive pithy messages about long-life light bulbs and how 'recycling just one aluminium can save enough energy to run a television for three hours'. After three days I sign off, because really living with Nicola is like having one long text message.

We return to London after a summer away and it becomes ever more obvious that we're creating changes we won't be able to halt. On the front page of the *Independent* the sons of Sir Edmund Hillary and Tensing Norgay, the conquerors of Mount Everest, Peter Hillary and Jamling Tensing, bemoan the effect climate change is having on the mountain. They say their fathers would no longer recognise it. The Himalayan glaciers are melting, the villages below will lose their drinking water and be subjected to catastrophic outburst floods affecting 40,000 people. Everest could be bare rock by 2050.

It gets worse. The Siberian permafrost will thaw and release huge amounts of methane (a much more potent greenhouse gas than carbon dioxide), says the geezer on a new TV series *Earth: The Power of the Planet*. London is at risk. The Eastern coast of Britain may disappear. My kids will never be able to holiday in Lincolnshire again – which is admittedly one of climate change's more appealing aspects. These days there are more tipping points than on the A13.

In November 2007 a report by the United Nations' top scientists in the snappily-titled Intergovernmental Panel on Climate Change (IPCC) warn of 'ecological catastrophe'. The IPCC (yes, the Greens are still at it with their acronyms) warned that temperatures could increase by 6 degrees centigrade by 2100. The IPCC says it is 90 per cent certain that global warming is down to human activity. Human greenhouse gas emissions grew by a whacking 70 per cent from 1970 to 2004. That's right, climate change is not caused by solar flares or natural cycles or left-wing conspiracies.

It reminds me of the classic *Doctor Who* story 'Inferno'. Professor Stahlman is determined to drill through to the Earth's core in pursuit of unlimited cheap energy. But Jon Pertwee's Doctor knows the sound of the drilling is the sound of the Earth crying out in protest. Only the Doctor's not around to save us now.

The IPCC urges a carbon tax and says the West must cut carbon emissions by almost a third by 2020 and at least 80 per cent by 2050. It warns that ice melting in Greenland could raise sea levels by several metres, sea ice could disappear from the summertime Arctic by the end of the century, warmer oceans will absorb less carbon, and England will probably never qualify for a World Cup again either. It's just a shame so many environmentalists and journalists have to fly to Bali for the UN conference that launched the report.

Something's changed in my life. When West Ham played away to Palermo in the Uefa Cup last season I was too guilty to book a flight to the match. Many Greens sound like puritans, they wear strange clothes, lack humour and come over as so earnest that you want to go straight into McDonald's and then book an internal flight. But they're on the right side.

Modern life is just too difficult. There are so many reasons to be fearful. Consuming is now one long fight with your conscience. You have to remember to buy refillable plastic containers of Ecover washing-up liquid, take your own bag when you shop, buy Fairtrade coffee, not drink bottled water, eat less meat, recycle everything, not accept too much packaging, use public transport, wear a jumper instead of turning on the heating, use public transport, stop flying and also pop into Black's to buy a moral compass.

But still, whatever climate chaos ensues, at least I pulled an eco-babe. Only in going Green to get the girl, I got Greener too. That wasn't meant to happen.

It's been a long journey lasting 14 years. We've been through a cold war, snake attacks in the Solomons, compost loos, hippos in cisterns, organic box schemes, overgrown allotments, festering compost bins, Green babies, downshifting, chickens and foxes, skip diving, cyber recycling and an eco-wedding. And really, for all my whinging, it's been quite some eco-trip.

The tunnelling, tin whistle and dreadlocks may have to wait. But this once-reluctant Green now hates Chelsea Tractors more than Chelsea FC. And that I guess, is progress.

Save Cash and Save the Planet

PUBLISHED IN ASSOCIATION WITH FRIENDS OF THE EARTH

ISBN 978-0-00-719420-9

Collins Gem Carbon Counter

MARK LYNAS

ISBN 978-0-00-724812-4

To order these titles please call our Customer Hotline number.

Tel: 0870 787 1724 • Fax: 0870 787 1725

CREDIT CARDS ACCEPTED

For further information about other books from Collins please visit

www.collins.co.uk